I0760188

# Historian in Chief

# Historian in Chief

## *How Presidents Interpret the Past to Shape the Future*

Edited by
Seth Cotlar
and Richard J. Ellis

University of Virginia Press / Charlottesville and London

University of Virginia Press

Printed in the United States of America on acid-free paper

*First published 2019*

9 8 7 6 5 4 3 2 1

Library of Congress Cataloging-in-Publication Data

Names: Cotlar, Seth, editor. | Ellis, Richard (Richard J.), editor.
Title: Historian in chief : how presidents interpret the past to shape the future / edited by Seth Cotlar and Richard J. Ellis.
Description: Charlottesville : University of Virginia Press, 2019. | Includes bibliographical references and index.
Identifiers: LCCN 2018051550 | ISBN 9780813942520 (cloth : alk. paper) | ISBN 9780813942537 (ebook)
Subjects: LCSH: Presidents—United States—Attitudes—History. | United States—Historiography. | Collective memory—United States—History. | Political culture—United States—History.
Classification: LCC E176.1 .H5556 2019 | DDC 306.20973—dc23
*LC record available at https://lccn.loc.gov/2018051550*

Cover art from Shutterstock.com/chemjc.

# Contents

# Acknowledgments

This volume emerged out of an October 2016 conference sponsored by the Center for Presidential History at Southern Methodist University. We would like to thank the Center's director, Jeffrey Engel, as well as Thomas Knock, who served as interim director during a pivotal time in the project's development. Our thanks are also due to the Center's associate director, Brian Franklin, and administrative coordinator, Ronna Spitz, whose work was crucial to making the conference a success.

We would also like to thank the contributors to this volume, who responded so positively and creatively to our unorthodox prompt. Presidential history often focuses on policy, politicking, and personalities, as it rightly should, but we wanted to shift the focus to the ways in which presidents have shaped the nation's collective memory and political culture. Roughly half of the contributors came to this project as scholars of American political culture who had only occasionally written about presidents, while the other half were presidential scholars who had only occasionally written about historical memory. This dichotomy is also reflected in the backgrounds of the organizers Jeffrey Engel tapped for this project—Seth Cotlar, a historian of popular political culture and collective memory, and Richard Ellis, a political scientist who has written extensively about the American presidency. We learned much from the innovative ways in which the contributors to this volume captured the distinctive voices of these eleven presidents, while also limning the powerful currents of American political culture in which their actions were embedded and by which they were constrained.

Finally, we would like to thank the folks at the University of Virginia Press. Editor Dick Holway saw the merit in this project from the beginning and was instrumental in bringing it to fruition. Dick solicited two excellent external reviewers, whose detailed and challenging comments helped to sharpen and enhance the book in countless ways. We would also like to thank Mark Mones and Robert Burchfield for their work in the final stages of production.

# Historian in Chief

# Introduction

Presidents shape not only the course of history but also how Americans remember and retell that history. Consequential decisions made in the Oval Office are typically accompanied by a justifying minihistory of who we are, who we have been, and who we can become as a people. Presidents draw attention to the parts of our history they want us to cherish and build upon, and repudiate or simply ignore facets of our collective memory that clash with their political objectives. They regularly invoke their presidential predecessors, encouraging us to admire some and revile or diminish others. The president of the United States, in short, is not just the nation's chief legislator, the head of a political party, or the commander in chief of the armed forces. The president is also, crucially, the nation's historian in chief.

Presidents forge collective memory not only through their words but through their symbolic actions as well. That is why presidents have often been quick to put up portraits and pull others down. Ronald Reagan famously took down Harry Truman's portrait in the White House Cabinet Room and replaced it with a painting of Calvin Coolidge with the hope of schooling the nation on the underappreciated virtues of the nation's thirtieth president and to signal his desire to roll back the "too active, intervening, interfering" government produced by the New Deal.[1] One of Donald Trump's first actions as president was to hang a portrait of the populist Andrew Jackson immediately to the right of his Oval Office desk, symbolically underscoring his inaugural address boast that his rise to power heralded "not merely transferring power from . . . one party to another but . . . transferring power from Washington, D.C. and giving it back to . . . the American people." Perhaps, too, giving the nation's most celebrated Indian fighter visual pride of place in the Oval Office was Trump's way of signaling his determination (again in the words of his inaugural address) to "protect our borders from the ravages of other countries" as well as to drive out those who do not belong here. Certainly, his predecessor, Barack Obama, sent a very different and more inclusive message about the nation's history by adding a bronze bust of the slain civil rights leader Martin Luther King Jr., the first African American to have his image adorn the Oval Office.

In describing presidents as historians in chief, we are not suggesting that they are the nation's only storytellers. The president's power to rewrite our past and reshape collective memory is significantly constrained. Presidential power to mold the nation's self-understanding, like most presidential powers, is the power to persuade, not the power to command. Presidents occupy the bully pulpit, but in a vast and fragmented nation there are many pulpits, and many of the audiences are inattentive if not hostile to the president's teachings.[2] In a pluralistic democracy no single person, not even the president of the United States, can single-handedly reconfigure the nation's historical memory. The essays in this volume explore how eleven American presidents navigated those constraints and deployed their power in their efforts to shape the nation's collective memory and its political future.

Labeling the president as the historian in chief does not mean that we are naive enough to think that presidents are aspiring professional historians. However, in casting the president as historian in chief—as opposed, say, to storyteller in chief—we wish not only to highlight the ways that presidents use the past to control the future but also to scrutinize the accuracy of the history that presidents tell. This book begins from the premise that presidents as the nation's historians in chief should be evaluated not only on how effective they are in persuading others to believe the historical narratives they tell—political scientists' conventional measure of presidential performance—but also on the veracity of those narratives. Good history is true to the archival record, and presidents who give more credence to "alternative facts" than established ones are failing in their role as historian in chief.

## *Presidents as Teachers*

"What is politics if it's not teaching?" asked longtime Missouri congressman Richard Bolling. "To me," Bolling added, "there's no difference between leadership and education." Of course, being a politician primarily involves formulating and voting on public policy, but as Bolling rightly points out, it also requires politicians to educate their constituents and the country. Not all members of Congress will share Bolling's understanding of their political calling. Some may see their job as simply doing whatever their local constituents desire or demand. Bolling himself expressed frustration that "too few congressmen are willing to accept a position of national leadership. . . . They are opinionated, and they vote their opinions. But not many try to lead their communities in ideas."[3]

Whatever truth there might be in this as a criticism of Congress, few would level the same complaint against presidents. All presidents, certainly all modern presidents, understand that they are educators of the American people. Most would agree with Franklin Roosevelt—one of the finest teachers ever to occupy the White House—that "the greatest duty of a statesman is to educate."[4] To be sure, some have chafed at what the political scientist Fred Greenstein has called "the teaching and preaching side of presidential leadership."[5] George Herbert Walker Bush, while still vice president, famously bristled at "the vision thing," an offhand private comment that, once made public, was continually thrown back at him by pundits and critics who faulted him for failing to convincingly articulate his guiding principles and ideas as president.

The first President Bush was not helped by the invidious contrast critics often drew with his predecessor, Ronald Reagan, whose dedication to the teaching side of presidential leadership helped to earn him the moniker "the Great Communicator." Of course, as Rick Perlstein emphasizes in chapter 10, being a skilled communicator does not necessarily make a president a good teacher if the information being taught is inaccurate. Presidents may tell a compelling story about the past, but if a democratic leader is, as Marc Landy and Sidney Milkis write, "one who takes the public to school," then one cannot avoid asking difficult and unavoidably contentious questions about the quality of the schooling the people receive from presidents.[6] In a 1984 presidential debate, Walter Mondale used the words of Will Rogers to criticize what he saw as Reagan's imperfect grasp of the truth: "It ain't what you don't know that gets you into trouble. It's what you know for sure that just ain't so."[7] Perlstein depicts Reagan as a historian in chief who often found himself in the sort of trouble Mondale described, claiming to know for certain things that just weren't so. Ironically, Mondale himself was not immune from falling into this same trap, for Will Rogers never said the words that Mondale confidently attributed to him.

History, of course, is about far more than brute facts. Some facts are undeniable: Barack Obama was not in fact born in Kenya; Abraham Lincoln really was fifty-one years old when he was elected president; Franklin Roosevelt is undeniably the only president to serve more than two terms; and Will Rogers never said what Walter Mondale claimed he did. However, most historical events are open to interpretation and are inherently contestable. Was the Civil War inevitable, and who was to blame for its coming? Was Jackson's war on the National Bank to blame for the economic depression during the Van Buren administration? Does the Reagan administration deserve credit for the collapse of the Soviet Union and the end of the Cold War? If professional historians disagree about such questions, we can hardly expect partisan politicians to agree.

Even more contestable are efforts to discern in the past the principles that should guide our present and future actions. Did the framers design the Constitution to be an evolving document that would enable the federal government to meet the changing imperatives of justice and the "general welfare," or were the framers most interested in avoiding the dangers of centralized political power? Lincoln taught Americans to regard the Declaration of Independence as the nation's core founding document, the "apple of gold" that the constitutional frame (the "picture of silver") was intended "to adorn and preserve."[8] Other historians in chief have placed the Constitution at the center of the nation's political tradition, arguing that fidelity to the past requires that we anchor ourselves to the original intentions or understandings of those "Founding Fathers" who wrote the Constitution. In contrast, Progressives such as Woodrow Wilson encouraged the American people to see the nation's history as a story of progress and development and to view the founders as men whose vision was necessarily blinkered by the primitive times in which they lived. Here, one person's education will be another's misinformation campaign.

Nonetheless, it seems obvious that some presidents are better teachers than others, their history lessons more memorable and consequential, their interpretations more compelling and enduring. Political scientists disagree about how much of this should be chalked up to individual attributes and how much to the historical moment. Some, like Fred Greenstein, emphasize the importance of a president's communication skills, cognitive style, and political gifts. Others, such as Stephen Skowronek, argue that the ability to reorder historical understandings and institutional arrangements depends also on the "historical time" in which presidents find themselves. Skowronek argues that presidents who come to power in opposition to a governing regime in which the core commitments of ideology and interest are being called into question (think FDR) are the presidents most likely to find a receptive audience for their historical revisions.[9]

Has it become more difficult for presidents to take the people to school? Some scholars think so, particularly because of partisan polarization and media narrowcasting. The percentage of people tuning in to the president's speeches, including the State of the Union address, has declined steadily. In the age of broadcasting, the president could count on a broad and diverse audience, but in the age of narrowcasting, presidents know that even their most visible speeches will reach far more supporters than opponents. On the other hand, partisan narrowcasting is hardly a novel phenomenon. Jefferson, Jackson, and Lincoln were all familiar with a press that was overwhelmingly partisan. And before television and radio, a president's ability to school the people was necessarily more limited and indirect.

Other scholars see the problem today quite differently. The problem, from this perspective, is not presidents' limited opportunities to communicate with the people but instead the nearly opposite one of presidents speaking too much. The problem is that presidents today are always trying to take the people to school, always going over the heads of Congress. The educative function is driving out the deliberative and governing function. Presidents shouldn't try to be the nation's teachers—that way is the path to demagoguery, a path that the framers of the Constitution tried to block, both through institutional mechanisms and informal norms, such as presidents not campaigning for their own reelection.[10]

For political scientists and historians, this is all familiar stuff. Of course, presidential leadership is about education, persuasion, communication, rhetoric. So what's new here? Is the idea of the president as historian in chief merely a new label for old wines? We think not. Conceptualizing presidents as historians in chief draws attention to a crucial aspect of the presidency that is too often slighted if not ignored: namely, that presidents are an extraordinarily history-conscious bunch with an outsized capacity for recasting the nation's historical memory. Obsession is not too strong a word to describe the ways that presidents think about their place in history, and that obsession and the power to act upon it set them apart from other politicians.

## *"The President Is Very . . . History-Conscious"*

One of the great puzzles of American politics is why Richard Nixon taped the Watergate conversations that led to his downfall. Entrapment is one thing, but laying the trap for yourself is quite another. Nixon aide Alexander Butterfield had a simple explanation: "*Everything*" in the Oval Office was taped, he informed the Senate Select Committee in 1973, because "the President is very history-oriented and history-conscious about the role he is going to play, and is not at all subtle about it, or about admitting it." Nixon wanted his every accomplishment and utterance recorded for posterity so future generations would remember him as a great president.[11]

There is no more room left on Mount Rushmore, but every president still wants to belong to the pantheon of great or at least near-great presidents. And if they can't be great, they certainly don't want to be cast as one of the failures. They want to be compared with Lincoln not Buchanan, FDR not Hoover. "Whatever their parties, whatever their personalities," the political scientists William Howell and Terry Moe have argued, "presidents have a burning desire to be remembered as great leaders. They want subsequent generations of citizens to look back on their time in office and pay homage to their accomplishments." If we are to understand presidential behavior, Howell and Moe suggest, we must take seriously presidents' "concern about legacy."[12]

As Ed Countryman shows in chapter 1, George Washington exhibited a particularly keen historical consciousness, informed primarily by the terrifying realization that his actions would have profound effects on the course of history. While the political theories that informed the political structure of the new nation had deep historical roots, the institutions themselves were sui generis and untested. Washington knew that there was no wind blowing from time immemorial to keep the ship of state moving steadily forward. He was painfully aware that it was his positive image, and his fellow citizens' investment in it, that provided the ballast that lent weight and substance to the edifice of the new American state. Just as generations of American citizens have looked back to Washington with a sense of wonder, if not always unqualified admiration, for his accomplishments as the nation's first president, Washington himself recognized how pivotal and potentially momentous every decision, every public interaction and utterance could be. This was not just a character trait of Washington's but also emblematic of his evolving understanding of himself as both a creature of and an actor in the unfolding and uncertain history of the new, fragile nation.

All presidents have exhibited, at least to some extent and in their own distinctive ways, the peculiar historical consciousness that comes with being the current holder of an office that traces its lineage back to Washington. Presidents have always invoked and measured themselves against past presidents, not only their immediate predecessors but all those who have taken the oath of office. Nixon's touchstone and "patron saint" was Woodrow Wilson. In Nixon's view, Wilson was the twentieth century's greatest president because he insisted on American leadership in the world and presidential control of foreign policy. One of Nixon's first presidential acts was to furnish the Oval Office with Wilson's desk—or what he thought to be the twenty-eighth president's desk; it turned out the "Wilson desk" belonged to Henry Wilson, Ulysses Grant's vice president. Speechwriter William Safire noted that Nixon used the Wilson desk "hundreds of times to get into points about idealism, about how Presidents can be misunderstood, [and] how peaceful men find themselves with need to do battle." It was from behind the Wilson desk that Nixon gave his 1969 "silent majority speech" defending U.S. military involvement in Vietnam. "Fifty years ago," Nixon reminded his television audience, "in this room and at this very desk, President Woodrow Wilson spoke words which caught the imagination of a war-weary world." Nixon did not claim to be fighting a war to end all wars—a dream that had been "shattered on the hard realities of great power politics" and left Wilson "a broken man"—but he did promise to "bring us closer to that great goal to which Woodrow Wilson and every American president in our history has been dedicated—the goal of a just and lasting peace." For Nixon, the road to presidential greatness ran through foreign policy, and he hoped that by tempering idealism with realism he would succeed where Wilson had failed.[13]

In the wake of Watergate, as his presidency unraveled, Nixon's thoughts turned from Wilson to Lincoln. He spent his final somber days in office reading *Abraham Lincoln: Theologian of Religious Anguish.* On his final night in the White House, he ushered Henry Kissinger into Lincoln's sitting room, where they "knelt down" and wept "in front of that table where Lincoln had signed the Emancipation Proclamation."[14] In his widely watched interviews with David Frost, broadcast in 1977, Nixon stressed what he had in common with Lincoln. They had both presided over an unpopular war that had sown protest and discord at home. He reminded the 45 million television viewers of President Lincoln's illegal acts, conscripting an army without congressional authorization, suspending the writ of habeas corpus, and arresting thousands of opponents of the war. And he invoked Lincoln's exculpatory words—that "actions which would otherwise be unconstitutional, could become lawful if undertaken for the purpose of preserving the Constitution and the nation." A proper understanding of Lincoln, Nixon suggested, would lead to a more sympathetic understanding of the dilemmas Nixon faced and the actions he took.

Aspects of Nixon's personality may have bordered on the pathological, but there was nothing unusual about his obsession with measuring himself against the words and deeds of his predecessors in the Oval Office. As John Milton Cooper Jr. shows in chapter 6, Wilson himself was haunted by Lincoln's specter, and Madison's too. Wilson, though, as befits the professional historian that he was, invoked these White House ghosts less to justify his own actions than to learn from the mistakes he believed they had made. Wilson was determined to prove himself a greater president than Madison by not allowing himself to be stampeded into a war the country was not prepared to fight.

Lincoln's ghost loomed particularly large in the active imagination of Theodore Roosevelt, the most prolific historian of all our presidents. In Kathleen Dalton's telling in chapter 5, Lincoln served a very different psychological and political function for Roosevelt than he did for Nixon. For Nixon, dragging Lincoln into the conversation was a way of justifying to himself and to others illegal or questionable actions. For Theodore Roosevelt, in contrast, the effort to live up to Lincoln's example helped to temper his jingoism and tame his impulsiveness. Remembering Lincoln, according to Dalton, made Roosevelt a more careful and patient president. Roosevelt's historical consciousness made for better decision making in the White House.

Lincoln has also figured prominently in the historical imagination of Barack Obama, as James Kloppenberg's close reading of *The Audacity of Hope* in chapter 11 makes clear. Obama announced his presidential candidacy in Springfield, Illinois, "in the shadow of the Old State Capitol, where Lincoln once called on a divided house to stand together." Obama vowed to be like Lincoln, a president who would bring us together, heal our divisions, and articulate "our common hopes and common dreams," to show, as he put it in his 2004 keynote address at the Democratic National Convention, that "there is not a liberal America and a conservative America—there is the United States of America. There is not a black America and a white America and Latino America and Asian America—there's the United States of America."[15]

When Obama failed to transcend the country's partisan and racial divisions, he did not abandon Lincoln so much as reinvent him. Obama replaced Lincoln the unifier and healer with Lincoln the forward-looking agent of historic progress. Obama's final State of the Union message took for its theme the famous admonition in Lincoln's storied second annual address to "disenthrall ourselves [from] the dogmas of the quiet past." The United States, Obama reminded his fellow Americans, had "been through big changes before: wars and depression, the influx of new immigrants, workers fighting for a fair deal, movements to expand civil rights. Each time, there have been those who told us to fear the future; who claimed we could slam the brakes on change; who promised to restore past glory if we just got some group or idea that was threatening America under control. And each time, we overcame those fears." We did so, Obama continued, because we "did not, in the words of Lincoln, adhere to the 'dogmas of the quiet past.' Instead, we thought anew and acted anew. We made change work for us, always extending America's promise outward, to the next frontier, to more people." Obama was asking to be remembered as a president who had, like Lincoln, stood on the side of progress against the backward-looking forces of reaction and bigotry.[16]

Of course, progressives might hope that any president would aspire to be remembered as a modern-day Lincoln, but neither Obama's Republican predecessor nor his Republican successor had much rhetorical use for the man Donald Trump has called "the late, great Lincoln."[17] George W. Bush, under the tutelage of his chief political strategist Karl Rove, ran for office in 2000 not by invoking the heroic mantle of Abraham Lincoln but by channeling the underappreciated William McKinley. The Bush campaign strove to emulate McKinley's success by winning not just one election but by expanding the appeal of the Republican Party to immigrants and working people so as to make it "the majority party for a generation."[18]

In 2016, the Trump campaign made no secret of its aim also to remake American politics for a generation, but whereas Rove followed the McKinley rule book (raise huge sums of money from large donors, smooth over divisions within the party, and reach out to new groups with "compassionate conservatism"), Trump's strategist Steve Bannon likened Trump to

McKinley's great populist opponent in 1896 (and 1900), William Jennings Bryan. Trump, gushed Bannon, is "probably the greatest orator since William Jennings Bryan." But the real affinity, in Bannon's mind, was with Andrew Jackson—and, like Jackson, Trump promised to defy a corrupt and self-dealing political establishment and "build an entirely new political movement" based not on out-of-touch elites but on the incorruptible common people.[19]

Trump told a story about the American past that was diametrically opposed to the one Obama told during his eight years as historian in chief. Obama spoke of an America that had slowly learned to embrace racial diversity, gradually acknowledged the rights of the LGBTQ community, and was working to make the promises of American prosperity and citizenship a lived reality for immigrants and historically marginalized groups. This audaciously hopeful vision for the future was rooted in an upward-sloping, Lincolnian narrative about the unfolding, egalitarian ideal at the core of American history and identity. In Trump's telling, though, Obama's inclusive, egalitarian story of America was a "politically correct" fairy tale. In its place Trump substituted a populist declension narrative in which a once strong and proud nation had become enfeebled by naysayers and weaklings who apologized for rather than celebrated America's past and by cosmopolitan elites who placed the interests of the world ahead of the interests of everyday Americans. For Trump, making America great again meant restoring the "forgotten" Americans—particularly white working-class males—to their former position of mastery and putting back in their place those who didn't look, speak, or worship like the "real" Americans of yesteryear.

As presidents try to move the nation toward different visions of the future, they constantly look backward for history lessons from their predecessors. They see history as "full of lessons and examples, information and cautions." Bill Clinton frequently stayed up "half the night" reading histories of past presidencies, seeking to better understand the opportunities for action in his own political time. Clinton was especially eager to discern how presidents like Theodore Roosevelt had made an enduring mark on the country even in the absence of an "empowering crisis." George W. Bush didn't have Clinton's "lifelong passion for history," but he reportedly read no fewer than fourteen books about Lincoln during his eight years in the White House. Obama even took to inviting a clutch of distinguished presidential historians—including Doris Kearns Goodwin, Robert Caro, and

Robert Dallek—for annual dinners in hopes that their knowledge of past presidents could help him do his job more effectively.[20] Not every president may be as inquisitive about presidential history as Clinton or Obama, but all have their eyes firmly fixed on their place in history. They rummage through presidential history for inspiration and justification, analogies and admonitions, the words they choose designed not only to sway the audience before them but the judgment of history ahead of them. The decisions they make (think, for instance, of Obama's decision to swing for the fences and continue to push for the Affordable Care Act while key advisers, including his chief of staff and vice president, advocated a less ambitious, more incremental approach[21]) are aimed not only at solving the problems of today but securing their reputation in the history books of tomorrow, their political strategies geared not only to winning elections and votes in Congress but to being crowned by historians as among the nation's most effective and influential presidents.

## *Presidents as Historians*

If every president becomes enthralled by presidential history—and even more by his place in that history—not every president sits down to write American history. A surprising number, however, have done just that. Some, like Obama (*The Audacity of Hope*) and John Kennedy (*Profiles in Courage*), did so before they became president. Others, like Martin Van Buren (*Inquiry into the Origin and Course of Political Parties in the United States*), John Quincy Adams (*Parties in the United States*), and Herbert Hoover (*The Ordeal of Woodrow Wilson*), did so after they left the White House. The reader will find chapters devoted to each of these histories in this book, but this is far from an exhaustive list of the historical works penned by U.S. presidents. John Adams, Thomas Jefferson, and James Madison were all careful students of history. Ulysses Grant's two-volume memoir is still read today for its lucid account of the Mexican War and the Civil War. Harry Truman was no scholar, but he wrote or dictated "a couple of thousand pages" of material on American history, particularly on the history of presidents he admired (Jackson was his favorite) and those he felt the country could have done without (a list that included the usual presidential "failures" like Pierce, Buchanan, Grant, and Harding as well as a president that historians have come to rate more highly, Dwight David Eisenhower).[22]

We have not attempted to include in this book every president who wrote or aspired to write a book on American history. Moreover, we have included in this volume four important presidents who never set out to write formal history: Washington, Lincoln, FDR, and Reagan. However, each of these presidents, at least the latter three, used rhetoric with great effect to tell his version of American history and to reshape the nation's historical consciousness. In that sense, these presidents were also our historians in chief—and indeed, measured by their impact on the nation's self-understanding, they must rank as among our most successful historians in chief. And for that reason, we include them in this volume.

We hope the reader will excuse our omission of Truman and Grant, not to mention Adams and Jefferson. Choices needed to be made. There are two presidents, however, who we could not omit: Theodore Roosevelt and Woodrow Wilson. They are not only among our most storied and influential twentieth-century presidents, they are also the two most prolific historians ever to occupy the White House. Neither man would have called himself a professional historian, but both were elected presidents of the American Historical Association (AHA), Roosevelt in 1912 and Woodrow Wilson in 1924. Roosevelt used his AHA presidential address to chastise professional or "scientific" historians for their obsession with compiling "a mass of dry facts and gray details" at the expense of "vivid," heroic writing that could "make dead men living before our eyes."[23] Wilson, who died before being able to deliver his AHA presidential address, also served as the president of the American Political Science Association (APSA) in 1909–10, at a time when the dividing line between political science and history was rather more fuzzy than it is today.[24]

Measured by the volume of history writing, Theodore Roosevelt is arguably in a class by himself. At the age of twenty-three, while studying law at Columbia, Roosevelt published an acclaimed history of the War on 1812 (*The Naval War of 1812*) that went through three editions in its first year.[25] He also wrote an ambitious six-volume history, *The Winning of the West,* as well as biographies of Thomas Hart Benton, Gouverneur Morris, and Oliver Cromwell. Roosevelt wrote with astonishing speed. *Cromwell* was dashed off during a one-month "vacation" at Sagamore Hill, while he was the governor of the nation's largest state, New York.[26]

Roosevelt may have written more history, but Wilson was the more accomplished scholar. Roosevelt took only one history course in his life—a required course on Anglo-American constitutional history at Harvard[27]—whereas Wilson was an undergraduate history major at Princeton (then called the College of New Jersey) and received a Ph.D. in history and political science at Johns Hopkins University.[28] In his chapter on Wilson, Cooper notes that historians today don't think much of Wilson's histories, which include a biography of George Washington, a two-volume history of the Civil War and Reconstruction (*Division and Reunion*), as well as the four-volume *History of the American People,* which netted Wilson the equivalent of $1 million in today's currency. Political scientists, in contrast, hold Wilson's work in the highest esteem. His first book, *Congressional Government,* published just four years before he became president, is still regarded as one of the seminal works in the field. Wilson's work as a political scientist powerfully reshaped the way Americans, at least Progressive Americans, thought about the Constitution and the American political system.

When Wilson ran for president in 1912, he elaborated his Progressive reading of American history, a reading that arguably set the terms for American debate for the following century. Wilson began from the premise that the country had entered "a new social age" that required new political institutions and theories. "The old political formulas," he said, no longer "fit the present problems; they read now like documents taken out of a forgotten age." In the "old-fashioned days when life was very simple," Americans believed that government only had "to put on a policeman's uniform, and say, 'Now don't hurt anybody else.'" The idea that prevailed in Jefferson's day, "that the best government was the government that did as little governing as possible," was no longer viable in a complex world of "great modern industrial enterprises." In the time of Jefferson, Wilson explained,

> it was no business of the law to come into my house and see how I kept house. But when my house, when my so-called private property, became a great mine, and men went along dark corridors amidst every kind of danger in order to dig out of the bowels of the earth things necessary for the industries of a whole nation, and when it came about that no individual owned these mines, that they were owned by great stock companies, then all the old analogies absolutely collapsed and it became the right of the government to go down into these mines to see whether human beings were properly treated in them or not; to see whether accidents were

> properly safeguarded against; to see whether modern economical methods of using these inestimable riches of the earth were followed or were not followed. . . . [I]n these great beehives where in every corridor swarm men of flesh and blood, it is the privilege of the government, whether of the State or of the United States, as the case may be, to see that human life is protected, that human lungs have something to breathe.[29]

Securing "The New Freedom," Wilson preached, required not only new laws and a new governing philosophy but rethinking the Constitution itself. The "makers" of the Constitution were brilliant Newtonians, crafting a mechanical system of checks and balances between the Senate, the House, the president, and the judiciary in "a sort of imitation of the solar system" in which "by the attraction of gravitation the various parts are held in their orbits." The Constitution may have been a scientific marvel for its day, but, according to Wilson, the theory behind it was archaic in the age of Darwin. Government was "not a machine, but a living thing" that needed to adapt to its changing environment in order to thrive. "No living thing," Wilson wrote, "can have its organs offset each other, as checks, and live." And no government could succeed "without the intimate, instinctive coordination of the organs of life and action." As good Darwinians, Progressives looked not to the framers' intent but to what Wilson called the "living political constitution"—one that could be amended to establish the direct election of U.S. senators by popular vote (as happened through the Seventeenth Amendment, ratified one month after Wilson's inauguration), reimagined to allow for a president "at liberty, both in law and conscience, to be as big a man as he can" (as he wrote in *Constitutional Government* after watching Theodore Roosevelt dramatically expand presidential power), and reinterpreted by the Supreme Court to enable the government to regulate a complex, modern economy.[30] It was upon the foundations of this Wilsonian reading of the Constitution that FDR's New Deal and LBJ's Great Society built. And it was largely in opposition to this living, Progressive, Wilsonian Constitution that the Goldwater and Reaganite Republican Party came to define itself. As the rise of constitutional originalism in the late twentieth century suggests, the Supreme Court and the nation more broadly remain divided over Wilson's reimagining of the Constitution's place in both the nation's past and its ever-unfolding present.[31]

Few readers will need to be persuaded of Wilson's importance as a historian in chief, but Van Buren? Certainly Van Buren had none of the facility for the English language possessed by Wilson or Roosevelt or Lincoln. Reading Van Buren's *Inquiry* is as laborious as writing it was for the minimally educated Van Buren. But Elvin T. Lim's original reading in chapter 3 finds in *Inquiry* the key to Van Buren's importance as a historian and political thinker. Van Buren not only elaborated a principled defense of political parties, he helped to recast the nation's understanding of the Constitution by reimagining it as an Anti-Federalist document enshrining states' rights and local control. It was the Little Magician's greatest if least appreciated conjuring trick. A Constitution written by Federalist state-builders intent on checking state and local power and strengthening the central government was reinterpreted as a compact dedicated to checking federal power and promoting local democracy. So stunning was Van Buren's success that when Wilson and many other Progressives at the turn of the twentieth century began to build the case for an energetic central government, they did so less by embracing the makers of the Constitution as kindred spirits than by rejecting the founders' vision and their handiwork as outdated relics of a simpler bygone era.[32]

As David Sehat shows in chapter 8, Franklin Roosevelt ran for president in 1932 echoing the same progressive understanding of history that Wilson had advanced in 1912. "The demands of the new time," Roosevelt taught, required fundamental change in the way the country thought about political economy and about the role of government. When in 1935 the U.S. Supreme Court ruled unconstitutional a key element of the New Deal (the National Industrial Recovery Act of 1933) that enabled the administration to regulate private industry, FDR offered scathing criticism of the Court for clinging to outmoded understandings of the Interstate Commerce Clause. "The country was in the horse-and-buggy age when that clause was written," Roosevelt told a press conference, and now, thanks to a backward-looking Court, the entire country had "been relegated to the horse-and-buggy definition of interstate commerce."[33]

But as Sehat also demonstrates, FDR found that the progressive understanding of history left him vulnerable to attack from conservatives who accused him of abandoning the country's founders. Sehat shows how the American Liberty League, formed in 1934 to combat New Deal policies, constructed a historical narrative that charged Roosevelt with wrecking the Constitution and forsaking the wisdom of the founders. To blunt the force of these attacks, Roosevelt increasingly developed alternative historical narratives that emphasized his affinity with the patriots of the Revolutionary era and the great presidents of the past. Instead of accenting the new demands of a new time, he framed the 1936 campaign as part of a perennial struggle in American history between the people and a "power-seeking minority." Far from being a radical departure from the past, the New Deal was only the latest effort, dating back to the American Revolution, "to restore power to those whom it rightfully belonged." Roosevelt used his second inaugural address, the 150th anniversary of the Constitutional Convention, to give the nation a different history lesson, but one that again emphasized the parallels between the founding period and the New Deal. Our "forefathers" at the convention, Roosevelt taught, were not the men of little faith that the American Liberty League (and Van Buren) made them out to be. Instead, they "found the way out of the chaos which followed the Revolutionary War" by creating "a strong government with powers of unified action sufficient then *and now* to solve problems utterly beyond individual or local solution." Just as the framers "established the Federal Government to promote the general welfare and secure the blessings of liberty to the American people," so the New Deal invoked "those same powers of government to achieve the same objectives."[34]

Challenged from the right, FDR found it necessary to get right with the founders. The nation's problems were not rooted in its eighteenth-century institutions but instead stemmed from losing touch with or falling away from the founders' animating vision. The rhetoric of politics became about restoration, not transformation. The job of the historian in chief was to reassure Americans that they had been here before, that their struggle was the same as that of their "forefathers," that policies and programs that might seem new were in fact consistent with the framers' deepest intentions.

This presidential tug-of-war over the Founding Fathers did not begin in the twentieth century. Indeed, the debate over the founders' intent began as early as the 1790s, while Washington was still in the White House. But David Waldstreicher in chapter 2 suggests that it is John Quincy Adams, the nation's sixth president and son of the second, who deserves to be remembered as the first great historical revisionist to occupy the White House. In *Parties in the United States,* written after his defeat in 1828, Adams put Jefferson and slavery at the center of what had gone wrong in American politics since the Constitutional Convention. In Adams's historical telling,

Jefferson's presidency, most especially the Louisiana Purchase, hugely enhanced the political power of the southern states and of slavery and thereby subverted the original nationalist vision that animated the Constitution and its creators. Whereas Jefferson told American history as a recurrent struggle pitting Whig against Tory, democrat against aristocrat, Adams painted the Jeffersonian Revolution as the moment in which the constitutional ideal of national sovereignty was subverted by a southern, agrarian planter elite dedicated to maintaining slavery and the "hallucination of State sovereignty."

The debate about slavery and the founders was also at the heart of the storied debates between Abraham Lincoln and Stephen Douglas. In chapter 4, Jonathan Earle shows that both Lincoln and Douglas were intent to enlist the founders on their side. But Earle draws a stark contrast between the "historical fundamentalism" of Douglas and the more careful, evidence-based history of Lincoln. He charges Douglas with searching for "scriptural antecedents" in the words of the framers, with little or no attention to historical context or contingency. He shows us Lincoln, in contrast, heading to the archives in the state capitol library in Springfield to research what would become the famous (and footnoted!) Cooper Union Address. Like a good historian, Lincoln dug into primary documents to find how the signers of the Constitution voted on other issues involving slavery, such as the Northwest Ordinance, which created the Northwest Territory where slavery was prohibited. In Earle's telling, Lincoln was not just the better politician, he was also the better historian.

So is there a connection between being a good historian and being an effective president? Certainly Lincoln went to the archive with a case to make, like the good lawyer and politician he was. But, like a good historian, he also brought to those primary sources a genuine curiosity about what he would find there. Moreover, his arguments about the centrality of equality to the American political tradition have been refashioned, refined, and recontextualized innumerable times, but they have never been fully repudiated. A long line of historians in chief, from Teddy Roosevelt to Obama, have sought to use their position to realize the Lincolnian ideal of a more perfect and just union. Each recognized the various failings and limitations of their predecessors, just as historians have noted and will continue to note the gap between the idealistic futures those presidents sought to create and the imperfect nations they left behind at the end of their terms.

Perlstein's chapter on Reagan, however, suggests that successful presidents need not be reliable historians. There is no denying that Reagan powerfully shaped the nation's political culture as well as its historical memory, fundamentally reorienting how millions of citizens remembered and felt about the pivotal eras of the 1930s and the 1960s. But it is equally difficult to deny that Reagan often had a cavalier relationship with historical facts. What Perlstein calls Reagan's "liturgy of absolution" made many Americans feel better about the nation's past while avoiding a reckoning with its more troubling impulses and actions. The inspirational stories lifted the spirits and swelled the nationalistic pride of Reagan's admirers, but they obscured the complexities of the nation's history. In this respect, Reagan fell short as a historian in chief.

The same could be said for JFK, whose self-serving recasting of political history celebrated the "courage" of the antipartisan "maverick." Although Kennedy prided himself on his "sense of history,"[35] Jeff Pasley shows in chapter 9 that Kennedy's *Profiles in Courage* created a tendentious and cherry-picked canon of the nation's past political leaders whose approach to politics just happened to resemble that of JFK, the aspiring presidential candidate. While Kennedy did not invent his history out of whole cloth like Reagan frequently did, his eagerness to burnish the reputations of certain leaders from the nation's past led him to downplay essential dimensions of their careers. JFK praised Republican congressman Edmund Ross for defying his party and casting the deciding vote to save Andrew Johnson from impeachment, for example, yet failed to note Ross's eventual switch to the Democrats and his participation in the racist backlash against the Republicans' Reconstruction efforts. One person's "maverick" was another person's sell-out, but JFK's works of history never considered such complexities. Like Reagan's, Kennedy's recasting of American history was politically efficacious, but it constructed an idealized, simplified past that was more mythical than real. Neither therefore should be counted as among the great historians in chief, despite their undeniable influence on the nation's collective memory.

## *Taking the Historian in Chief Seriously*

The term "historian in chief," then, is more than just a catchy title. It is instead, we maintain, a crucial part of how we should think about the president's role in the American political system—and how we as citizens and scholars should evaluate presidential performance. Policies passed and elections won are of course hugely important, as is securing peace and prosperity. But in evaluating presidents, we must also critically assess the history that presidents tell.

Taking the historian in chief seriously does not require adopting a naive version of history as the uncovering of fixed and immutable truths. We acknowledge, as Arthur M. Schlesinger Jr. has written, that all historians are "prisoners of their own experience" and that those experiences and preconceptions shape the questions they ask. We recognize, too, that "conceptions of the past are far from stable" and that "they are perennially revised by the urgencies of the present." And of course it is true that "when new urgencies arise . . . the historian's spotlight shifts, . . . throwing into sharp relief things that were always there but that earlier historians had carelessly excised from the collective memory." Every generation writes history anew.[36]

But we can recognize that an omniscient, objective history is unattainable without succumbing to a reflexive historical relativism that treats every interpretation of the past as equally valid or plausible. Liberal democracy requires a respect for different ways of viewing the world, but it also depends on being able to distinguish between truth and falsehood, between facts and lies. The historian David Blight has suggested that the Trump administration's brazen disregard for historical facts has had the salutary effect of compelling historians "to use words like 'truth' and 'right or wrong.'" As Blight notes, "there are some things that are just not true. . . . And [as historians] we've got to point that out."[37]

Trump's ignorance and misuse of history underscore the importance of taking seriously the notion of the president as historian in chief.[38] It is a role every bit as important as the more familiar jobs of commander in chief, chief of state, chief diplomat, chief executive, chief legislator, and party chief.[39] If "history is to the nation as memory is to the individual," then it is vital that presidents be assessed for the ways they have distorted or clarified the nation's collective memory of its past. A nation denied an accurate understanding of its past will, as Schlesinger points out, "be disabled in dealing with its present and its future."[40]

Our greatest presidents have been our greatest historians in chief because they have grounded an understanding of the present in a conception of the past that enabled the nation to learn from its failings and to build on its successes. The great historians in chief have given the American people an honest reckoning of the nation's past injustices, a reckoning that in turn has enabled the country to better live up to its liberal democratic principles.[41] Admittedly, serious evidence-based history is a high bar for politicians who are only too willing to use history instrumentally, if not cynically, to justify their political objectives. But the future health of our democracy demands that scholars of the presidency and American citizens measure our presidents by how well they help us to understand and accurately assess our past. Presidents who tell us fairy stories about the past fail to fulfill their most basic duty as our nation's historian in chief.

## *Notes*

1. Reagan's words are from an interview published in *Newsweek,* Jan. 26, 1981, quoted in Steven F. Hayward, *The Age of Reagan: The Conservative Counterrevolution, 1980–1989* (New York: Three Rivers Press, 2009), 72. On Reagan's admiration for Coolidge, see Charles C. Johnson, *Why Coolidge Matters: Leadership Lessons from America's Most Underrated President* (New York: Encounter Books, 2013), 2–3. Also see Alan Brinkley, "Calvin Reagan," *New York Times,* July 4, 1981; David Greenberg, "Hot for Coolidge: Why Are Republicans So Obsessed with Silent Cal?" *Slate,* Nov. 10, 2011, http://www.slate.com/articles/life/history_lesson/2011/11/calvin_coolidge_why_are_republicans_so_obsessed_with_him_.html.

2. George C. Edwards III, *On Deaf Ears: The Limits of the Bully Pulpit* (New Haven, CT: Yale University Press, 2003).

3. Richard Fenno, "Congressman and Constituency: Richard Bolling of Missouri," http://www.lib.rochester.edu/IN/RBSCP/ATTACHMENTS/D359-Box36-Folder7-unpublished-manuscript-2014.pdf. Also see Richard F. Fenno Jr., *Home Style: House Members in Their Districts* (Boston: Little, Brown, 1978), 162. Bolling served in the U.S. House of Representatives from the late 1940s through the early 1980s.

4. Franklin D. Roosevelt, Commonwealth Club Address, Sept. 23, 1932, http://www.heritage.org/initiatives/first-principles/primary-sources/fdrs-commonwealth-club-address.

5. Fred I. Greenstein, *The Presidential Difference: Leadership Style from FDR to Clinton* (New York: Free Press, 2000), 195.

6. Marc Landy and Sidney M. Milkis, *Presidential Greatness* (Lawrence: University Press of Kansas, 2000), 4, also see 6. Milkis and Landy derive the phrase "take the people to school" from a letter Felix Frankfurter wrote to FDR on August 9, 1937, in which he urged the president to "take the country to school" about the Supreme Court's place in the American constitutional system and how the conservative justices were overstepping those bounds. See Milkis and Landy, *Presidential Greatness,* 158;

Jeff Shesol, *Supreme Power: Franklin Roosevelt vs. the Supreme Court* (New York: Norton, 2011), 334.

7. The serious point embedded in the quip is explicated at book-length in Jennifer Hochschild and Katherine Levine Einstein, *Do Facts Matter? Information and Misinformation in American Politics* (Norman: University of Oklahoma Press, 2015).

8. Abraham Lincoln, "Fragment of the Constitution and the Union," [ca. Jan. 1861], in Roy P. Basler, ed., *The Collected Works of Abraham Lincoln* (New Brunswick, NJ: Rutgers University Press, 1953), 4:169. This fragment can also be accessed at http://quod.lib.umich.edu/l/lincoln/lincoln4/1:264?rgn=div1;view=fulltext.

9. Greenstein, *Presidential Difference;* Stephen Skowronek, *The Politics Presidents Made: Leadership from John Adams to George Bush* (Cambridge, MA: Belknap Press of Harvard University Press, 1993). Also see the debate between Skowronek and Greenstein ("Resolved, presidential success and failure have more to do with political time than with a president's character and leadership qualities") in Richard J. Ellis and Michael Nelson, *Debating the Presidency: Conflicting Perspectives on the American Executive,* 4th ed. (Washington, DC: CQ Press, 2018), 113–36.

10. See Jeffrey K. Tulis, *The Rhetorical Presidency* (Princeton, NJ: Princeton University Press, 1987).

11. Stanley I. Kutler, ed., *Abuse of Power: The New Nixon Tapes* (New York: Free Press, 1997), xiv. President John Kennedy was more selective in his taping, but the motive was the same: to help ensure that history remembered him as among the great presidents. See Thurston Clarke, *JFK's Last Hundred Days: The Transformation of a Man and the Emergence of a Great President* (New York: Penguin Books, 2014), 131–32.

12. William G. Howell and Terry M. Moe, *Relic: How Our Constitution Undermines Effective Government and Why We Need a More Powerful Presidency* (New York: Basic Books, 2016), 107.

13. Michael Paul Rogin, "The King's Two Bodies: Lincoln, Wilson, Nixon, and Presidential Self-Sacrifice," in J. David Greenstone, ed., *Public Values and Private Power in American Politics* (Chicago: University of Chicago Press, 1982), 80–81, 90; William Safire, *Before the Fall: An Inside View of the Pre-Watergate White House* (New York: Doubleday, 1977), 104–5; Richard Nixon, Address to the Nation on the War in Vietnam, Nov. 3, 1969, The American Presidency Project, http://www.presidency.ucsb.edu/ws/?pid=2303.

14. Rogin, "King's Two Bodies," 73.

15. Illinois Sen. Barack Obama's Announcement Speech, Feb. 10, 2007, http://www.washingtonpost.com/wp-dyn/content/article/2007/02/10/AR2007021000879.html. Obama reflected on his "passion for Lincoln" in an "exit interview" with presidential historian Doris Kearns Goodwin in *Vanity Fair,* Sept. 21, 2016, http://www.vanityfair.com/news/2016/09/barack-obama-doris-kearns-goodwin-interview.

16. Barack Obama, Address Before a Joint Session of the Congress on the State of the Union, Jan. 12, 2016, The American Presidency Project, http://www.presidency.ucsb.edu/ws/index.php?pid=111174. Also see Katharine Q. Seelye, "The Abraham Lincoln Analogy," *New York Times,* Feb. 12, 2009.

17. Donald Trump's reference to the "late, great Lincoln" occurred in the second presidential debate between Trump and Hillary Clinton in which Clinton attempted to explain why, in a closed-door speech to banking executives that she had refused to release, she had said that you sometimes need a "public and a private position" to be effective in politics. Asked about the comment (which had been made public by WikiLeaks following the hacking of Clinton's campaign chairman John Podesta's emails), Clinton explained that it was made after she had viewed Steven Spielberg's 2012 movie *Lincoln,* which portrayed the thirteenth president strategically deploying different arguments with different audiences in order to secure passage of the Thirteenth Amendment. Trump ridiculed Clinton's answer: "Now she's blaming the lie on the late, great Abraham Lincoln." He added, "Honest Abe never lied. . . . That's the big difference between Abraham Lincoln and you." In truth, during the campaign Trump showed limited knowledge of what made Lincoln an effective president. In an interview with Bob Woodward in April 2016, Trump explained that Lincoln succeeded because "he was a man of great intelligence, but he was also a man who did something that was a very vital thing to do at that time. Ten years before or 20 years before, what he was doing would never have even been thought possible. So he did something that was a very important thing to do, and especially at that time" ("Transcript: Donald Trump Interview with Bob Woodward and Robert Costa," *Washington Post,* Apr. 2, 2016). The Clinton-Trump exchange over Lincoln is discussed in Amy B. Wang, "Being Truthful Isn't What Made Abraham Lincoln a Great Politician," *Washington Post,* Oct. 10, 2016.

18. David Von Drehle, "Republicans Admire Bill . . . McKinley, That Is," Washington Post, July 24, 1999. Bush's failure to measure up to McKinley did not dim Rove's admiration for McKinley's party-building achievements, and in 2015 he published *The Triumph of William McKinley: Why the Election of 1896 Still Matters* (New York: Simon & Schuster, 2015).

19. Daniella Diaz, "Steve Bannon: 'Darkness Is Good,'" CNN, Nov. 19, 2016, http://m.cnn.com/us/2016/11/19/steve-bannon-darkness-is-good?fullarticle=true. The Jackson analogy is critically scrutinized by Jackson biographer H. W. Brands in "Trump as the New Andrew Jackson? Not on Old Hickory's Life," *Politico Magazine,* Jan. 29, 2017, http://www.politico.com/magazine/story/2017/01/andrew-jackson-donald-trump-populist-president-history-214705. Trump's vice president, Mike Pence, in a speech at the Panama Canal, tried on a different comparison, likening Trump to Theodore Roosevelt. Both TR and Trump, according to Pence, exhorted their fellow Americans to "dare to be great," and both were builders of "boundless optimism" and monumental ambition who sought to "break new ground and break new records" and "usher in a new era of shared prosperity all across the new world" (Philip Rucker, "Pence Likens Trump to One of His Heroes: Teddy Roosevelt," *Washington Post,* Aug. 17, 2017).

20. Edward Isaac Dovere, "President Obama: Historian in Chief," Politico, July 4, 2012, http://www.politico.com/story/2012/07/obama-historian-in-chief-078110; Russell L. Riley, "Introduction: History and Bill Clinton," in Michael Nelson,

Barbara A. Perry, and Russell L. Riley, eds., *42: Inside the Presidency of Bill Clinton* (Ithaca, NY: Cornell University Press, 2016), 1–2; Peter Baker and Jonah Engel Bromwich, "With Civil War Remark, a President Who Doesn't Go by the (History) Book," *New York Times,* May 2, 2017; Jodi Kantor, "Now a Chance to Catch Up to His Epochal Vision," *New York Times,* Nov. 7, 2012; David M. Kennedy, "Dinners with the President," *Chronicle of Higher Education,* Sept. 25, 2016, http://www.chronicle.com/article/Dinners-With-the-President/237861/.

21. Jonathan Cohn, "How They Did It," *New Republic,* May 20, 2010.

22. The materials were edited and compiled into a book by his daughter Margaret Truman, and published as *Where the Buck Stops: The Personal and Private Writings of Harry S. Truman* (New York: Warner Books, 1989); the quotation is from Margaret Truman's introduction (ix).

23. Roosevelt's AHA address ("History as Literature"), delivered in Boston on Dec. 27, 1912, https://www.historians.org/about-aha-and-membership/aha-history-and-archives/presidential-addresses/theodore-roosevelt.

24. Between 1909 and 1933, three other men—Albert Bushnell Hart, William Dunning, and Charles Beard—were elected presidents of both the AHA and the APSA; since 1933 no historian or political scientist has been similarly honored.

25. Jean M. Yarbrough, *Theodore Roosevelt and the American Political Tradition* (Lawrence: University Press of Kansas, 2012), 50, 53.

26. Ibid., 133.

27. Ibid., 28.

28. Wilson remains the only president of the United States to earn a doctorate in any field, though the 1972 Democratic nominee, George McGovern, also had a Ph.D. in history.

29. Woodrow Wilson, *The New Freedom: A Call for the Emancipation of the Generous Energies of a People* (New York: Doubleday, Page, 1913), 3–4, 7, 19–20, 23–24. Also available at http://bonevac.info/303/Wilson.pdf. Wilson's disdain for "the standpatter" whose gaze remained fixed on the past is nowhere clearer than in his complaint that "[s]ome citizens of this country have never got beyond the Declaration of Independence, signed in Philadelphia, July 4th, 1776. Their bosoms swell against George III, but they have no consciousness of the war for freedom that is going on to-day." In Wilson's view, it was plain that since the Declaration of Independence "did not mention the questions of our day . . . [u]nless we can translate it into the questions of our own day, we are not worthy of it, we are not the sons of the sires who acted in response to its challenge" (48–49).

30. Ibid., 46–48; Woodrow Wilson, *Constitutional Government in the United States* (New York: Columbia University Press, 1908), 70.

31. Lawrence B. Solum, "What Is Originalism? The Evolution of Contemporary Originalist Theory," 2011, http://scholarship.law.georgetown.edu/cgi/viewcontent.cgi?article=2362&context=facpub. According to Solum, the term "originalism" was first used in 1981, and the phrase "original meaning" was first used in 1966.

32. This theme of the antifederal appropriation of the founding is fruitfully explored in Jeffrey K. Tulis and Nicole Mellow, *Legacies of Losing in American Politics* (Chicago: University of Chicago Press, 2018), esp. chapter 2.

33. FDR Press Conference, May 31, 1935, The American Presidency Project, http://www.presidency.ucsb.edu/ws/index.php?pid=15065.

34. A close reading of Wilson shows the same ambivalence about the founding's relationship to the present. In the preface to *The New Freedom,* written after his election as president, he described the New Freedom as "only the old revived and clothed in the unconquerable strength of modern America" (viii). He spoke there too of the need to "restore our politics to their full spiritual vigor again." Here was a historical narrative less of a new progressive organization of society rendering irrelevant the old political formulas than of a restoration or recovery of American values. It was about making American great again by restoring a world of small producers and fair competition.

35. When asked during the 1960 campaign in an interview with CBS's Roger Mudd "what single quality do you think will be the most important that you take into the White House," Kennedy fumbled: "Well, I think it's . . . well, I think you would probably . . . well, I think you'd probably find my sense of history. It's my sense of history. I have a sense of history" (Clarke, *JFK's Last Hundred Days,* 136).

36. Arthur M. Schlesinger Jr., "Folly's Antidote," *New York Times,* Jan. 1, 2007.

37. Philip Bump, "Historians Respond to John F. Kelly's Civil War Remarks: 'Strange,' 'Sad,' 'Wrong,'" *Washington Post,* Oct. 31, 2017.

38. Donald Trump generally appears to know so little about American history that he avoids talking about it as much as possible. In those moments when he has either invoked dimensions of American history or spoken about specific historical figures or events, he has gotten the story wrong in significant ways. On August 17, 2017, he tweeted, "Study what General Pershing of the United States did to terrorists when caught. There was no more Radical Islamic Terror for 35 years!" This was a reference to the long-discredited story that General John Pershing dipped fifty bullets in pigs' blood and then shot forty-nine prisoners to deter Muslim fighters in the Philippine-American War. Trump also made public statements during Black History Month in February 2017 that talked about Frederick Douglass, who passed away in 1894, as if he were still alive. Trump also claimed that few Americans knew that Lincoln was a Republican, a statement that perhaps applies to Trump himself but would not be true for most Americans who have a passing familiarity with American history. Finally, in a CNN interview Trump claimed that Andrew Jackson could have made a deal to end the Civil War, even though he had died in 1845. See Stephen Collinson, "Trump's Wacky History Lessons Continue," *CNN Politics,* May 1, 2017, http://www.cnn.com/2017/05/01/politics/donald-trump-andrew-jackson-us-history/index.html. Like Reagan, Trump has little regard for the actual historical record, but he lacks Reagan's ability to spin a compelling and believable yarn about the past.

39. For a conventional accounting of presidential roles, see Edward S. Corwin, *The President: Office and Powers, 1787–1957* (New York: New York University Press,

1957); Clinton Rossiter, *The American Presidency* (New York: Harcourt, Brace & World, 1960).

40. Schlesinger, "Folly's Antidote."

41. Our conclusion parallels in some ways Arthur M. Schlesinger Jr.'s conclusion based on a 1962 poll of seventy-five historians who were asked to rank the performance of each U.S. president. One of Schlesinger's chief conclusions based on the historians' responses was that "the foremost Presidents possessed a profound sense of history, a rooted dedication to time-sanctioned principles which each, in his own day and way, succeeded in reinvigorating and extending" ("Our Presidents: A Rating by 75 Historians," *New York Times Magazine,* July 29, 1962, 43).

# I Slavery, Political Parties, and the Making of a New Constitution

# 1 George Washington

## *His Own Historian*

Edward Countryman

George Washington was no intellectual. Unlike his immediate successors, he lacked a degree from Harvard, William and Mary, or Princeton. He felt both that lack and his ignorance of French, the language of the eighteenth-century "Republic of Letters," though his wide-ranging interests mark him as among that unbounded republic's citizens, and the fame of his actions places him among its contributors.[1] Perhaps, as with Lyndon Johnson surrounded by Ivy Leaguers, the absence rankled him. More likely, Washington accepted himself, valued having bright people around him, and made sure that he was in charge.

Washington did not have Benjamin Franklin's playful spontaneity, John Adams's introspection and self-doubt, Thomas Jefferson's ability to dream big and to cloak his dreams in soaring rhetoric that often obscured their problems, Alexander Hamilton's capacity for economic thought, or James Madison's insights about human fallibility in public life. Nor could he approach the eloquence of Abraham Lincoln. To borrow a bit of Lincoln's best prose, Washington did come to realize as he developed into a world figure that "the dogmas of the quiet past are inadequate to the stormy present," that "as our case is new, so we must think anew," and that "we cannot escape history," only deal with it and live within it. In one important historic way, the problem of slavery, he finished his life not far from his own time's leading edge, though it took him his whole lifetime to get there.

Borrowing again, this time from the great Cornell historian Carl Becker's 1932 American Historical Association presidential address, Washington became his own historian.[2] Becker's point was that people live in history of necessity and that they think historically too. So in suggesting that

Becker's idea helps us understand Washington's life, I am not thinking just about what Washington learned from books, although he did read widely. He certainly understood that republics continually had failed to govern themselves, lurching into civil war and tyranny. He showed as much in his Farewell Address of 1796. He shaped both his mature self and his large role in history within a framework of "Whig" or "Atlantic Republican" language and ideas that placed the American Revolution's leaders within a problem of historical understanding as a guide to action that stretched from Niccolo Machiavelli to James Madison. That problem was how republics could be founded and could thrive, and why they seemed doomed to fail.

How people lived within the flow of time was central to such thinking. Revolutionary intellectuals' early colonial predecessors, whether in Puritan New England or in Counter Reformation New Spain and New France, had understood themselves as operating at the edge of Sacred Time, with the Millennium close at hand and their own actions perhaps helping to bring it about. Washington's era understood instead that the Millennium was nowhere near; that they were living in contingent, secular time; and that their actions would have lasting worldly consequences.[3] Washington took this republican language for granted, just as someone now who speaks in terms of social class, evolution, personality, and relativity is invoking Marx, Darwin, Freud, and Einstein, without, perhaps, even knowing it.

Republicanism's secular-historical language helps explain Washington's actions as his public career took shape: his earliest involvement in Virginia protests against British taxation, his not-so-subtle seeking command of the Continental army; his resignation as its general in 1783; his importance for the Federalist movement that led to the Constitution; his presidency; and his second great departure from public office in 1796. It helps explain much of his personal life, in which he demonstrated his lifelong belief that the ways of a liberty-loving English gentleman offered the best possible model for a good human existence. It pervades one of the two great documents in which he explained himself to his people and to the world. This was the Farewell Address of 1796. But the Farewell Address was just one of his two late-life statements that linked what he had done and learned during his life to the American Republic's future. The other, only months prior to his death in 1799, was his will, in which he freed his slaves and set forth the idea of a national university. The Farewell Address is a statement about living in history as the thinkers of his time understood that project. The will drew on the course of his own development during a transformative, revolutionary time. It presented a statement about living in the future in a way that drew upon Washington's personal life, rather than upon what the European thinkers had taught.

Looking backward, we can be dazzled by the glittering prose of Washington's Virginia contemporaries Thomas Jefferson, James Madison, George Mason, Patrick Henry, and Richard Henry Lee. But, as with most people, including elite eighteenth-century Virginians, Washington's inner life of thought and attitude displayed itself in what he did, as much in what he had to say.[4] His flat day-to-day journal is nothing like the two great self-revealing eighteenth-century Virginia diaries by William Byrd II and by Landon Carter.[5] He read books and pamphlets but published almost nothing; he voted for resolutions but did not propose them; he listened and pondered while others debated in the House of Burgesses, the Continental Congress, at councils of war with his staff officers, in the Federal Convention of 1787, or even when Jefferson and Hamilton went at it in his cabinet. And then he would decide what to do. Only at the very end of his life did he venture onto the ground of high statements.

Washington's own books, now housed at Mount Vernon and the Boston Athenaeum, show the scope of his mental world. His shelves held very little of the antimonarchical "Whig history" that the historian H. Trevor Colbourn found in Revolutionary-era college and society libraries, in the catalogs of booksellers, and in individuals' holdings.[6] But many such writers did figure among the 500 volumes that his stepson Jacky Custis inherited from his grandfather. That collection was at Mount Vernon until Jacky left for schooling, college, and his short, unhappy adulthood.[7] Washington bought books throughout his life, including many volumes on the American Revolution. He had a few on its French counterpart, including both Edmund Burke's hostile *Reflections* and the British historian Catharine Macaulay's defense of revolutionary France. Washington had books on the era of the Columbian encounter and on American Indians, on geography and biography. He bought two studies of Frederick the Great, Edward Gibbon's *Decline and Fall of the Roman Empire,* and Adam Ferguson's *History of the Progress and Termination of the Roman Republic.* Probably realizing that he never would leave the United States, he purchased travel accounts that ranged around the globe. He also owned three copies of *Don Quixote,* including an elegant edition in Spanish given to him by the Spanish minister to the

United States, as well as the Earl of Chesterfield's letters to his son, Henry Fielding's *Tom Jones,* and volumes by Jonathan Swift, Tobias Smollett, and now-obscure American novelists and poets. He bought books on scientific agriculture and on general science. He acquired a small collection on slavery, including pamphlets that he read with interest and had bound together, and others that he never opened, leaving their pages uncut.[8]

In his late-life fame, Washington welcomed historians to Mount Vernon. They included Catharine Macaulay, who had defended the American movement in 1775 and whose monumental history of England figured strongly in shaping Whiggish historical imagination.[9] One can only wonder what they discussed. He opened the house to writers who wanted to use his enormous Revolutionary archive. But he declined invitations to write the Revolution's history. He could compose vivid prose, but he was no latter-day Julius Caesar telling the story of the Gallic Wars in classic Latin. Nor did he prefigure Ulysses S. Grant, whose autobiography is one of the great narratives by any man of arms. Instead, until nearly the end of his life, Washington expressed his historical awareness in his possessions and his actions. These demonstrate his ever-growing sense that he was living within a developing and distinctively American context, and that his own actions would change his time's course. Had Washington written incessantly, we could trace the development of his thoughts in his words. Instead, we have to assemble discrete deeds and objects, asking whether they display a developing pattern. But Thomas Jefferson did much the same when he built the Declaration of Independence around the historically based assertion that a set of separate "facts" fitted together into evidence of malign intent and conspiracy that justified deposing King George III.

First, consider Mount Vernon. The house is a statement, displaying its owner's sense of how English country gentlemen lived. But built as it is of rusticated wood rather than stone or brick, Mount Vernon imitates rather than replicates an English gentleman's manor house. This is not just a matter of building materials. The whole estate represented wealth accrued from the unpaid labor of slaves, not from rent paid by free tenant farmers, and accrued as well from Washington's lifelong speculation in land that Native people had every right to believe was theirs. Its seeming Englishness is just a veneer, as deceptive as the imitation blocks of stone beveled into its exterior planks and coated with heavy sandy paint to complete the illusion. It is a colonial American wooden building set within a colonial American social landscape, as Washington came to realize.

That may connect with two major points in his own development. The first was abandoning the distinctively Virginia crop of tobacco in favor of the characteristically English and northern-colonial crop of wheat, early in the 1760s. The second was attempting in 1797 to bring in English tenant farmers who would work the estate and pay him rent.[10] Getting out of tobacco was a practical gesture, because Mount Vernon's soil could not produce a good crop. But it meant abandoning one of the prime signifiers of a man's worth in Virginia's all-defining tobacco culture. Bringing in English tenants would have meant freeing himself from the institution of slavery. Having that idea was a penultimate step on his long trudge to finally realizing that freeing his slaves was better. The house and the surrounding estate present a record of his historical thinking.[11]

Turn to his portraits. Taken one by one, they show the issues and situations that defined his life: overcoming supposed colonial inferiority and genuine Virginia provincialism, emerging to military heroism and world fame, creating the American Republic, and slavery's emergence as a public problem. Artists created those portraits, most notably Charles Willson Peale, John Trumbull, Edward Savage, and Gilbert Stuart. But with one exception among the canvasses that I have in mind, Washington either commissioned the paintings or responded to requests that he pose, which meant that he had the ultimate say over how the artist represented him to the world. After fame came to him, engravers copied the originals and invented images of their own, turning the living man into an icon but also presenting capsule versions of his story, which came to stand for his people's history.[12] Washington could not control the engravers and copiers, but it is safe to assume that he did approve how Peale, Savage, and Stuart crafted his image. He would have approved what his former aide-de-camp John Trumbull painted in London in 1780 for European viewers, if he saw it. Almost certainly he did see it in print form, since Trumbull, who had preceded Hamilton as a member of his military "family," returned to America and did another major Washington portrait sometime between 1792 and 1794.

Washington's earliest portrait, done by Peale in 1772, is charming in its naïveté.[13] It shows an untroubled man who had gone about as far as he could expect to go in Virginia provincial life and who could afford Peale's commission. In it, he might be just one more prosperous colonial, of the sort that Pennsylvanians Peale and Benjamin West, Connecticut Yankee Trumbull, and Bostonian John Singleton Copley all traveled to England to transcend so they could turn to history painting, the premier genre of their day. Peale had just returned from West's studio in London when he visited Mount Vernon, and he had to have seen West's masterwork *The Death of General Wolfe,* completed in 1770 and shown to such acclaim that it catapulted West to the pinnacle of the London art world. Central to that painting's message was that history was not just an inheritance from ancient Rome; people wearing eighteenth-century dress, rather than togas and sandals, were making important history in the Western Hemisphere, whence the aptly named West had come.[14]

Peale turned what could have been just another wealthy-colonial portrait into a subtle history painting, by posing Washington in his uniform as colonel of militia, against a vague forest background. Perhaps these were at Washington's suggestion; perhaps the idea was Peale's. Either way, they called up remembrance of how a callow, youthful, inexperienced Washington had launched the global war that culminated in both Wolfe's death and France's loss of its claim to American empire, when he blundered into a firefight near modern Pittsburgh in 1754. But though the 1772 portrait evoked Washington's martial past, which had brought him to the attention of King George II, it conveyed no public lessons-of-history of the sort that West clearly intended with *General Wolfe;* or with his toga, sword, and sandal canvasses; or with his other modern-dress history paintings. This Washington was not for public display; it would simply hang at Mount Vernon.

Peale's *George Washington after the battle of Princeton, January 3, 1777,* first done in 1779 and replicated several times, imagines him just after the Revolutionary War's darkest moment, when he had lost New York City and his army seemed on the edge of dissolution. This is a history painting in the grand eighteenth-century manner. Now Washington wears the Continental army's blue-and-buff, with the epaulettes of its commanding general on his shoulders. This time he had not blundered; fallen British standards are at his feet. He leans casually on the barrel of a cannon. His crossed legs and the way he places his hand on his hip convey relaxation and confidence. Proud of his record, he looks straight out of the frame at the viewer. Wolfe had died in triumph at Quebec, but this Washington had triumphed both at Trenton a few days earlier and at Princeton, and he was very much

Charles Willson Peale, *George Washington as First Colonel in the Virginia Regiment,* 1772, oil on canvas. This first portrait of Washington, done for display at Mount Vernon, presents him as a somewhat naive but also very successful Virginia planter. His uniform reminds viewers of the fame he won during a firefight near the Forks of the Ohio River in 1754. (University Collections of Art and History, Washington & Lee University, Lexington, Virginia; gift of George Washington Custis Lee; HIP/Art Resource, NY)

Charles Willson Peale, *George Washington after the Battle of Princeton, January 3, 1777*, 1779, oil on canvas, 234.5 × 155 cm. Peale's second Washington portrait shows its subject as a confident man of arms who realizes that he is stepping onto the stage of world fame. (Chateaux de Versailles et de Trianon; photo: Gérard Blot; © RMN-Grand Palais/Art Resource, NY)

John Trumbull, *George Washington,* 1780, oil on canvas, 36 × 28 in. (91.4 × 71.1 cm). Artist Trumbull had been Washington's aide-de-camp before he left for London to study with noted American artist Benjamin West. His portrait of the general, done for European viewers, shows Washington with his enslaved valet William Lee. The two rode together throughout the Revolutionary War. (Image copyright © The Metropolitan Museum of Art; bequest of Charles Allen Munn, 1924 [24.109.88]; image source: Art Resource, NY)

Gilbert Stuart, *George Washington* (Lansdowne Portrait), 1796, oil on canvas, 247.6 × 158.7 cm (97½ × 62 in.). Stuart's full-length Washington is a quasi-regal figure in its iconography and in how Washington posed. But Washington was on the very point of showing that he was a citizen, not a would-be-monarch, by stepping down from the presidency. (National Portrait Gallery, Smithsonian Institution; acquired as a gift to the nation through the generosity of Donald W. Reynolds Foundation, NPG.2001.12; National Portrait Gallery, Smithsonian Institution/Art Resource, NY)

alive to achieve more. This was not a painting to decorate Mount Vernon; Peale meant it to be displayed, engraved, and copied. Through the figure of Washington, it offered a new history lesson to the world, about the success of American arms and the American cause, and it presaged a different kind of future.

Turn next to the portrait that Trumbull painted in London in 1780 (which may seem remarkable, but it was the eighteenth century and his mentor West had become a friend of the king).[15] Again Washington is on foot, with his sword by his side. He holds a document. Both objects are signs of his power to give the orders. It seems much like Peale's Washington after Princeton. But Trumbull was broaching a new theme: Washington's relationship with black people and thus with slavery. To Washington's left, enslaved valet William Lee holds the reins of the general's horse, which itself signifies Washington's rank and power over both the man and the animal. The placement also partially obscures Lee. Washington is brightly lit; a cloud shadows Lee. The date is vague but the site is specific: West Point provides the background. Lee also may be the black man who appears in Edward Savage's enormous Washington family group, painted slowly over the course of Washington's two-term presidency. Most likely, however, that figure was Christopher Sheels, who belonged to the Custis estate rather than to Washington himself, both because Lee was doubly crippled by that time and because this man looks nothing like Lee as Trumbull, who had seen him daily while he was serving on Washington's staff, had portrayed him. Sheels also is at the margin of the canvas and shadowed, rather than central and fully lit.[16]

Washington stands alone in my final image of him, Gilbert Stuart's great Lansdowne Portrait of 1796.[17] He wears a sword, subtly calling up his military past, and he extends his right arm, betokening authority. A proclamation or bill lies on a table to his right for him to sign with the feather pen that is just beneath his extended hand. Behind him are an ornate chair reminiscent of a throne, two columns, and a red curtain pulled back to reveal the view through an open window. This view is not over the woods of Washington's early fame, or over wartime West Point, or over the Potomac as in Savage's family group. Instead, Washington's extended arm underscores and emphasizes a view of the westward-stretching republic. Both the iconography and Washington's identity offer the clear implication that the view behind him presents the Republic's future.

Despite the sword, Stuart's Washington wears civilian clothing. Even during his presidency, the living Washington still knew the value of his uniform. Savage painted him wearing it, and as the historian T. H. Breen shows, he donned it and mounted his white charger each time he entered a town during his national tours of 1791 and 1792. This was history-as-theater, and he had been the star. He was conjuring up shared memories of the "glorious cause" that he had led and which linked his generalship to the office that he now held.[18] But his black suit and sword in the Lansdowne Portrait are the costume of a gentleman, not a uniform. The war was long over, and this is the sort of thing he wore to address Congress or at his notoriously stiff levees. Stuart presents him as a statesman, not a general, and as the president, not the hero.

Nonetheless, the Lansdowne image reaches beyond dignity to present Washington as nearly regal. Stuart's Washington does not need elaborate raiment to establish who he is in the world. In fact, the mature George III did much the same, presenting himself to portraitists as the First Gentleman of England rather than in his gaudy monarchical regalia, though often, like Washington and like modern British royal figures, in uniform.[19] How regal, then, was George I of America? How much had American history actually left monarchy behind?

Accusations of quasi-monarchy arose in the intensely partisan press of Washington's second term,[20] and if there is truth to them, one possible model existed. This was Viscount Henry St. John Bolingbroke's *Idea of a Patriot King,* first published in London in 1738 and available in an American imprint from Benjamin Franklin's Philadelphia printing house as early as 1749. Bolingbroke's idealized prince, who is no tyrant but rather the protector of his people's liberties, offers a plausible model for Washington's self-presentation, both in the flesh and in the great character-portraying portraits. The historians Stanley Elkins and Eric McKitrick suggest that the fit was deliberate.[21] Bolingbroke's description of what a British king ought to be and to do also fits with Jefferson's agonized, last-ditch, defiant advice to King George in 1774 on the king's duty to respect and protect "the rights of British America."[22] It fits with Alexander Hamilton's six-hour speech at the Constitutional Convention, arguing the need for a lifetime monarchy and senate. It fits with John Adams's clumsy attempt in 1789 to create titles for the new federal offices—"His Highness, the President of the United States and Protector of their Liberties"—and even with Richard Nixon's brief attempt to put Ruritanian uniforms on the White House guards. More dangerous to the Republic, it fits with our own time's idea of a so-called unitary presidency whose occupant supposedly is totally above the law.[23]

Most recently, the political scientist Eric Nelson has argued that rather than rejecting kingly power, the Revolution created "[a] New Monarchy in America," in the form of the presidency.[24] Would Washington have agreed? Despite all these points, I think not. Bolingbroke does not appear among the books in his surviving library. He contributed to the cost of publishing Jefferson's piece of 1774, and some of Jefferson's argument appears in the Fairfax County Resolves, which he apparently cowrote with George Mason. But the Resolves contained no reference to Jefferson's call on George III to be the good king many of his American subjects still thought they needed.[25] Washington heard Hamilton's oration, and the two very probably discussed it. His demeanor was remote and dignified, the more so as he rose to high office; this was not a person to share a beer. But he rejected all of monarchy's possible justifications: that kings were ordained by God or given legitimacy by history, that somebody who had conquered power would hold on to it, and that a monarch was born to reign and to rule for life. George III could not fathom such an attitude, exclaiming when he learned (from Benjamin West, who frequented the king's table) that Washington had resigned the command of the Continental army that the action made Washington "the greatest man in the world."[26] Washington wanted neither a crown for himself nor a monarchy for his republic. The English romantic poet Lord Byron got it right in his "Ode to Napoleon Buonaparte" (1814, set to music by Arnold Schoenberg in 1942). In eighteen acid-etched verses, Byron contrasts the fallen emperor's betrayal of the ideals of revolutionary France with "the first, the last, the best, the Cincinnatus of the west [who] bequeathed the name of Washington. To make man blush there was but one." This was the historical image that Washington had crafted and which he had offered as a model to the future.[27]

I am suggesting that Washington indeed developed a strong historical consciousness. He drew it from what he read and what his peers discussed, but much more from realizing that fortune had assigned him the premier role in great historical events. What he came to think would have astonished his fawning, youthful self, hungry for British recognition, or his midlife provincial self, satisfied enough with how things were if only the distant ministry would cease its foolishness about parliamentary taxation. How he grew through these to what he had become by the end of his life explains the two documents where he did show himself to be his own historian, the Farewell Address and his will.

The Farewell Address is public, addressed in the first-person singular to a collective "you," as its author's life approaches its conclusion. Admittedly, Madison and then Hamilton presented drafts at Washington 's request, but his own language is in it. All of it was Washington's document, issued in his name. He would not have published what did not express his mind.[28] He was nobody's marionette. The first part of the will also is a public document. Being who he was and doing what he was doing, he knew that the will was likely to circulate just as widely as the Farewell Address. Both documents are valedictions. Each sums up one dimension of what he had learned as he lived through his time within American history, and of what ought to be done for the sake of the Republic's future. They make more sense taken together, completing and declaring his assessment of his life, himself, and his republic, than if we read them separately.

First, take the Farewell Address. Its language is pure Atlantic republicanism tempered by his experience of eight years in the presidency: "baneful effects of the spirit of party . . . cherish public credit . . . the insidious wiles of foreign influence . . . vicissitudes of fortune . . . overgrown military establishments which, under any form of government, are inauspicious to liberty . . . every reflecting and virtuous mind." Washington did not have to cite the great writers of the Republican canon. He could take them for granted. He was offering a review lesson that he drew from what Whig historians had taught his whole reading generation; he also was offering a practicum.

Whether in Madison's draft for a possible retirement in 1792 or in Hamilton's later version, or in words that were his own, Washington's concern about political partisanship drew on the history through which he was living, and which he knew he was making. He had taken up the presidency expecting that the best and the brightest of his time would bring their minds together for the sake of a public good upon which all could agree. By 1792, it was clear that his two chief cabinet secretaries, Jefferson and Hamilton, barely could agree that the sun rises at dawn. When Washington ended his public life four years later the political nation was riven with mutual suspicion, intense anger, and public vituperation that reached Washington himself. Here, he believed, was a historical lesson that the Republic needed to learn: partisanship could destroy what the Revolution had wrought.

In fact, the Republic's subsequent development demonstrates that on this count he was wide of the mark. As Elvin T. Lim shows in chapter 3 of this collection, Martin Van Buren, not Washington or even Madison, came to understand that the realities of American public life required unashamed partisanship and political organization if the Republic's political institutions were to operate. The constitutional crises of 1800 and 1824, when the Electoral College deadlocked and the presidential election went to the House of Representatives, offered clear evidence by Van Buren's time.

Republicanism in its distinctively American form, as the Revolution had shaped European ideas into American reality, was central. The Revolution had wrought a great republic, created in a time of weakness and out of the wreckage of an empire, and now possessed of power. In words that were his own whoever first penned them:

> The unity of government which constitutes you one people is . . . now dear to you. It is . . . a main pillar in the edifice of your real independence, the support of your tranquility at home, your peace abroad; of your safety; of your prosperity; of that very liberty which you so highly prize. But as it is easy to foresee that, from different causes and from different quarters, much pains will be taken, many artifices employed to weaken in your minds the conviction of this truth; as this is the point in your political fortress against which the batteries of internal and external enemies will be most constantly and actively (though often covertly and insidiously) directed, it is of infinite moment that you should properly estimate the immense value of your national union to your collective and individual happiness; that you should cherish a cordial, habitual, and immovable attachment to it; accustoming yourselves to think and speak of it as of the palladium of your political safety and prosperity; watching for its preservation with jealous anxiety; discountenancing whatever may suggest even a suspicion that it can in any event be abandoned; and indignantly frowning upon the first dawning of every attempt to alienate any portion of our country from the rest, or to enfeeble the sacred ties which now link together the various parts.

Here was one great lesson, drawn not just from the history he had read but from the history he had lived. What his people had done, they had done together: "the independence and liberty you possess are the work of joint counsels, and joint efforts of common dangers, sufferings, and successes." North, South, East, and West differed greatly, but they shared a common interest, and they would reap common benefit from working together. What his epoch had achieved during its encounter with historical time was fragile; what his people had wrought needed now to be preserved. Foreign alliances, divided loyalties, religious rivalries, "the alternate domination of one faction over another, sharpened by the spirit of revenge, natural to party dissension," all posed dangers. Worse might lie in store: "The disorders and miseries which result gradually incline the minds of men to seek security and repose in the absolute power of an individual; and sooner or later the chief of some prevailing faction, more able or more fortunate than his competitors, turns this disposition to the purposes of his own elevation, on the ruins of public liberty."

History had taught Washington that the shared strength, not the weakness, of the nation was the safeguard of its peoples' liberty. In a line of thought that runs from Washington through Lincoln, both Roosevelts, Dwight Eisenhower, and Lyndon Johnson to Barack Obama, the power created in the Constitution existed to be used, not to be feared. He remained an elitist and he believed in authority. He disparaged "self-created societies," and he was tone-deaf to the raucous, boisterous sounds of American public liberty. But he was invoking the ancient recognition of any republic's fragility, warning Americans that they were not exempt from the fate that had befallen ancient Athens and Rome, renaissance Florence, and Cromwellian England. In his historical judgment, his people needed to deploy rather than fear what the framers of the Constitution had wrought. Starting with Jefferson, many others have disagreed, in an argument that still goes on.

Now turn to the will. What Washington said as he bade farewell to his public career was heartfelt, but it also was conventional in terms of Atlantic Republican historical thinking. By the time he gave the address, another problem, the distinctively American one of slavery in the land of the supposedly free, was on his mind. Slavery had been universal in his colonial America. Now it was becoming his South's "peculiar institution," as he was fully aware. That may explain why he raised the problem of sectionalism in the Farewell Address. When the Revolution had begun decades earlier, slavery existed everywhere that colonizers of any sort had settled, and most white people, including the leaders, just did not see it as a problem. About the only exception among the Revolution's early leaders, Boston lawyer James Otis raised the issue, in his 1764 pamphlet "The Rights of the British Colonies Asserted and Proved."[29] English literary figure Samuel Johnson, who despised the Revolution, put it much more forcefully than Otis when he asked a dozen years later "how is it that we hear the loudest *yelps* for liberty among the drivers of negroes."[30] Frederick Douglass, who admired the Revolution and its leaders, famously posed the same problem on July 5, 1852: "what to the slave is the Fourth of July?"[31]

By the time of the Farewell Address Washington was coming to understand that the slavery issue, rather than classical republicanism's fear of overweening power turning into tyranny and dominating a corrupted citizenry, formed the Republic's greatest threat. The revolutionary era had opened the public, political problem of slavery, but the problem had not become part of the national agenda, as happened in all of the hemisphere's other emerging new nations and in its remaining empires, except for imperial Brazil and Spanish Cuba and Puerto Rico. In this dimension, the American Revolution stalled, and the stall was to prove nearly fatal to the whole project. Washington saw the danger.

Biographer James Thomas Flexner quotes Washington as foreseeing a national split on slavery, in which case he, Washington, would have to "move and be of the northern" part.[32] Washington might or might not have said it; the quote is not documented.[33] But the will was not ambiguous; it was emphatic, detailed, and direct. Washington had to have known that by freeing his slaves he was tying the slavery issue to his life and experiences ("I George Washington of Mount Vernon—a citizen of the United States, and lately Pr[es]ident of the same") and to his people's great achievement ("You have in a common cause fought and triumphed together; the independence and liberty you possess are the work of joint counsels, and joint efforts of common dangers, sufferings, and successes"). What to do about slavery was the final lesson drawn from history that he could offer to the people whom he had led through so much.

The problem had been gnawing at his mind for years, perhaps decades. Revolutionary soldiers (John Laurens, Thaddeus Kosciusko, the Marquis de Lafayette), his postwar associates (Tobias Lear, David Humphreys), and admirers both domestic and foreign all had urged him to act on slavery.

Hamilton had joined the New York Manumission Society. Washington had tried and failed to free himself from the institution of slavery by bringing tenant farmers to Mount Vernon. He had presided over the Federal Convention, which came closest to rupture when the slavery question emerged. The historian Henry Wiencek sees the problem as beginning to open for Washington as early as 1769, when he took part on behalf of his stepchildren in the settlement a bankrupt estate. His duty included raffling off the slaves in separate lots, which meant breaking up families for the sake of his own family's benefit. Wiencek calls it a "moral nadir."[34]

Without Washington realizing it, the issue may have begun to confront him as early as 1758, when Joseph Addison's play *Cato* was performed at Belvoir, home of Washington's patron family, the Fairfaxes. As much as any toga-and-sandal painting or as West's *Death of General Wolfe,* the play presents a history lesson. Set when Julius Caesar was in the final stages of subverting the Roman Republic, the title character is a hero of stern republican virtue who disembowels himself rather than submit to the tyrant. *Cato* inspired both Patrick Henry ("Give me liberty or give me death") and Nathan Hale ("I only regret that I have but one life to lose for my country"). But there is another dimension to the drama.

At the 1758 staging the mistress of Belvoir, Sally Fairfax, took the role of Marcia, Cato's daughter. Young Colonel Washington was thoroughly besotted with her. Marcia is beloved and courted by Juba, a prince of Numibia. After the performance, Washington flirted with her about "playing a part in *Cato* with the company you mention and myself doubly happy in being Juba to such a Marcia as you must make."[35]

Many students of Washington's life have noted the importance of Addison's play for his thinking and self-modeling, citing the sternness of the title character in the face of Caesar's imminent takeover.[36] Washington came to love the theater, and he owned a copy of the play. He had it staged at Valley Forge. Martha Washington, who was with him, probably was blissfully ignorant of what Sally Fairfax, playing Marcia, had meant to her husband two decades earlier. Though Fairfax had gone permanently to England with her Loyalist husband, the general probably recalled it and perhaps saw new meaning within it. Such suspicions must remain a matter of speculation; no commentary or production notes seem to survive. Without question, Washington wanted to encourage his soldiers, including black ones, and perhaps himself as well, with the play's message of stern patriotism. But now its context was entirely different from the staging at Belvoir.

Only three literary scholars—Lisa Freeman, Jason Shaffer, and Randall Fuller—have paid serious attention to the love-story subplot, which actually fills much of the stage time.[37] Freeman posits that the love theme sets up a feminized counterpoint to the title character's stern masculine virtue, which would explain why a version appeared from which the subplot was excised. Shaffer and Fuller do note that Juba is a prince of Numibia, but they miss the character's full import, which is that he is clearly and repeatedly identified as African (act 1, scene 1, lines 89–91; scene 3, lines 43–44; scene 4, lines 18–27). He is "tawny," not black, but he and his fellows definitely are not white (act 1, scene 4, line 19). Juba is as capable of civic virtue as Cato himself, and his actions count in the play's development. If he were to abandon Cato, it would give Caesar control of Africa (act 1, scene 3, lines 28–31), and Caesar's agents tempt him with the thought that he could have Marcia should he do so. Juba's late father's power had reached deep into the continent, whence "black ambassadors" had come "loaden with gifts." If those diplomats only knew Cato, Juba speculates, Africa's "remotest kings would pour multitudes about him; their swarthy hosts would darken all our plains, doubling the native horror of the war, and making death more grim" (act 2, scene 4, lines 23–39). Cato fully approves Juba's courtship of Marcia, and the two are united at the end.

Only teacher Jon Gubera, a participant in a summer seminar whose essay found its way onto the Internet, seems to have spotted the subplot's full import.[38] Here, performed openly on makeshift Virginia and Pennsylvania stages, are any slaveholder's twin nightmares: a determined army of black men and an open, legitimate sexual union of masculine Africa and feminine Europe. Unlike both the historical and the theatrical unions of Cleopatra with Caesar and Mark Antony, Juba and Marcia embody civic virtue. He is a prince, and on the Augustan stage being a prince could overcome every other social quality. But to repeat and to emphasize, he is African; she is European; his royal father's connections reach from Numibia on the Mediterranean to far south of the Sahara; black African soldiers conceivably could come to Cato's rescue.

Did Washington see this dimension in 1758? Most likely not. He was a young man in love, and not perceiving something that has been in plain sight all along is common enough, even without love's ability to blind the lover to everything else. The historians who have cited Addison's Cato in relation to Washington's self-image present no exception. But when Washington had the play staged at Valley Forge, it may have been another matter. The youthful Washington had been smitten with Sally Fairfax, and he had cast himself as her African lover; the mature Washington definitely had slavery on his mind.

How he responded early in 1776 to the ode that black Bostonian, former slave, and internationally famous poet Phillis Wheatley penned in his honor, addressing her as "Miss Phillis" and inviting her to visit camp in Cambridge, is one sign; such politeness to any black person from any Virginia master seems almost unthinkable. His recognition before the end of 1775 that he needed black soldiers, after first trying to drive them out of the Continental army, is another sign. So were the parts that black Rhode Islanders played in rescuing Washington's army from entrapment at Brooklyn in 1776 and in the siege of Lord Cornwallis at Yorktown five years later, where he gave them pride of place in the final assault. His joining the financial backers of Mother Bethel African Methodist Episcopal Church in Philadelphia during his presidency is still another.

He was anything but perfect on the matter. When the British army was evacuating New York City, triumphant General Washington had pressed the final British commander in chief, Sir Guy Carleton, to send back the thousands of black men and women who had found their freedom under the Union Jack, as Article VII of the Treaty of Peace required. To his great credit, Carleton refused. Instead, they departed on British transports.[39] As president, Washington carefully rotated slaves from Philadelphia back to Mount Vernon so they could not take advantage of Pennsylvania's act of 1780 for beginning slavery's destruction, keeping them ignorant of his reason for doing so, which was that the statute mandated that if they remained within the Commonwealth for longer than six months they would gain freedom. But the problem of slavery was on his mind.

Return for a moment to the John Trumbull portrait of 1780 and the Edward Savage Washington family group from the presidential years, and specifically to the inclusion of black men in both canvasses. Taken just as images, both figures are ambiguous. Their being in the frames at all could be mere convention. The art historians David Dabydeen and Hugh Honour show that eighteenth-century English imagery abounds with black men and women. In William Hogarth's London street scenes, they are part of a raucous crowd. When they appear in images of the Great and the Good, their iconography is the same as in the Trumbull and Savage paintings, to the side of the main figure and clearly subordinate.[40] Even Dido Elizabeth Belle Murray, Anglo–West Indian niece and ward of Lord Chief Justice Mansfield, whose 1771 decision in *Somersett v. Steuart* earns him a place in antislavery history, is placed behind Mansfield's other niece and her fellow ward, Lady Elizabeth Murray, in their double portrait, probably done in 1779.[41] Trumbull and Savage might merely have been following English convention in their placing of Lee and Sheels with Washington.

But in the context of Washington's own development, the trans-Mediterranean and interracial love plot in Addison's play, the possible self-disgust at being involved in breaking slave families for the sake of a lottery, the response to Phillis Wheatley, and his change of mind about black soldiers, the portraits are at least suggestive. Among the slaveholding early presidents (which means all of them except John Adams), Washington alone appears in paintings from his own time that also show slaves. There are no painted images at all of James or Sally Hemings or of her children with Jefferson, or of any other Monticello slaves. No slaves appear in portraits of James Madison and James Monroe. Unlike Lee, Sheels, and the Hemingses of Monticello, we do not even know such presidential slaves' names.

Is it, then, merely happenstance that among all the statesmen-slaveholders of the revolutionary era, Washington alone took a direct step against slavery, by freeing his own slaves in his will? He did not write about the matter; he did not make speeches. He did not pat his own back, as did Pennsylvania's state legislators in 1780, when they started slavery's destruction in their state by a method so slow that it was not complete until 1845. As was his way, he waited, listened, considered, and finally acted. Nonetheless, he was trying to set an agenda for the Republic itself to follow. It was the very last public action of the intensely public life that he had lived. He had only five months and five days remaining to him. It completed his valediction. Friends, well-wishers, and advisers had been urging him for years to take a public step on slavery. Now, finally, he took it, and because he was George Washington, he knew that his action was historic.

The slavery directive fits with what followed immediately in the will, in the form of five separate bequests to foster education for the sake of inculcating civic virtue. He had raised the question of public virtue in the Farewell

Address, linking it vaguely to "religion and morality." Now he was more specific, addressing not a loose sense that dissipation was bad, but rather his fears about dissolution, particularly in what he had to say about:

> the establishment of a UNIVERSITY in a central part of the United States, to which the youth of fortune and talents from all parts thereof might be sent for the completion of their Education in all the branches of polite literature; in arts and Sciences, in acquiring knowledge in the principles of Politics & good Government; and (as a matter of infinite Importance in my judgment) by associating with each other, and forming friendships in Juvenile years, be enabled to free themselves in a proper degree from those local prejudices & habitual jealousies which have just been mentioned; and which, when carried to excess, are never failing sources of disquietude to the Public mind, and pregnant of mischievous consequences to this Country.

In this national university a young man from anywhere within the Republic would find a peacetime equivalent to what Washington had found among his fellow officers of the Continental army. Southerners like himself would mingle with northerners, easterners with westerners, and the Republic would benefit. All would be sons of the elite. Higher education for women waited decades into the future. Large-scale, low-cost public higher education would not come until the Lincoln administration's Morrill Land Grant Act in 1862 made it possible. Ending slavery within the Republic took just as long. Both actions required the party of Lincoln's determination to use rather than fear federal power in order to bring them about. But clearly the bequest represented Washington's desire that the Republic as a whole should complete what he proposed to inaugurate.[42]

The fate of the Republic as an entity in space and time, ending slavery within it, continuing via the projected university with the formation of a national elite that had begun in the revolutionary officer corps—all these were on Washington's mind as he prepared to step out of life and into eternity. He knew full well whatever he did became part of history, and he wanted his indubitably historic example to influence his republic's and his people's future. He had been born into a world that a person would inherit, accept, and pass on, no matter what that person's supposedly static "sort" or "station in life." He was on the point of departing from a world that had become open to profound change. He had led two great demonstrations that the past did not have to control the future. One was destroying an empire. The other was creating a republic.

Could slavery's cycle of timeless endurance also be broken? Freeing his own slaves, which post-independence Virginia law allowed (but which had not been possible in the colonial order), meant the former slaves entering contingent historical time as actors, something that Washington had been all his life. He knew that black Americans were doing so already, without his say-so, including both Mount Vernon slave Ona Judge, who, like Christopher Sheels, belonged to the Custis estate and whom he could not have freed but who freed herself and defied his efforts to bring her back, and his cook Hercules, whom he could have freed but who did not wait and freed himself as well.[43]

By the end of his life, Washington had learned that historical cycles could be broken. Britain's Parliament could not carry through on its boast in 1766 that it had power to legislate for its colonies "in all cases whatsoever." British arms had not prevailed in the War of Independence. The separate states had not gone their own ways or formed smaller regional confederacies. He himself had walked away from power, twice. These were the lessons he had learned from his own history, and he wanted to see them applied beyond his own life. The Farewell Address, full of foreboding that the whole republican project could fail, and the freeing of his own slaves set, he hoped, an example. So did a national university as a publicly sponsored place where young men could learn to think in national terms. All of these fit together.

Without doubt, George Washington drew on lessons he had learned from books, though he owned and read fewer than his immediate successors in the presidency. Without doubt, he drew on conversations with people who read more than he. His actions in stepping down from command and then from the presidency, his self-presentation in his life and in his portraits, his understanding that he had to make it all up as he went along, and his two deeply personal late-life statements all are in accord with the civic humanism in which he and his fellows were steeped. But he grew on the slavery question, onto ground that European civic humanism and Whig history did not reach. He made himself his own historian, interpreting both the past that he had learned about and the past that he had made with the hope of guiding the future. Probably more clearly than any of his successors until Lincoln, he understood what it meant to live in history, to try to shape it, and to be ready for its endless capacity to surprise.

## *Notes*

I owe thanks to my colleagues Tom Knock and Jeff Engel for inviting me to take part in the Historians in Chief Conference at Southern Methodist University in October 2016; to my fellow participants, particularly David Waldstreicher, Jonathan Earle, and James Kloppenberg; to volume editors Seth Cotlar and Richard Ellis for suggestions about my manuscript; to the anonymous readers for the University of Virginia Press; to Beth Newman and Rhonda Blair for Addison references and suggestions; and to my introductory-level undergraduate student Holden Maney for raising a point in a term paper that enriched what I had to say.

1. See Kevin J. Hayes, *The Books in George Washington's Life* (New York: Oxford University Press, 2017). For the idea of the republic of letters, see Martin J. S. Rudwick, *Bursting the Limits of Time: The Reconstruction of Geohistory in the Age of Revolution* (Chicago: University of Chicago Press, 2005); Martin J. S. Rudwick, *Worlds Before Adam: The Reconstruction of Geohistory in the Age of Reform* (Chicago: University of Chicago Press, 2008). For its practice in the young American Republic, see James Morton Smith, ed., *The Republic of Letters: The Correspondence Between Thomas Jefferson and James Madison, 1776–1826,* 3 vols. (New York: W. W. Norton, 1995).

2. Abraham Lincoln Second Annual Message, Dec. 1, 1862, http://www.presidency.ucsb.edu/ws/?pid=29503; Carl Becker, "Everyman His Own Historian," *American Historical Review* 37, no. 2 (Jan. 1932): 221–36.

3. This republican way of thinking is explored in Clinton Rossiter, *Seedtime of the Republic: The Origin of the American Tradition of Political Liberty* (New York: Harcourt, Brace, 1953); Caroline Robbins, *The Eighteenth-Century Commonwealthman: Studies in the Transmission, Development, and Circumstance of English Liberal Thought from the Restoration of Charles II until the War with the Thirteen Colonies* (Cambridge, MA: Harvard University Press, 1959); J. R. Pole, *Political Representation in England and the Origins of the American Republic* (New York: St. Martin's Press, 1966); H. Trevor Colbourn, *The Lamp of Experience: Whig History and the Intellectual Origins of the American Revolution* (Chapel Hill: University of North Carolina Press, 1965); Bernard Bailyn, *The Ideological Origins of the American Revolution* (Cambridge, MA: Harvard University Press, 1967); Gordon S. Wood, *The Creation of the American Republic, 1776–1787* (Chapel Hill: University of North Carolina Press, 1969); Joyce Oldham Appleby, *Economic Thought and Ideology in Seventeenth-Century England* (Princeton, NJ: Princeton University Press, 1978); Joyce Oldham Appleby, *Liberalism and Republicanism in the Historical Imagination* (Cambridge, MA: Harvard University Press, 1992); J. G. A. Pocock, *The Machiavellian Moment: Florentine Political Thought and the Atlantic Republican Tradition* (Princeton, NJ: Princeton University Press, 1975); J. G. A. Pocock, *Virtue, Commerce, and History: Essays on Political Thought and History, Chiefly in the Eighteenth Century* (Cambridge: Cambridge University Press, 1985); J. G. A. Pocock, *Barbarism and Religion, vol. 4, Barbarians, Savages, and Empires* (Cambridge: Cambridge University Press, 2005).

4. See Rhys Isaac, "A Discourse on the Method: Action, Structure, and Meaning," in *The Transformation of Virginia, 1740–1790* (Chapel Hill: University of North Carolina Press, 1982), 323–58.

5. Kenneth A. Lockridge, *The Diary and Life of William Byrd II of Virginia, 1674–1744* (Chapel Hill: University of North Carolina Press, 1987); Rhys Isaac, *Landon Carter's Uneasy Kingdom: Revolution and Rebellion on a Virginia Plantation* (New York: Oxford University Press, 2004).

6. Colbourn, *Lamp of Experience;* Appleton P. C. Griffin, *A Catalogue of the Washington Collection in the Boston Athenaeum* (Cambridge, MA: University Press, J. Wilson and Son, 1897); http://www.librarything.com/catalog/GeorgeWashington.

7. Hayes, *Books in Washington's Life,* chapter 8.

8. François Furstenberg, "Atlantic Slavery, Atlantic Freedom: George Washington, Slavery, and Transatlantic Abolitionist Networks," *William and Mary Quarterly* 68 (2011): 247–86.

9. Catherine Macaulay, "An address to the people of England, Ireland, and Scotland, on the present important crisis of affairs" (New York: John Holt, 1775); Catherine Macaulay, *The History of England from the Revolution to the Present Time, in a Series of Letters to the Reverend Doctor Wilson* (Dublin: printed for John Exshaw, and William Hallhead, 1779); Catherine Macaulay, "Observations on the Reflections of the Right Hon. Edmund Burke, on the revolution in France: in a letter to the Right Hon. the Earl of Stanhope" (repr., Boston: I. Thomas and T. Andrews, 1791); see also Robbins, *Eighteenth-Century Commonwealthman;* Colbourn, *Lamp of Experience.*

10. See Robert E. Dalzell Jr. and Lee Baldwin Dalzell, *George Washington's Mount Vernon: At Home in Revolutionary America* (New York: Oxford University Press, 1998).

11. T. H. Breen, *Tobacco Culture: The Mentality of the Great Tidewater Planters on the Eve of Revolution* (Princeton, NJ: Princeton University Press, 2001); Henry Wiencek, *An Imperfect God: George Washington, His Slaves, and the Creation of America* (New York: Farrar Straus Giroux, 2003); Edward Countryman, "Getting to Know George Washington," *Southwest Review* 94 (2009): 132–46.

12. Marcus Cunliffe, *George Washington: Man and Monument* (Boston: Little, Brown, 1958); Mark Edward Thistlethwaite, *The Image of George Washington: Studies in Mid-Nineteenth-Century American History Painting* (New York: Garland, 1979); Barry Schwartz, *George Washington: The Making of an American Symbol* (New York: Free Press, 1987); Wendy C. Wick, *George Washington: An American Icon, the Eighteenth-Century Graphic Portraits* (Washington, DC: Smithsonian Institution, 1982).

13. For both Peale images, see http://www.mountvernon.org/george-washington/artwork/life-portraits-of-george-washington/.

14. See Emily Ballew Neff and Caitlyn H. Weber, eds., *American Adversaries: West and Copley in a Transatlantic World* (Houston: Museum of Fine Arts, 2013); Jane Kamensky, *A Revolution in Color: The World of John Singleton Copley* (New York: W. W. Norton, 2013).

15. https://www.metmuseum.org/toah/works-of-art/24.109.88/.

16. https://www.nga.gov/Collection/art-object-page.561.html.

17. http://www.georgewashington.si.edu/portrait/.

18. T. H. Breen, *George Washington's Journey: The President Forges a New Nation* (New York: Simon & Schuster, 2016).

19. Contrast Allan Ramsay's coronation portrait (https://www.npg.org.uk/collections/search/portrait/mw02455/King-George-III) with later portraits by Thomas Gainsborough (https://www.royalcollection.org.uk/collection/401406/george-iii-1738–1820), Johan Zoffany (https://www.royalcollection.org.uk/collection/400501/george-iii-1738–1820-queen-charlotte-1744–1818-and-their-six-eldest-children), and Peter Edward Stroehling (https://www.royalcollection.org.uk/collection/404865/george-iii-1738–1820).

20. Richard N. Rosenfeld, *American Aurora: The Suppressed History of Our Nation's Beginnings and the Heroic Newspaper That Tried to Report It* (New York: St. Martin's Press, 1997).

21. Stanley Elkins and Eric McKitrick, *The Age of Federalism: The Early American Republic, 1788–1800* (New York: Oxford University Press, 1993), 18.

22. Thomas Jefferson, *A Summary View of the Rights of British America* (1774), http://avalon.law.yale.edu/18th_century/jeffsumm.asp.

23. In general, on the idea of monarchy in the British colonies, see Brendan McConville, *The King's Three Faces: The Rise and Fall of Royal America, 1688–1776* (Chapel Hill: University of North Carolina Press, 2006); see also J. G. A. Pocock, "1776: The Revolution Against Parliament," in Pocock, *Virtue, Commerce, and History*, 73–88. For Jefferson, see "A Summary View of the Rights of British America," http://avalon.law.yale.edu/18th_century/jeffsumm.asp; for Adams, Elkins and McKitrick, *Age of Federalism;* for the White House guards' uniforms, https://www.bloomberg.com/view/articles/2013-08-16/richard-nixon-s-palace-guard.

24. Eric Nelson, *The Royalist Revolution: Monarchy and the American Founding* (Cambridge, MA: Harvard University Press, 2014).

25. [George Mason and George Washington] "Fairfax County Resolves," July 18, 1774, http://press-pubs.uchicago.edu/founders/documents/v1ch17s14.html.

26. Countryman, "Getting to Know George Washington."

27. http://www.bartleby.com/333/543.html; https://www.youtube.com/watch?v=5dT6LI9BiE0.

28. My thanks to one of the anonymous readers for the University of Virginia Press for pointing out that Washington's own language pervades the Farewell Address.

29. James Otis, "The Rights of the British Colonies Asserted and Proved" (Boston: Edes and Gill, 1764).

30. http://hcl.harvard.edu/libraries/houghton/exhibits/johnson/later/8_3.cfm.

31. Frederick Douglass, "What to the Slave Is the Fourth of July?" http://teachingamericanhistory.org/library/document/what-to-the-slave-is-the-fourth-of-july/.

32. Countryman, "Getting to Know George Washington," 145.

33. Flexner repeated the point in "Washington and Slavery," *New York Times,* Feb. 22, 1973, http://www.nytimes.com/1973/02/22/archives/washington-and-slavery.html?_r=0. See also http://www.historynet.com/george-washington-hero-of-the-confederacy.htm.

34. Wiencek, *Imperfect God,* 178–88.

35. Henry C. Montgomery, "Addison's Cato and George Washington," *Classical Journal* 55, no 5 (Feb. 1960): 210–12.

36. Clinton Rossiter, *The First American Revolution* (New York: Harcourt, Brace and World, 1956), 203; Bailyn, *Ideological Origins,* 44; Wood, *Creation of American Republic,* 14, 450; Wood, *Radicalism of the Revolution,* 197–98, 216–17; Jay Fliegelman, *Prodigals & Pilgrims: The American Revolution against Patriarchal Authority, 1750–1800* (Cambridge: Cambridge University Press,1982), 60, 152–53; Forrest McDonald, "Foreword" to Joseph Addison, *Cato: A Tragedy and Selected Essays* (Indianapolis, IN: Liberty Fund, 2004), vii–x. See also James Thomas Flexner, *George Washington: The Forge of Experience, 1732–1775* (Boston: Little, Brown, 1965), 199; Ron Chernow, *Washington, A Life* (New York: Penguin, 2010); John E. Ferling, *First of Men: A Life of George Washington* (Knoxville: University of Tennessee Press, 1988).

37. Lisa Freeman, "What's Love Got to Do with Addison's 'Cato'?" *Studies in English Literature 1500–1900* 59, no. 3 (Summer 1999): 463–82; Lisa Freeman, *Character's Theater: Genre and Identity on the Eighteenth-Century English Stage* (Philadelphia: University of Pennsylvania Press, 2002); Randall Fuller, "Theaters of the American Revolution: The Valley Forge 'Cato' and the Meschianza in Their Transcultural Context," *Early American Literature* 34, no. 2 (1999), 126–46. My deep thanks to Beth Newman and Rhonda Blair for suggesting these and other studies.

38. Jon Gubera, "Observations on the Influence of Joseph Addison's Play, Cato a Tragedy, on George Washington's Character," N.E.H. Summer Seminar Paper, Boston University, 2005; http://www.georgewashingtonmythsymbolandreality.org/Gubera.pdf.

39. Cassandra Pybus, *Epic Journeys of Freedom: Runaway Slaves of the American Revolution and Their Global Quest for Liberty* (Boston: Beacon Press, 2006); Simon Schama, *Rough Crossings: The Slaves, the British, and the American Revolution* (New York: Harper Collins, 2007). Amid all the entirely justified excitement about Lin-Manuel Miranda's *Hamilton,* it is worth noting another major contemporary artistic meditation on slavery in the revolutionary era. This is Canadian writer Lawrence Hill's novel *The Book of Negroes,* published in 2008 and broadcast in 2015 as a miniseries that Hill wrote. The title has raised some controversy, and it first was published in the United States as *Somebody Knows My Name.* The original *Book of Negroes* is the record that Carleton ordered to be kept of the black people whom he refused to return to their enslavement. The novel and miniseries follow a strongly realized fictional woman from her enslavement as a young girl to old age when she is working in London with British abolitionists. Significantly, the miniseries was broadcast in Canada on the Canadian Broadcasting Corporation but in the United States on BET, and even white

professional historians of the American Revolution seem, impressionistically, to be completely ignorant of it.

40. David Dabydeen, *Hogarth's Blacks: Images of Blacks in Eighteenth Century English Art* (Athens: University of Georgia Press, 1987), esp. 17–39; Hugh Honour, *The Image of the Black in Western Art,* gen. ed. Ladislas Bugner, vol. 4 (New York: W. Morrow, 1976).

41. https://www.theguardian.com/artanddesign/2014/may/27/dido-belle-enigmatic-painting-that-inspired-a-movie. The painting is held at Lord Mansfield's family home, Scone Palace, Scotland, whose website could not be accessed.

42. Compare Eric Foner, *Free Soil, Free Labor, Free Men: The Ideology of the Republican Party Before the Civil War* (New York: Oxford University Press, 1970), with James Oakes, *Freedom National: The Destruction of Slavery in the United States, 1861–1865* (New York: W. W. Norton, 2013).

43. Erica Armstrong Dunbar, *Never Caught: The Washingtons' Relentless Pursuit of Their Runaway Slave Ona Judge* (New York: 37 Ink/Atria Books, 2017).

# 2 Slavery, Voice, and Loyalty

## *John Quincy Adams as the First Revisionist*

David Waldstreicher

Like the early republic political culture out of which it developed, the institution of the presidency promoted an awareness of historical change. Electing, defending, and criticizing presidents involved intensive investigations into origins, close readings of documents, and attempts at encompassing narrative—as well as the more often remarked upon weaker historicisms such as conspiracy theories, founder worship, and calls for counterrevolutionary clean-up operations by putative outsiders. Historicizing impulses and practices may have even intensified with the seeming modernization of the party system and the presidency in Jackson's time, accompanied as that was by a renewed profusion of print. The central figures in such efforts included not only George Bancroft—the partisan politician as epic historian—but also John Quincy Adams, the very model of the scholar as statesman, whose very name sounds like a grudging revision. The first son of the first president to have a son, Adams became, in several senses, the first revisionist: the first president to have to struggle not only with his father's legacy but also—like his father—with his place in history after losing a bid for a second term.[1]

Both John and John Quincy Adams's politics exemplified the structurally time-heightening aspects of the presidency that Stephen Skowronek has so lucidly explained. With elections every four years and a change in incumbent at least every eight, the presidency and two-party system "institutionalize[d]" the cycles of republican politics. Successful mandates require a kind of electoral revolution and the attendant skeptical attitude toward the recent past. Consequently, it is difficult for presidents to "articulate"—to continue or renew—the revolutions of their predecessors. The junior Adams in particular inherited the "disjunction" stage of the national Republican ascendancy, after James Monroe's somewhat successful "articulation" of the regime.[2] It might be added that with several regimes under bridge by the 1820s, the process of getting right with the past raised the stakes for historical and constitutional argument even outside presidential successions.[3] This could be an opportunity as well as a burden. In the case of John Quincy Adams, it ultimately required a reinterpretation of the founding and a body of historical work to support that interpretation. We might especially wish to consider the interpretation—and revision—of the past offered by "the professor" derided in Jacksonian polemic at a time when Adamsian interpretations of the early republic have become respectable again.[4] His antislavery revisions, as well as his own astounding archive, inform current, and perhaps ascendant, perspectives on the early national past, and some reflection on how it came to be seems in order.

For better or worse, Adams helped develop a tragic as well as triumphalist understanding of his era, an interpretation that eventually formed a core of antislavery politics in its Lincolnian mode. He did so by transforming his loyalty to the American Revolution and its stewards, to national expansion under the National Republicans, and to the attendant sidelining of slavery, into a dissenting antislavery nationalism. His new ethos, and new voice, required a new narrative, which he haltingly constructed during the first years after his presidency.[5] We marvel now at the junior Adams's dexterity and sheer persistence, admiring his final career as an antislavery tribune in Congress as a crowning achievement. Biographers and pundits who have promoted him to honorary Founding Father status, however, have not often paused to consider the implications of his unusual political journey, or the implications of our new preference for his revisionism over the narratives and acts, including his own, that made the revisions necessary in the first place.

John Quincy Adams was predisposed to think about politics historically and to conceive of writing as part of his political practice. His father served the patriot movement in multiple capacities and devoted himself especially to the study of past republics, ancient and modern, for the lessons history offered. Some of John Adams's most famous quotes are those that sought to fix the historical significance and nature of the Revolution: on July 3, 1776, he wrote home that the day Congress declared independence "will be the most memorable Epocha, in the History of America." During a long retirement, he also obsessed about his place in the revolutionary pantheon.[6]

John Quincy's deep identification with American independence and nationhood has been traced both to witnessing the Bunker Hill battle with his mother and to serving as his father's secretary while representing the American Union abroad during and after the Revolutionary War. But he first made a name for himself in the United States by developing his father's revolutionary nationalism publicly and eloquently, in a historical argument. In a July 1787 commencement address at Harvard published in the fledgling *Columbian Magazine,* he coined the era as the "critical period, when the whole nation is groaning," and ascribed it to the failure of "national credit," the foundation of "national grandeur." Economic distress in Massachusetts could ultimately be understood as a consequence of the "erosion of the bands of union which connected us to our sister states, [which] have been shamefully relaxed by a selfish and contracted principle," namely, an unwillingness to pay taxes to retire the Revolutionary War debt. Localism was the problem, thinking bigger the solution. When Massachusetts folk abided by their agreements, the "radiant sun of our union" would not only reappear but begin again to protect "the wretched object of tyranny and persecution in every corner of the globe."[7]

The years John Quincy Adams spent abroad confirmed his nascent American exceptionalism as well as his sense that what Americans had in common trumped any relationship that might be forged with particular European nations. At a time when his father, now vice president, was being attacked as a closet monarchist, Anglophile, and old-fashioned champion of "balanced" and to some insufficiently democratic constitutions, John Quincy insisted in his first published newspaper essays that the U.S. Constitution had the virtues of both the British and new French constitutions "without the evils of both." He gained the attention of the rest of the Washington administration with carefully reasoned pseudonymously published defenses of neutrality as the only sure guide against partisanship and "foreign usurpation," a folly of past republics. Earlier than most, and more consistently, he defined both British and French influence in America as "the shameful fetters of a foreign bondage" and the French Revolution as a tragic rather than heroic story. These writings, as much as his famous name and prior apprenticeship in Europe, led directly to his first diplomatic appointments. While serving in Europe, he translated and wrote an introduction for Friedrich Gentz's comparative history of the U.S. and French Revolutions, which he commended to Americans "because it contains the clearest account of the rise and progress of the revolution which established their independence, that has ever appeared within so small a compass; and secondly, because it rescues that revolution from the disgraceful imputation of having proceeded from the same principles as that of France."[8]

Biographers of John Quincy Adams have often focused on what seems to be a series of reverses and vocational crises during these years, as his father lost the election of 1800 and the son returned to the United States, served in the Massachusetts legislature, and joined the Yankee Federalists' bitter opposition, writing for one of its most ambitious venues, the *Port Folio.* He was sent to the Senate but did not fulfill partisan expectations. Instead, he became a lonely apostate who supported the administration on Louisiana and the embargo, only to be forced out of office and find himself accepting an honorable if once again strenuous exile as minister to Russia under Madison.

One might, however, view these years as those in which he further developed his intellectual as well as political method: revisiting the classics regularly, keeping a more extensive diary that recorded both political events and his reading, and periodically recalibrating his sense of the relationship between the recent and distant past in writing projects. He consistently positioned the nation as the sympathetic protagonist of his historical narratives. In an 1802 oration on the anniversary of the Plymouth landing, he argued for the close relationship of New England's founders to Grotius and his theories of just international relations. No European settlement had ever been kinder and fairer to natives: American Indian rights of possession rested "upon a questionable foundation" because native hunters acted as "lordly savages" wasting land. Plymouth settlers in particular landed on the "territory thus free" of a tribe wasted by "disease." Proof of American virtue lay in expansion itself: in two more centuries American numbers would surely exceed that of Europe. Later, Adams wrote in his diary of his pride in this argument "which was afterwards useful to me at Ghent and which after the lapse of more than twenty years I still think unanswerable." Adams did not think his recapitulation of the doctrine of res nullius, or the just occupation of vacant land, was original: it seems to have been more important to him that it seemed timely and effective as well as historically sound, developed in an oration and put to use in diplomacy for the national good.[9] Settlement was improvement, north or south. The lesson would apply to the Louisiana territory, and ultimately inform his reemergence at the center of National Republicanism.

Despite the criticisms of New England Federalists that the Louisiana Purchase would imbalance the Union, Adams did not try to argue his way out of the implications of the Louisiana Purchase, which he was known to have supported. New England's present and future decline in power was "founded in nature." The real question was whether southern power would be "enjoyed with moderation." Things had not worked out as anticipated in 1787: slaveholders reaped their representation but without the federal taxation that had been part of the deal, since no direct tax had been passed except during the war scare of 1798, during the John Adams administration.[10] The speech he had drafted for the Senate debate on the Ely amendment—an attempted rollback of the three-fifths clause—made a historical argument for constitutional change even more pointedly. The compromise of 1787 was no longer fair. The South was more than safe: it was in the saddle. All sections had "a deep a permanent and a paramount interest in *Union.*" Planter interest in the Union should allow for an adjustment. For his own part, he avoided politicizing slavery with respect to other issues that came before the Senate, including trade with Haiti and slave trade abolition. Impressed by a young Henry Clay's speech against the slave trade, he wrote in his diary that "I took, and intend to take, no part in the debates on this subject."[11]

Adams's neutrality on increasingly politicized questions relating to slavery may seem in retrospect surprising. But it is less so when we realize that his thoroughgoing nationalism informed both his career strategy and his famously antipartisan and his perhaps less well known antisectionalist preferences. Adams took Fourth of July pieties about the role of the United States in world history deadly seriously; the first son of the founders, he aspired to live up to a reputation for republican virtue on the national stage that was already mythical. And while his father, John Adams, has recently gained an exaggerated reputation as an antislavery Founding Father, the son knew better. John Adams had actually helped tamp down slavery issues in the Continental Congress and never tried to resuscitate them as vice president or president.

At a time when sectional and partisan interests dovetailed for many statesmen, John Quincy supported the administration, he told a friend, because the nature of the Federalists' opposition, in time of war, could lead to civil war and the subservience of the Atlantic states to Britain. Hearing rumors of a secession plot, he wrote to Harrison Gray Otis, an alleged plotter, of the need to consider the whole Union objectively. This, in addition to republicanism and independence from foreign influence, was the meaning of the founding for Adams during his formative years in politics. For Adams, New England disunionism was not only misguided, it was "British usurpation," a deliberate effort to divide the sections and undermine the nation. The recurrent "Essex Junto" controversy, which has since seemed mythical or even comical, was very serious for Adams. He went directly to President Jefferson with news of a New England secession plot (later to be disputed), arguing that the embargo be repealed to combat the secret Federalist-British negotiations. His efforts in 1806–7 were particularly appreciated by Secretary of State James Madison, who compared Massachusetts's rapid unseating of Adams as senator to the backbiting he and Jefferson received from the likes of John Randolph, who repeatedly called them soft on federal threats to the South and slavery. Before it became clear that he would be consoled with a diplomatic post, Adams wrote in his diary that he had "sacrificed" himself to "the Constitution."[12]

His "exile" to Russia as foreign minister confirmed his identity as a national as opposed to regional statesman. John Adams had been more consistently concerned about how too much democracy or aristocracy could corrupt a republic, but "*Union* is to me what the *balance* is to you" wrote his son in 1811.[13] Ultimately, John Quincy Adams's loyalty and consistency, as well as his diplomatic experience, earned him the coveted State Department post in Monroe's administration. The prior two secretaries of state—Virginians—had proceeded directly to the presidency. There was considerable irony in the structural position Adams had come to play among National Republicans. He was the New England man in the cabinet, there for sectional balance as well as his manifest skills, and thus suspect; but he was also a one-man argument for the flourishing of nationalism, and the end of partisanship and sectionalism, in the would-be "Era of Good Feelings." His more famous antipartisanship was also a canny appreciation of the role that he in particular could play as the embodiment of the unionist founding.

This had particular implications for what he did and did not say and do about slavery. Adams's Transcontinental Treaty with Spain remained at stake in Congress when Representative James Tallmadge offered his famous amendment to make Missouri statehood conditional upon abolition. Indeed, Adams's immediate diplomatic success at growing the nation in a southwesterly direction is part of what made the question of slavery in a new state so momentous.[14] In discussions within the cabinet, Adams took the position that slavery restriction was unconstitutional and inconsistent with the Louisiana Purchase treaty. He continued to worry that Missouri would derail the Spanish treaty. The pressures mounted. On February 4, 1820, he wondered if restrictionist senator Rufus King was thinking disunion, for any politician so willing to condemn slavery in public should realize "it must end in that." Yet a week later he wrote that he would have to be prepared for an active role in the crisis.[15]

The orator and statesman felt himself drawn in. The problem with the restrictionists' arguments was that they were not bold enough. All the passion lay with the proslavery side, he mused. He foresaw a new arrangement of parties—never a good thing to an Adams. Still, "this is a question between the rights of human nature and the Constitution of the United States. Probably both will suffer by the issue of this controversy." During a gripping evening with John C. Calhoun, he came face to face with the emerging positive good argument on behalf of slavery expansion. The founding fiction that slavery would die of its own accord or wither from the end of the international slave trade had clearly faded if the cabinet colleague he most admired for his intelligence and devotion to the Republic found a neocolonial dependence on Great Britain preferable to a union in which slavery existed on sufferance, banned from the western future. A few days later, on March 4, Adams joined a cabinet majority advising the president that slavery restriction was, in fact, constitutional.[16] His own position had flipped, but clarified. Slavery questions were restricted to the states where slavery existed; where it did not yet exist was a different matter. Missouri was ambiguous, so a deal was inevitable. "The fault is in the Constitution of the United States, which has sanctioned a dishonorable compromise with slavery." The dishonor lay in the conflict with the Declaration of Independence, which had grounded the American Revolution in the consent of the governed. Yet now it was clearer than ever that "slave representation has governed the Union." Maybe he should not have signed on to the compromise, failing to object in the cabinet meetings. Maybe he could propose a constitutional convention.

In public, however, he stayed out of the line of fire. Revealingly, in his diary he expressed increased admiration for Rufus King's stance while (in a striking instance of projection) noting that it scotched any hopes the sixty-nine-year-old New York Federalist might still have of becoming president. Meanwhile the debates in Congress continued to slow consideration of the Spanish treaty. Missouri was "a flaming sword that waves round on all sides and cuts in every direction" as questions suddenly arose about slavery in Florida or, someday, Texas. What did he think? It mattered less than what he said—and did not say. He spoke differently to different colleagues on the matter, or literally divided himself: as a "servant of the whole union" he had to represent the interests of all, but as an "eastern man" he certainly expected resolutions against slavery in the next wave of territories. It was only the second Missouri crisis, over the new constitution that banned free blacks, that made Adams sure which side he was on, though he was hardly more forthcoming or public about it. The new Missouri Constitution that deprived free blacks of rights was unconstitutional and had to be resisted, he said to a congressman privately. His now oft-quoted predictions of "servile war" and the end of slavery date from this period: "if the dissolution of the Union must come, let it come from no other cause than this." But it did not come, and three months later he could write that while constitutional conflict would return, this was not the proper time.[17]

Instead, 1821 became the year of his most famous, defining statement of America's exceptional identity, a July 4th address in Washington, D.C., that depicted "conquest and servitude" as "mingled up in every part of the social existence" of Great Britain. The rebellions of the seventeenth century indexed this British history. The settlement of New England, by contrast, which stood in for the entire nation, involved the purchase of American Indian lands and a social compact "in which conquest and servitude had no part." The Declaration of Independence represented a new epoch in history because it delegitimized foundings based "upon conquest." The United States stood for natural and equal rights; "her glory is not dominion, but liberty." This historical interpretation undergirded the Monroe Doctrine he developed: Europe must not interfere in the Americas because the United States "abstained from interference" abroad and refused the "Imperial diadem."[18]

Adams was developing and publicly articulating a sense of U.S. history in which slavery represented a problem needing adjustment by far-seeing, historically informed statesmen like himself. His differences with Madison and Monroe seem less important than the aid he provided to the Monrovian or National Republican moment. (With Adams's urging, Monroe had accepted Jackson's aggression in Florida; Monroe also seems to have worked behind the scenes to broker the Missouri Compromise.) The ascent of Adams epitomizes the "shutdown" of formal antislavery politics during the 1820s, but during these same years the all too apparent politics of slavery also exposed the limits of his vision. Expropriation of native lands in the South and Southwest could not be seen as proslavery by Adams because he had become the most prominent exponent of the blame-the-British school—literally providing continuity to the founding historical narrative of the United States, in which the Americans liberated themselves from a "servitude" about to be imposed by colonial overlords craven enough to set the natives (and slaves) against them.

His room for maneuver narrowed. In the lead-up to the presidential election of 1824, in which he was much more active than traditional interpretations allow, he repeatedly found himself immersed in documents, to contest partisan accusations about his own past. Jonathan Russell, a fellow negotiator at Ghent, went public with an accusation that Adams had tried to sell claims to Mississippi River navigation in exchange for access to North Atlantic fisheries—a damning accusation to southwesterners. Supporters in the South wanted to hear that he had opposed the Tallmadge Amendment, contrary to reports in newspapers that supported other candidates, so he went back to his earliest diary entries for proof, ignoring what had come after. He told the South Carolinian George McDuffie that his opinions had been greatly misrepresented: he had never favored restriction, he was just against the Missouri Constitution as a violation of both the U.S. Constitution and the Louisiana Purchase treaty. Making a point that subsequent political historians seem to have missed, Samuel Flagg Bemis, his greatest biographer, noted that Adams avoided all comment on slavery-related matters in 1824: when friends, northern and southern, wrote to him for a statement on the matter, "he would not even answer their letters." Adams, in other words, remained confident that "slave representation" and expansion could be managed—and that he was the one to manage them.[19]

But the new partisan alliances of the 1820s, which brought sectional interests even more out into the open, made John Quincy Adams's attempts at crafting an antipartisan nationalism increasingly untenable. The Clay-Adams "corrupt bargain" to resolve the deadlocked Electoral College in Congress was all too obviously a sectional bargain, allowing Jackson to look like the man of the people and the nation. The Jacksonian opposition was itself essentially cross-sectional, as Martin Van Buren proposed, an urban worker–southern planter alliance, to be led by the southerners. The fact that

Van Buren wanted to create it as a revival of the old Jeffersonian alliance is important, however, because Adams was its rather unlikely victim. He had made his peace with second-wave, nationalist Jeffersonianism against the New England Federalists, with an eye toward international as much as domestic issues, and in the hope that National Republicans would be less partisan and more unionist than either their Federalist or Democratic-Republican predecessors. The new partisan dispensation threatened to leave him out even as he sat in the White House: to make a mockery of his principled postpartisanship and instead to make a principle of opposition to a stronger national government.[20]

It was, in other words, the very nightmare he might seem to have prevented by serving, and to some extent influencing, Jefferson, Madison, and Monroe. The Jacksonians proceeded to turn him into the very shadow of the Yankee Federalism he had run all the way to Russia to escape. But there was no easy way out, no divorce of sectional from seemingly more substantial or important issues, not during the 1820s. The improvements, the stronger federal government he advocated, did threaten slavery in an era when not only canals and banks but also African colonization using federal revenues could be contemplated. The antigovernment, retrenchment-happy opposition held special appeal for many slaveholders, who increasingly insisted upon states' rights and the unconstitutionality of any legislation touching slavery. And Adams was suspected of being antislavery—or at least it became useful for planters and their representatives to paint him as such.[21] Nevertheless, as president, he refused to see the opposition as particularly southern. That would concede too much. He could not advocate for union and a vigorous, activist state as president while drawing regional distinctions.

At this point, Adams's historical narrative, with its emphasis on British perfidy, Anglophile and Francophile follies at home, expansion, American exceptionalism, and studied inattention to slavery, did not help him. If anything, it paralyzed him to the meaning of the double-whammy that ruined his presidency: the rise of proslavery sectionalism and its enabling if occasionally antagonistic counterpart, Jacksonian "democratic" nationalism. Much as Van Buren said he only wished to revive the good old alliance against Federalist aristocrats, Adams too continued to see the mix of partisan and sectional posturing through the lens of the first party system, writing in his diary during the summer of 1828 that rumors of secession in South Carolina amounted to a mere gambit to carry state elections, a precise counterpart to Yankee Federalism between 1803 and 1815. National Republicanism had triumphed then; why not now? Playing the slavery card was what partial, irresponsible politicians did. No redemptive narrative could support it. If he sensed that Jackson and Van Buren had trumped him by constructing a populist, antigovernment nationalism that kept its proslavery leanings quiet whenever possible in the interest of an intersectional alliance, he did not admit of the dangers, perhaps precisely because he recognized in them a kind of inverted mirror image, not only of Yankee high Federalism but of National Republicanism itself. Slavery remained off-limits for as long as he remained in the White House, including in the campaign of 1828. To admit that his own strategies had been co-opted by his opponents would have belied the very conditions of his existence as president. On the eve of Jackson's inauguration, he could still complain that although "the North assails me for my fidelity to the Union; the South for my ardent aspirations of improvement . . . [p]assion, prejudice, envy and jealousy will pass. The cause of Union and of improvement will remain, and I have duties to it and to my country yet to discharge."[22]

The president actually spent part of the 1828 election season responding to his old New England nemeses. Electioneering had inspired some Adams supporters to claim that the late Thomas Jefferson had not only despised Andrew Jackson but also supported internal improvements. William Branch Giles, a former Senate colleague and now states' rights governor of Virginia who had objected to the new president's call for "energy" in government, badgered an aging and forgetful Thomas Jefferson for support in an attempt to rewrite Adams's career trajectory. After Jefferson's death, Giles selectively published parts of these exchanges, suppressing the praise but highlighting Jefferson's criticisms of the Adams administration. After considerable back-and-forth in the press in which Adams tried to show he had been a faithful National Republican, not a Federalist, former Hartford Convention types jumped into the fray, denying that they had ever plotted disunion and demanding proof otherwise.

Adams then devoted even more of the first months of 1829 writing a book-length "Reply to the Appeal of the Massachusetts Federalists," which he did not publish. Here he began for the first time to lay the blame for his political failures on the slave power. The whole "cabalistic watch-word of 'state-rights'" of the "Virginia oligarchy" hid darker motives that had wrecked his presidency.

> The lurking jealousies of slave-holders were enlisted against the nature of a state wholly free. The bone-bred dislikes of the cavalier race for the stock of the Pilgrim Puritans were summoned to the array against him; and the Virginian and Southern and slave-holding mind was thus predisposed to receive falsehood for truth, to ruin the reputation and paralyze the power of a President of the United States elected by one-third of the suffrages of the people, already basely slandered by infamous imputations upon the mode of his election.

In his part of this revival of the controversy over New England disunionism between 1804 and 1815, Adams tried to make it clear that he was the nationalist who had worked with Jefferson and Madison. The die-hard Federalists—some of whom had now allied with Jackson—had "deserted their country." In his own way he was trying to revive the party split of old by rewriting history. He had helped save the Union, in part from the somewhat rational (he admitted) protests of a coalition who feared France, democracy, and slave representation. Now the very beneficiaries of slave representation sought to ally with the likes of Harrison Gray Otis against him.[23]

The newly retired president apparently realized that the form of the "Reply" got him too deep into the weeds of personal exchanges and motives. Instead, he attempted to write a more analytical and encompassing political history of the United States. In February 1828, anticipating defeat, he had told a visitor at the White House that he planned "to write Memoirs of the Life of my father; and perhaps a History of the United States from the formation of the present Constitution of the United States," a plan he reiterated a year later and worked on intensively in May 1829, beginning two weeks after his son George's death. Because he gave this manuscript the title "Parties in the United States" and remained critical of them in the era of their supposed triumph, it has been overlooked by historians as just another anachronistic Adamsite wail against parties as a corruption of republican virtue.[24] But it was actually a serious attempt to come to terms with national politics during his long career, with slavery considered as a major part of the story.

At the very outset Adams theorized slavery as one of the six causes of the rise of parties. His definition of the other five causes, including "the character of the different settlements," ethnic and religious differences, and preexisting local structures of government, made it clear that the workings of slavery in politics had been the epitome, or typification, of the other party-making engines as well. He proceeded to note that under the Articles of Confederation, the state governments in the South were based on property—with one-third of the people considered to be property—rather than on persons, as in the North. At its origins, the Union had already had two versions of republicanism: slavery aristocracy and democracy. Sectional differences over slavery reinforced and re-created the original material and cultural bases of partisan differences, yet also complicated national politics by creating another, cross-cutting basis for them.

What saved the Republic, temporarily, from the implications of these multiple sources of partisan division was the highly contingent, yet wise, creation of a supreme "national government" with "a closer union between the whole people than ever yet existed between the members of any other confederacy." Indeed, the United States was not even a confederacy, strictly speaking, but rather "a national government complicated with a federation. The national character predominated even throughout." Antifederalists had the "advantage of numbers" in 1787, but "aristocracy" fortunately won out, only to sacrifice itself during the next decade to its "Tory" tendencies—by which he meant Anglophilia to the point of disunionism. Here Adams backdated New England plotting against a "slave representation" all the way to 1796–98, adapting his growing sense of slavery's importance to national politics, including the history of his father's administration.[25]

Another innovation in Adams's history emerged in his self-distancing from Jefferson. In passages that anticipate his grandson Henry Adams's *History of the United States during the Administration of Thomas Jefferson,* Adams describes how Jefferson "quickened into life" the New England confederacy when he eviscerated the federal government through budget cuts while approving the Louisiana Purchase, "at an immense price, not of money, but of principle." Jefferson gave "immense preponderance" to the South, aggravated the "slave representation," and ultimately upended a federal Constitution that had been formed to protect international and interstate commerce. The third president's seeming concession to commerce as the "handmaid" of agriculture in his inaugural address "exhibited two great and equal interests in the community in the relative position of master and slave. It could have originated only on a tobacco plantation." Jefferson liked the partisan division of "Whig" and "Tory" because it magnified his power and clothed the dominance of agriculture—actually a Tory doctrine in England—as a matter of agrarian democracy versus urban aristocracy.[26]

Here lay the nature and the lesson of American political history. In the American Revolution and its aftermath, as John Adams had insisted, the classic battle of aristocracy and democracy had reemerged, and it had been openly admitted. But slavery created a "hideous contrast" in the context of such battles. As a result, in the federal system, the relation between the general and state governments became the issue, and a source of continuing hypocrisy. Practice would violate principle, as aristocrats and democrats rallied to states or the federal government depending on who held power. American politics was a struggle of principles and men, but the principles and men were ever "transitory" and mutable. What was permanent material? The differences between the sections that warped neoclassical republicanism and its prospects for healthily moderating class politics.[27]

Adams's narrative broke down when he tried to come to terms with the National Republicans and what had happened to them. A long passage on Calhoun the nationalist at the War Department sought to capture the promise of the new era circa 1817 yet could not but hint at the troubles to come. He leaped ahead to the problem of presidential succession in the Monroe administration yet stumbled when he remembered the sacrifice of House Speaker John W. Taylor, an ally and a Missouri restrictionist, to "slaveholding resentments" in 1821. He put aside the manuscript.

He had similar difficulties with a biographical/memoir project about his father, although he made some progress. He began to catalog John Adams's papers (a project, along with the biography, to which his son Charles Francis would return after his defeated bid for the vice presidency in 1848). He found he could not begin to tell his father's story without a "look into history" to discern the transit of liberty—and empire—from Rome and its failure in Carthage, to Britain and its failure in America. This was what John Adams had understood on the eve of the Seven Years War, and prophesied long before the Revolution: Britain's empire could only last until the colonies united. John Quincy had less trouble summarizing his father's intellectual development, and his understanding of the necessity of union of the colonies, than dealing with the politics of slavery, especially after noticing a later deleted sentence in the manuscript of the 1765 *Dissertation Upon Canon and Feudal Law* that stated unequivocally that "I always consider the settlement of America with reverence and wonder, as the opening of a grand scene and design in Providence for the illumination of the ignorant, and the emancipation of the slavish part of mankind." If the elder Adams could write such lines without thinking of Africans, his son, sixty-five years later, could not read them that way. The biographical narrative leaves off with the Boston Massacre, a few years before the Continental Congress, with its sectional politics, would have begun.[28]

Adams's election to Congress in 1830 also slowed these ambitious projects, and led him away from book-length narrative and back toward other favored genres to revise the historical record. By 1831–32, the ex-president had developed a historical analysis positing the irreducible conflict between slavery and national sovereignty, and he had begun to elaborate its implications on specific public occasions as well as privately with selected interlocutors, such as Alexis de Tocqueville, whom he told that slavery lay at the core of the nation's various and complex woes. He devoted a widely read Fourth of July oration in Boston in 1831 to a historical demolition of "the South Carolina doctrine." The occasion allowed him to go public selectively with his reading of political history without having to attack the administration, or slavery, head on. Union, he insisted, even preceded American independence in 1776; the states were not preexisting entities, as "the colonies are not named" in the Declaration. The "hallucination of State sovereignty" was based on the same error of undivided sovereignty that had misled the British parliamentarians into declaring their power to legislate for Americans "in all cases whatsoever." There was no such thing as complete sovereignty or power. American history proved it: the powers of the national government had been expanded by either party when in power. "Our collisions of principle," then, "have been little, very little more than conflicts for place." But worst of all, nullification "strips us of that peculiar and unimitated characteristic of all our legislation—free debate. It makes the bayonet the arbiter of law," and could only lead to civil war. Some weeks later in his lengthy eulogy on James Monroe, Adams tried out a new argument about the origins of sectional controversy during the Confederation period, observing that the structure of the Articles of Confederation government required delegates to the Congress to represent their states, which led to sectional enmities over Mississippi River navigation and "a coldness and mutual alienation between the north and the southern divisions of the Union which is not extinguished to this day."[29]

The freshman congressman also completed and published a long historical narrative poem begun as he worked on his histories, entitled *Dermott MacMorrogh, or the Conquest of Ireland.* The subject was a thirteenth-century local Irish prince who, in a farcical reenactment of *The Iliad,* sold out his larger nation as a result of his ill-conceived lust. Adams saw contemporary Ireland as a republican, antimonarchical and anti-imperial cause, akin to the contemporary Greeks, whom he had also written about in a series of magazine articles. Careful readers would have noticed the echoes of anti-Jackson critique in *Dermott,* though Adams insisted that his poem was a history in verse, a rebuke to David Hume's account of Irish and British history and to hero-worship generally. He tried to keep at the level of allegory the apparent parallel of an imperial president from the backcountry who was accused of an illegitimate marriage. (He even excised a canto on a hanging for desertion, no doubt as too evocative of the famous anti-Jackson "coffin handbill.") If nothing else, *Dermott* allowed John Quincy Adams to imagine himself anew as the nation's leading critic of Britain, monarchy, and tyranny, and as a champion of resistance to imperial servitude and slavery, notwithstanding the pretensions of a planter of Scots-Irish descent.[30]

In the coming years, however, Adams gradually found in congressional oratory, eulogies, and celebratory occasions something akin to the Ciceronian revival he had trumpeted as the first Boylston Professor of Rhetoric and Oratory at Harvard between 1805 and 1808. Moreover, his seemingly failed self-reinvention as a historian between 1829 and 1831 informed his return to real politics in the eventual guise of conscience and prophet. As an "Old Man Eloquent" with less than presidential political ambitions, he could further develop the notion of a slave power perversely pushing the Union toward civil war by resisting the natural rights and nationalist doctrines of the Declaration of Independence. He may not have fully succeeded as a "literary gentleman," but he did resurface as a "bruiser," as his contemporary Ralph Waldo Emerson put it—a polemical, political writer with one eye on the past and the other on the future.[31]

What's striking about these later years is how often Adams as the great orator and scourge of the slave power returned to historical modes of critique—in his eulogies on Madison and Lafayette, in several Fourth of July orations, and in intensive arguments about the course of recent federal policy vis-à-vis Texas and Mexico. Bewailing the selectivity of states' rights at home and empire abroad, he repeatedly went back to 1776 to argue that the

Declaration of Independence founded a nation-state. That Union, dedicated to human rights, had not been superseded by the Articles of Confederation, the revolutionary state constitutions, or the compromises of 1787. The Union may be an unprecedentedly "complicated machine," he remarked in his lengthy 1837 Independence Day oration-cum-treatise, but it was still a Union with a sovereign national government, not "a mere cluster of sovereign confederated States." Because that "heresy" came from the South, it needed to be confronted with an antislavery interpretation of the founding, also going back to 1776 and a new appreciation of Jefferson.

> The inconsistency of the institution of domestic slavery with the principles of the Declaration of Independence, was seen and lamented by all the southern patriots of the Revolution; by no one with deeper and more unalterable conviction, than by the author of the Declaration himself. No charge of insincerity or hypocrisy can be fairly laid to their charge. Never from *their* lips was heard one syllable of attempt to justify the institution of slavery. They universally considered it as a reproach fastened upon them by the unnatural step-mother country, and they saw that before the principles of the Declaration of Independence, slavery, in common with every other mode of oppressor, was destined sooner or later to be banished from the earth. Such was the undoubting conviction of Jefferson to his dying day. In the Memoir of his Life, written at the age of seventy-seven, he gave to his countrymen the solemn and emphatic warning, that the day was not distant when they *must* hear and adopt the general emancipation of their slaves.

He continued to develop his specific account of revolutionary nationalism frustrated in the 1780s and then renewed, with a fatal compromise, in the Constitution. In other speeches-turned-pamphlets like *The Jubilee of the Constitution* (1839) he went even further, calling the sovereignty of states established in the Articles of Confederation a "usurpation upon the rights of the people of the United States," and extended his account into the 1790s and beyond to the nation-making ("if not eventually leading to the dissolution of the Union") Louisiana Purchase. As secretary of state, he had put considerable time into the same documents that contemporary historians of the Constitution pore over, helping to preserve and publish records of the

Continental Congress. Combined with the family archive he was cataloging and extending, he had, in other words, unusual access to evidence as well as an increasingly well-honed, revised narrative to buttress his appeal to "the fathers."[32]

His family members constantly remarked on his remarkable energy during these years—quite a contrast to his own complaints about his laziness during the brief retirement period. What they, and he, meant was that he found the cycle of reading, writing, and politicking to be mutually sustaining. Certainly there was always another Jacksonian revision of history to rouse him, as when Jackson himself floated the notion in 1845 that Adams had given away much of Texas to Spain as secretary of state. Speaking to Whigs in Boston, Representative Adams brought his 1819 diary to the rostrum and had a young man read from the primary source to prove that Jackson himself had approved of the Transcontinental Treaty at the time. Confronted repeatedly by what he saw with considerable justification as the Big Lies of the day, Adams wrote more history even while continuing to build his diary as an archive. As late as 1846, he planned to write a history of the U.S. Patent Office, probably as another proof that a wise federal government could evenhandedly promote economic growth, because it already had.[33]

Adams's self-assessment during the congressional years we now see as his heroic era tended to swerve from the grandiose to the tragic and back. The tragic theme was often an antislavery jeremiad, a call to arms. He was winning some battles to define the past and the present, and losing others—losing and then finally winning with the Gag Rule; and not unrelatedly, in the case of Texas annexation, winning and then losing. Having raised one son (Charles Francis) who embraced the dual role of politician and historian but lost others (George Washington, John II) who felt burdened by the family legacy, he inspired ambivalence in the next generations much as he did in the twentieth century. Henry Adams discouraged his brother Brooks from publishing his biography of their grandfather after reading a draft that struck him as hero-worship. He cited an 1837 letter in which John Quincy had called his political career a failure, as the nation failed to coalesce or put slavery on the road to extinction. Henry did much to distance himself, as a literary artist and scholar, from partisan politics as well as from any aura of hagiography. The first university teacher of U.S. history and introducer of the German historical research seminar, Henry Adams cut his teeth as a historian with biographies of mavericks John Randolph and Albert Gallatin, later devoting his master work to the period between the two Adams's administrations, 1801–17.[34] But his devastating sense of the limits and necessities of politics, of the ironies of history, and his clear awareness that slavery lay at the heart of the hypocrisies of Jefferson's America may have derived far more from his apprenticeship sorting family papers, and from his grandfather's interpretation of the early Republic, than the author liked to admit.

And so does our own historiography. Just as John Adams remains the first source of quotes on the nature of the American Revolution, so John Quincy Adams's diary has reemerged as the locus classicus for understanding the politics of slavery in the early republic, no less than for events like the Treaty of Ghent and the Monroe Doctrine. The leading synthesis of the period 1815–48 is dedicated to Adams, and the leading rival quotes him almost as often even while relying on a curiously inverted interpretation of him as politically naive if not craven until he suddenly became a sage and a hero.[35] We would like to separate his careers into successes and failures, or into politics and good intentions, or into doing and writing, and so did he; but he also knew better. Moreover, both his historical interpretation of a proslavery Republic and his consequently anguished, revisionist search to square nation-building and empire with America's inspiring opposition to tyranny resonate strongly today, leading to what can only be called an Adams revival. Did the Revolution, or the Constitution, make a nation? Did the Revolution or the Constitution undermine, or advance, slavery? What is the relationship between the answers to those questions? We have not revised perhaps as much as returned to our founding revisionist, the president whose very loyalty to the regime of the father first suppressed, and then enabled, an antislavery nationalism.

## *Notes*

1. For the significance of Washington's lack of a biological son, which made it easier for him to serve as consensual father to all, see Francois Furstenberg, *In the Name of the Father: George Washington, Slavery, and the Making of the Nation* (New York: Penguin, 2006).

2. Stephen Skowronek, *The Politics Presidents Made: Leadership from John Adams to George Bush* (Cambridge, MA: Harvard University Press, 1993), 33, 110–27.

3. See the classic analysis of "getting right with Lincoln" in David Donald, *Lincoln Reconsidered,* 2nd ed. (New York: Vintage, 1961), 3–18.

4. For the election of 1824 as an opposition of "the plowman and the professor," see John William Ward, *Andrew Jackson: Symbol for an Age* (New York: Oxford University Press, 1955), 46–78.

5. Here and in the title of this essay I refer to the classic delineation of these qualities as aspects of politics in Albert O. Hirschman, *Exit, Voice, and Loyalty: Responses to Decline in Firms, Organizations, and States* (Cambridge, MA: Harvard University Press, 1970).

6. David Waldstreicher, *In the Midst of Perpetual Fetes: The Making of American Nationalism, 1776–1820* (Chapel Hill: University of North Carolina Press, 1997), 17; Joseph J. Ellis, *Passionate Sage: The Character and Legacy of John Adams* (New York: Norton, 1993), 56–83, 143–73.

7. John Quincy Adams, "An Oration, Delivered at the Public Commencement in the University of Cambridge, in New England," *Columbian Magazine* 1 (Sept. 1787), 625–28.

8. John Quincy Adams, "Publicola," "Marcellus," and "Columbus," in *Writings of John Quincy Adams,* ed. Worthington Chauncey Ford (New York: Macmillan, 1913) [hereafter cited as *WJQA*], 1:91, 159; Robert A. East, *John Quincy Adams: The Critical Years, 1785–1794* (Cambridge, MA: Harvard University Press, 1962), 31, 142; Friedrich Gentz, *The Origin and Principles of the American Revolution, Compared with the Origin and Principles of the French Revolution, Translated by John Quincy Adams,* ed. Peter Koslowski (Indianapolis, IN: Liberty Fund, 2010), 3. In his first Fourth of July oration in 1793, he provided a textbook example of that new genre, recounting the causes and exceptionally positive consequences of a reasonable revolution that he hoped would inspire other nations, like France, to embrace liberty but hopefully to abjure democratic and reactionary excesses. John Quincy Adams, *An Oration, Pronounced July 4th, 1793, at the Request of the Inhabitants of the Town of Boston* (Boston, 1793).

9. John Quincy Adams, *An Oration Delivered at Plymouth* (Boston, 1802), 25; John Quincy Adams, "Ecce Iterum" [1825?], *WJQA,* 3:11. For earlier uses of res nullius, see Anthony Pagden, *Lords of All the World: Ideologies of Empire in Britain, Spain and France, 1500–1800* (New Haven, CT: Yale University Press, 1995); Andrew Fitzmaurice, *Sovereignty, Property, and Empire, 1500–2000* (New York: Cambridge University Press, 2014).

10. For an analysis that supports Adams's reasoning, see Robin Einhorn, *American Taxation, American Slavery* (Chicago: University of Chicago Press, 2006).

11. "Publius Valerius," *WJQA,* 3:49–50, 59, 70–71, 73; "Proposed Amendment to the Constitution on Representation" [Dec. 1804], *WJQA,* 3:88; JQA Diary, Dec. 17, 1804, Jan. 21, 1805, Feb. 20, Dec. 24, 1806, Jan. 15, 1807, Massachusetts Historical Society, The Diaries of John Quincy Adams: A Digital Collection, http://www.masshist.org/jqadiaries/php/. Many of the entries cited here also appear in the annotated collection *John Quincy Adams and the Politics of Slavery: Selections from the Diary, ed.* David Waldstreicher and Matthew Mason (New York: Oxford University Press, 2017), or in *The Diaries of John Quincy Adams, 1779–1848,* ed. David Waldstreicher, 2 vols. (New York: Library of America, 2017).

12. JQA to Harrison Gray Otis, Mar. 31, 1808, to Orchard Cook, Nov. 25, 1808, to Nahum Parker, Dec. 8 and 15, 1808, to William Plumer, Oct. 16, 1809, *WJQA,* 4:193, 255–56, 258–59, 340–41; Henry Adams, ed., *Documents Relating to New England Federalism,* 1807–1815 (1877; repr., Boston: Little, Brown,1905), 11–13, 107–330; JQA Diary, Jan. 20, Apr. 23, 1808, May 31, 1820.

13. JQA to William Plumer, Aug. 16, 1809, to Abigail Adams, June 30, 1811, to John Adams, Aug. 31, Oct. 31, 1811, *WJQA,* 3:341, 4:127–28, 208–9, 267.

14. James E. Lewis Jr., *John Quincy Adams: Policymaker for the Union* (Wilmington, DE: Scholarly Resources, 2002), 62–63.

15. *Diary and Autobiographical Writings of Louisa Catherine Adams,* ed. Judith S. Graham et al. (Cambridge, MA: Belknap Press of Harvard University Press, 2013), 2:472, 462, 464; JQA Diary, Feb. 4, 11, 27, 1820.

16. Adams to James Monroe, Feb. 24, Mar. 4, 1820, *WJQA,* 7:1–2; JQA Diary, Mar. 3, 1820; Chandra Miller, "'Title Page to a Great and Tragic Volume': The Impact of the Missouri Crisis on Slavery, Race and Republicanism in the Thought of John C. Calhoun and John Quincy Adams," *Missouri Historical Review* 94 (2000): 365–88.

17. JQA Diary, Feb. 23, Mar. 3, 5, 31, Apr. 9, Nov. 29, 1820; Adams to Jonathan Jennings, July 17, 1820, to John D. Heath, Jan. 7, 1822, *WJQA,* 7:53, 191–93; Miller, "Title Page to a Great and Tragic Volume," 380–85; Matthew Mason, "John Quincy Adams and the Tangled Politics of Slavery," in David Waldstreicher, ed., *A Companion to John Adams and John Quincy Adams* (Malden, MA: Wiley-Blackwell, 2013), 406–7.

18. JQA Diary, Feb. 28, 1821; John Quincy Adams, *An Address Delivered at the Request of the Committee of Citizens of Washington; On the Occasion of Reciting the Declaration of Independence, on the Fourth of July, 1821* (Washington, DC, 1821), 9–10, 21, 28, 31. For an analysis that compares the logic of the July 4th address with the Monroe Doctrine, noting that both simultaneously separated American Indians from foreign policy and made slavery a foreign problem, see Gretchen Murphy, *Hemispheric Imaginings: The Monroe Doctrine and Narratives of U.S. Empire* (Durham, NC: Duke University Press, 2005), 33–60.

19. David Callahan, "The Elections of 1824 and 1828," in Waldstreicher, *Companion to John Adams and John Quincy Adams,* 325; David Callahan, "The War of the Giants: The Presidential Election of 1824 and the Reshaping of American Politics" (Ph.D. diss., Temple University, 2017); Waldstreicher and Mason, *John Quincy Adams and the Politics of Slavery,* 120–30; Samuel Flagg Bemis, *John Quincy Adams and the Union* (New York: Knopf, 1956), 26–27, 70–71.

20. Padraig Riley, "The Presidency of John Quincy Adams" in Waldstreicher, *Companion,* 335–36; William W. Freehling, *Prelude to Civil War* (New York: Oxford University Press, 1966), 141; JQA Diary, Sept. 11, 1826. For the structural constraints Adams faced in trying to consolidate Monrovian policies, see especially Skowronek, *Politics Presidents Make,* 110–27.

21. Robert Pierce Forbes, *The Missouri Compromise and Its Aftermath* (Chapel Hill: University of North Carolina Press, 2007), 9, 190–92, 195–96; Richard R. John, "Affairs of Office: The Executive Departments, the Election of 1828, and the Making of

the Democratic Party," in Meg Jacobs, William J. Novak, and Julian Zelizer, eds., *The Democratic Experiment: New Directions in American Political History* (Princeton, NJ: Princeton University Press, 2003), 50–84.

22. JQA Diary, July 10, 1828, Feb. 28, 1829; Donald J. Ratcliffe, "The Decline of Antislavery Politics, 1815–1840," in Hammond and Mason, *Contesting Slavery,* 280.

23. Henry Adams, ed., *Documents Relating to New-England Federalism* (Boston: Little, Brown, 1905), 11–13, 52–53, 144–45, 285; Bemis, *John Quincy Adams and Union,* 161–74; Arthur Scherr, *Thomas Jefferson's Image of New England: Nationalism versus Sectionalism in the Young Republic* (Jefferson, NC: McFarland, 2016), 316. Jackson supporters had earlier accused Adams of being a member of the Essex Junto, a claim revived in 1829 when he appointed Rufus King as minister to Great Britain. Dinah Mayo Bobee, "Understanding the Essex Junto: Fear, Dissent and Propaganda in the Early Republic," *New England Quarterly* 88 (Dec. 2015): 650–51. Bemis, *John Quincy Adams and the Union,* 174, maintains that the comments on slavery were the reason Adams ultimately decided not to publish the "Reply."

24. JQA Diary, Feb. 1, 1828, Jan. 19, 1829; John Quincy Adams, *Parties in the United States* (New York: Greenberg, 1941); Fred Kaplan, *John Quincy Adams: American Visionary* (New York: Harper, 2014), 442. The Adams Papers project dates the manuscript at 1829. In the Diary, he first mentions its existence in at least a partial draft on May 14, 1829. On May 26, he wrote: "My observations upon parties in the United States now absorbs all my time, and have swollen to a much greater extent than I had intended—I must break off writing further on them now or postpone my return to Quincy, and I fear if I do break off that I may never resume them—They lead me over much of the same ground that I have already traversed in the Reply to the Appeal—These compositions upon the past abstract one from contemplations of the future, and alone preserve me from despondency, which I cannot controul. I had foreseen evil enough—All that I had foreseen has come, and it is nothing—Nothing to that stroke which I did not foresee, and which has unman'd me." On December 29, he mentions resuming it for the first time since the spring, and on May 26, 1830, calls it "yet unfinished" upon loaning it out. This manuscript and that of the "Reply to the Massachusetts Federalists" appear to derive from copies made and bound in one volume, probably at the behest of Charles Francis Adams Jr. or Henry Adams. Adams Family Papers, Reel 246, Massachusetts Historical Society, Adams Family Papers collection guide, http://www.masshist.org/collection-guides/view/fa0279.

25. Adams, *Parties in the United States,* 2–4, 6, 9, 25.

26. Ibid., 32, 39.

27. Ibid., 108, 119–21.

28. John Quincy Adams and Charles Francis Adams, *John Adams* (1855; repr. New York: Chelsea House, 1980), 1:30, 91, 123.

29. JQA Diary, Jan. 18, 27, June 29, 1831; John Quincy Adams, *An Oration Addressed to the Citizens of the Town of Quincy, on the Fourth of July, 1831* (Boston, 1831), 6–7, 14, 23, 29, 36; Olivier Zunz, ed., *Alexis de Tocqueville and Gustave de Beaumont in America: Their Friendship and Their Travels* (Charlottesville: University of Virginia

Press, 2010), 242–43; Bemis, *John Quincy Adams and the Union,* 233; John Quincy Adams, *An Eulogy on the Life and Character of James Monroe* (Boston, 1831), 37–38.

30. Kaplan, *John Quincy Adams,* 455–57; John Quincy Adams, *Dermott MacMorrogh, Or the Conquest of Ireland,* ed. Martin J. Burke, Elizabeth Fitzpatrick, and Olivia Hamilton (1832; repr. Dublin: Maunsel, 2005), 64, 112, 148, 150, 155, 178. For Adams's view of the Irish question, see Martin J. Burke, "Medieval Irish History and American Epic Poetry" in Burke, Fitzpatrick, and Hamilton, *Dermott MacMorrogh,* 19.

31. John Quincy Adams, *Lectures on Rhetoric and Oratory* (1810; repr. New York: Russell and Russell, 1962), 1:19–23; Emerson in Bemis, *John Quincy Adams and the Union,* 195.

32. John Quincy Adams, *A Eulogy on the Life and Character of James Madison* (Boston, 1836), 8; John Quincy Adams, *An Oration Before the Inhabitants of the Town of Newburyport . . . July 4th 1837* (Newburyport, MA, 1837), 6, 12, 24–25, 49–50; John Quincy Adams, *The Jubilee of the Constitution: A Discourse Delivered at the Request of the New-York Historical Society in the City of New York, the 30th of April, 1839* (New York, 1839), 12–23, 98–99; Bemis, *John Quincy Adams and the Union,* 233; Paul C. Nagel, *John Quincy Adams: A Private Life, a Public Life* (New York: Knopf, 1997), 361–62, 371–72; Charles N. Edel, *Nation Builder: John Quincy Adams and the Grand Strategy of the Republic* (Cambridge, MA: Harvard University Press, 2014), 262–63, 280, 297.

33. Lynn Hudson Parsons, *John Quincy Adams* (Madison, WI: Madison House, 1998), 263; James Traub, *John Quincy Adams: Militant Spirit* (New York: Basic Books, 2016), 518.

34. Michael O'Brien, *Henry Adams and the Southern Question* (Athens: University of Georgia Press, 2005), 6; Garry Wills, *Henry Adams and the Making of America* (Boston: Houghton Mifflin, 2005), 12–28; Paul C. Nagel, *Descent from Glory* (New York: Oxford University Press, 1983), 352–53; Adams to Charles Upham, Feb. 2, 1837, in Adrienne Koch and William Peden, eds., *Selected Writings of John and John Quincy Adams* (New York: Knopf, 1946), 389; Henry Adams, *The History of the United States during the Administration of Thomas Jefferson, 1801–1809* (New York: Library of America, 1984); Henry Adams, *History of the United States during the Administration of James Madison, 1809–17* (New York: Library of America, 1984).

35. Daniel Walker Howe, *What God Hath Wrought: The Transformation of the United States, 1815–1848* (New York: Oxford University Press, 2007); Sean Wilentz, *The Rise of American Democracy* (New York: Norton, 2006).

# 3 Martin Van Buren, the Democratic Party, and the Jacksonian Reinvention of the Constitution

Elvin T. Lim

Parties seem like an established and uncontroversial feature of American democracy today, but nowhere in the Constitution does the word "party" appear. In a formal sense, then, the parties and party system that exist today are extraconstitutional, perhaps even unconstitutional. Most of the framers of the Constitution, especially the Federalists, understood parties to be obstacles to the harmony of the body politic. Even the Republicans who organized to expel the Federalists from office in the "Revolution of 1800" operated under this understanding, and envisioned their party more as a temporary movement to undo the excesses of the Washington and Adams administrations—"a party to end all parties." But Martin Van Buren, vice president under Andrew Jackson and, later, eighth president of the United States, would go further than the Republicans ever did, tapping into Anti-Federalist reservations still widely held by Republicans about the dangers of consolidated power wielded by the federal government to defend the idea of a permanent opposition and a competitive party system—in effect, creating and dressing up an initially illegitimate form (the party) with historically resonant and legitimate ends (limiting government) inherited from the Revolution. And so, as Richard Hofstadter observed, "for all his desire to be a sound Republican in the Jeffersonian tradition, Van Buren was a heretic on one vital count: he accepted, he even welcomed, the idea of a permanent opposition."[1] If the Federalists had persuaded the nation that the separation of powers was enough of a check on the perils of consolidated power, Van Buren would permanently introduce a further, extraconstitutional check on it, the political party. By padding the Constitution with an institution that was deliberately written out of it, Van Buren would create an informal constitution, thereby also rewriting a Federalist text with Anti-Federalist ink. He was an astute, if political, historian who artfully embraced the deeper past to rewrite the recent past.

So successful was Van Buren's integration of party to the constitutional edifice that James Ceaser has argued that Van Buren offered both a partisan and a constitutional defense of the party. Ceaser observed, in "proposing party competition" as a solution to the problem of controlling ambition, "it may well have been that Van Buren, and not [John Quincy] Adams, was the true heir to the Founders' intentions."[2] This is an extraordinary claim because the framers were avowedly antiparty. Yet Ceaser's observation can be robustly defended if we understand that Van Buren was indeed a "true heir," but not one of the ideas of Alexander Hamilton and the Federalists, but the "Other Founders," or the people who feared the "consolidation" of the Union and opposed the ratification of the Constitution, the Anti-Federalists.[3] If so, the birth of the Democratic Party and the two-party system that eventually emerged from it may be understood as another Anti-Federalist concession, perhaps less glamorous than but arguably as transformative as the Bill of Rights, extracted from the Federalists—these are rare examples of when the "losers" got to rewrite history, twice. As a reaction to Federalist understandings of the Constitution along distinctly Anti-Federalist lines, the Democratic Party was part repudiation and part reformation of what was accomplished in 1787, both weakening and, for its proponents, supplementing the Constitution as the framers passed the revolutionary torch to the second generation of political leaders.

Operating in an era steeped in a strong tradition against parties, Martin Van Buren and his followers invoked criticisms that the Anti-Federalists and Republicans had made of the Constitution to create and justify the Democratic Party as its necessary supplement. By simultaneously borrowing from while challenging the Constitution's legitimacy, Van Buren and Jacksonian Democrats would create an extraconstitutional institution to secure a latter-day victory for Anti-Federalism by another name. "The Democracy," as the party was called, became the organizational reincarnation of Anti-Federalism, giving structure and organization to the dissenting movement that was only temporarily vanquished in 1789. The Democratic

Party would put organizationally and tangibly into place the states-centered, grassroots democratic paradigm that the Anti-Federalists had defended a generation ago.

## *The Birth of the Democratic Party*

By the War of 1812, the elite patrician generation that led the Revolution was passing on, and with them, the classical reservations about party and democracy. A new type of political man emerged on the scene, men who did not come from great families but who understood the need for organization if they were to compete with the ruling elites of the time. These men were the first "outsiders" of many more to come in American politics. In 1817, Martin Van Buren created the Bucktails, a statewide political organization in New York consisting of Democratic Republicans united against Governor Dewitt Clinton and the patrician class and the values the latter represented. The Bucktails formed the core of the Albany Regency, which would eventually become the Democratic Party in New York.[4] Elected to the Senate in 1821, Van Buren would bring his ideas about party and party organization to Washington, and from there, to other states. By 1824, the size of the Union had almost doubled to twenty-four states, and most states had moved away from the original legislative selection of presidential electors, abolished property qualifications for voting, and moved toward adult white male suffrage. There was an increasing sense of disconnect between what the Constitution had promised and what it delivered, and an expanded electorate presented an opening for men who understood the popular passions and the arts of political organization and mobilization to make a vocation of politics and to revisit some of the terms of the revolutionary settlement.[5] As a keen observer of national politics, Van Buren believed that the existing way of conducting politics produced faction and chaos. He especially distrusted President Monroe, who, though Republican, was also an old-school patrician who still held on to the old hopes of unity and standing above party. Van Buren believed that Monroe's "fusion policy" of making appointments in an even-handed manner was dividing the Republican Party into personal factions, producing the chaos of 1824.[6]

The election ("corrupt bargain") of 1824, which delivered an unexpected victory to John Quincy Adams, would be a watershed election for the development of parties. First, it provided the impetus to seriously reconsider the existing system of presidential selection. That election had operated exactly by the letter of the Constitution as it proceeded from the Electoral College to the House of Representatives, and yet appeared illegitimate in denying the presidency to Andrew Jackson, who garnered the most popular and Electoral College votes (though not a majority). The results persuaded Van Buren that the existing presidential selection system privileged candidates culled from the elite patrician class, which reduced politics to a divisive clash of major personalities. Second, and resultantly, the election of 1824 clarified in Van Buren's mind the necessity of party organization to guarantee popular control of election outcomes, and he would soon come to the conclusion that the congressional caucus had to give way to partisan nominating conventions. Though initially a supporter of William Crawford and not of Jackson, who he thought represented a continuation of personalized politics, Van Buren came to the conclusion that the best way to eradicate personalized politics was to subsume these personalities in a regular, partisan nomination process. If candidates sought the nomination of parties, then they would be governed and united by a platform greater than themselves. By emphasizing the need for party discipline and regularity, and dangling his control of New York's thirty-six electoral votes to presidential aspirants, Van Buren hoped to bring order to the messy, personality-centered politics of the 1820s.[7] In the 1828 contest between the plowman versus the professor, the popular rejection of the highly credentialed John Quincy Adams, who was adamantly antifaction like his Federalist forebears, in favor of a frontier duelist with little education and even less political experience was the clearest sign that the antidemocratic, patrician era of the Federalists was at its twilight, and that Van Buren's vision was coming to pass.

If the early republic's patricians were committed to the idea of political society as an organic whole that could not afford to be divided by faction, Martin Van Buren explicitly broke from the Madisonian framework that was designed to contain conflict *within* the institutions of government, specifically, by way of the separation of powers. The difference between the Democratic Party and its predecessor is that while Jefferson had only summoned Anti-Federalist rhetoric and ideas to combat Federalist excesses, Van Buren and his followers formed a permanent organization, formally *outside* of the Constitution, to make up for the perceived defect of democracy in the Federalists' Constitution. This creation was a much more full-throttled iteration of the Anti-Federalist spirit than even Jefferson had envisioned, and one that we have not fully appreciated. Indeed, organization was arguably the missing link that explained the Anti-Federalists' loss in 1787/88. There may well have been more Anti-Federalists than Federalists across the various states,[8] but the Federalists were better organized and used the "heresthetics" of agenda setting and rule manipulations to forge a majority in their favor.[9] Martin Van Buren would resurrect the reservations and arguments of the Anti-Federalists, and put a machine behind them to secure a restoration of some of their core principles.

## *"To Revive the Old Contest between Federals and Anti-Federals"*

There is ample proof of Van Buren's sympathy to Anti-Federalism, though it is revealingly unsung in our history textbooks today—a testament to his contribution to melding Anti-Federalist to Federalist thought widely ascribed to the typically undifferentiated generation we now collectively call the "founders."[10] Writing to a fellow member of the Albany Regency in 1822, Van Buren announced that it was "the proper moment to commence the world of a *general resuscitation of the old-democratic party.*"[11] When he left for Washington, Van Buren expressly told his friend Charlemagne Tower that his purpose was "to revive the old contest between federals and anti-federals and build up a party for himself on that."[12]

The spirit of Anti-Federalism was alive and well in the 1820s. That the Jeffersonian-Republican and then later the Democratic Party took its inspiration from the ideas of the "other founders" was a common view among contemporaries at the time. At the dawn of the Jacksonian era, near the end of his life, an old but still partisan Thomas Jefferson wrote to Albert Gallatin to rigorously denounce the claim that the debate between the Federalists and the Republicans was no more. In defiance of his own words in his first inaugural address, "We are all Republicans, we are all Federalists," he now wrote:

> You are told indeed that there are no longer parties among us, that they are all now amalgamated in peace, the lion and the lamb lie down together in peace. Do not believe a word of it, the same parties exist now as ever did.[13]

Jefferson was saying that the quarrel between the two conceptions of union and republicanism that occupied his generation had been passed on, by a different set of names, to the next. So the conventional view that the framers were antiparty, and the Van Burenites, proparty, needs to be clarified, for *both* were highly partisan, even if the first generation of leaders saw parties only as temporary movements to restore constitutional order.[14] The framers', or more specifically, the Federalists' antiparty stance was not merely a position inherited from Bolingbroke and those of the "Country" persuasion in England, for their antiparty position was a partisan position directed specifically to the challenge of their time and space. Specifically, the Federalists' disdain of party was in itself partisan in its nationalistic bias. For them, to be partisan or factious was to be overly zealous for states' rights. "An over-scrupulous jealousy of danger to the rights of the people" prevented the Anti-Federalists from seeing the benefits of a stronger Union.[15] As one scholar put it, "for Hamilton, state sovereignty under the Articles of Confederation meant nothing but rule by party."[16] The noblest advocates of this view were trying to cultivate a national partisanship or patriotism, in place of local jealousies and attachments which, in their mind, prevented obstacles to union.[17] It was this attitude that persuaded the Madison of the 1780s, writing in *Federalist* 10 and still on board with this view, that majority tyranny was a problem for which the extended sphere, and the multiplication of factions, was the answer.

But Madison would soon reverse his position and embrace the Republican and Anti-Federalist cause. As soon as the new government began business, Secretary of Treasury Alexander Hamilton began to push his ambitious nationalist economic program, and it became clear to his detractors that the ancient quarrel between aristocracy—reborn as financial aristocracy—and democracy was far from over, and that contrary to *Federalist* 10, popular majorities were not to be feared, but were rather still in need of protection from aristocracy. Republicans, who emerged from among the ranks of former Anti-Federalists, saw the Federalist economic program as a fulfillment of the Anti-Federalist prophecies of "consolidation" and the evisceration of states' rights. Although Madison had once thought that majority tyranny was the greatest threat to republicanism, by the early 1790s he had come to accept Jefferson's view that the will of the majority had to be protected against the intrigue of the financial aristocracy.

This much Van Buren inherited from his heroes. But while both Jefferson and Madison still harbored hopes that the Constitution was capable of producing sound government that would work in the interest of the majority as long as the Federalists did not monopolize power, Van Buren would take the idea of party one step further, by advancing the heretical view that a permanent party was necessary to ensure that the majority could be organized to win elections that would otherwise always be vulnerable to elite capture. Van Buren was very conscious of the fact that while Democrats split their vote between William Crawford and Andrew Jackson in the election of 1824, "the 'high-minded' espoused the cause of Mr. [John Quincy] Adams zealously" behind the "federal ranks" of a generation ago.[18] Like his eighteenth-century predecessors, Van Buren understood societies as constituted by separate estates; but unlike his predecessors, he believed that whereas members of the financial aristocracy or "money power," aligned in their interests, banded together naturally, the "landed interest," comprising mostly self-reliant framers, would not do so in the absence of a disciplining institutional framework such as the political party. In a new spin on the idea of "ambition counteract[ing] ambition," he would argue that the only way to check the factious financial aristocracy was to organize a vigilant army of democracy against it in a perpetual constitutional struggle. Van Buren, therefore, was a proponent more of organized democracy as the permanent opposition to financial aristocracy than of the idea of a symmetrical two-party system that would follow in the ensuing decades. His contribution to the development of the latter was only indirect. Indeed, for him, to accomplish the former was in some ways to render obsolete the need for the latter. Though he is often credited as the founder of not only the Democratic Party but also the two-party system, Van Buren never envisioned two great parties each equal in legitimacy and electoral success, for this would not have comported with his view of the Federalists as the party of the monied interests and aristocracy, and the Democracy as the party of the people and therefore the only truly legitimate party.

Indeed, Van Buren spent his retirement writing an entire book, *Inquiry into the Origins and Course of Political Parties in the United*, to explicate the debt the nation owed to the Democratic Party for preserving its republican form of government. His record of history, it turns out, had a heavy influence on the history that transpired after him. After a lengthy discourse on the failures of the Federalists, Van Buren concluded *Inquiry* on a triumphant and revealing note: "the course of events to which I have referred has had the effect of breaking up as a national organization the party so long opposed to the Democratic Party, leaving the latter the only political association coextensive in its power and influence with the Union."[19] Standing where he did in history, he was right. With the exception of 1824, the party of Jefferson and Jackson dominated American politics from 1800 until the election of Abraham Lincoln, which would inaugurate another era of domination, this time by the Republican Party. This was a fact that Van Buren took pleasure in. He had watched with great pain the fragmentation of the Republican Party into personal factions under Monroe and Adams, both of whom had tried to reconcile the party with the Federalists. The cost of reconciliation with the Federalists far outweighed the benefits for Van Buren because of his view that party unity disproportionately benefited the Democratic Party. He wrote, "[i]t is a striking fact of our political history that the sagacious leaders of the Federal party . . . have always been desirous to bring every usage or plan designed to secure party unity into disrepute with the people, and in proportion to their success in that has been their success in the elections."[20] Because he saw the battle between financial aristocracy and self-government (understood as democratic, states' rights constitutionalism) in very stark terms, his campaign for the presidency in 1836 "rested on the principle that only one party under a democratic constitution could stand for popular sovereignty and that in the United States the Democrats were it."[21] Van Buren favored an asymmetric two-party system, and he did not accept that the governing principles of the Federalists or the Whigs could be squared with the Constitution. His vision of an asymmetric two-party system laid out in his *Inquiry*—not two parties alike in strength and dignity as they have become in the era of divided party control of government, but of one dominant party winning most elections and a minority party usually losing—would persist well into the twentieth century.

In keeping with his thesis through *Inquiry,* Van Buren characterized the Federalists as factious and partial to commercial interests and Jefferson, Madison, and his own party as upright and constitutionally steadfast. His open denigration of the Federalists made it, arguably, easier for later generations to conflate Federalists with the Anti-Federalists, or at least to elevate the "other" founders to the same plane as Publius and the Federalists. Indeed, Van Buren's partisan account of the origins of parties had as its foil another partisan account, that of John Quincy Adams's *Discourse* on the occasion of the Constitution's Jubilee, where the former president, for his part, had shared more than a few jibes "at the party opposed to the administration of Washington" and the "great antagonist" to the Constitution,

Thomas Jefferson.[22] While Van Buren could not make much of the Anti-Federalists' vote against the adoption of the Constitution, since that was a battle fought and long lost, he honored them by resuscitating the substantive theory on which their objection was based. He wrote:

> The most auspicious prospects beamed upon the opening administration of the new government, and it is fair to presume that the anticipations thus inspired would have been triumphantly realized if those who had been selected to conduct it, and their successors for the ensuing twelve years, had accepted the Constitution in the sense in which it was known to have been understood by those who framed it, and by the people when they adopted it. A course thus right in itself . . . would not have failed to conciliate large portions of the Anti-Federal party.[23]

If Van Buren's most significant contribution to American politics was his justification of the political party in a culture predisposed against "faction," his method to this end was by insinuating an Anti-Federalist reading of the largely Federalist Constitution. As a defender arguably closer to the Article of Confederation's conception of union, and yet bound to a text predominantly written by Federalists, Van Buren would attack the new, more centralized federalism by indirection, characterizing the Federalists in *Inquiry* not as winners of the ratification debate but as one-sided partisans who perverted the views of those who helped to "frame" the Constitution. According to him, "Alexander Hamilton, the able and undisputed leader of the Federal party, from its [the Constitution's] origin to his death, did comparatively nothing either toward its formation or adoption by the Federal Convention."[24] Though Hamilton was indeed absent from the Federal Convention in July and August 1787, this characterization conveniently obscures the very significant role Hamilton played, if not in the adoption of the Constitution by the Federal Convention, then certainly the ratification of the Constitution by the several states. It also obscures the alliance between Hamilton and Madison, one that the latter showed no evidence of disavowing until after the Constitution was ratified.[25] The author of more than two-thirds of the *Federalist Papers* (indeed, the man who convinced Madison and Jay to join him in coauthorship) would probably have received more credit had he not been "the leader of the Federal party." One reason why Van Buren could not accept Hamilton's contribution to the character of the Constitution is clear: as a prominent member of George Washington's cabinet who was also there at the Philadelphia Convention, Van Buren's argument that post-ratification Federalists failed to execute "the Constitution in the sense in which it was known to have been understood" becomes less tenable.

Whereas Van Buren trivialized Hamilton's role in the creation of the Constitution, he extravagantly praised Madison's. Indeed, Van Buren played a major role in raising Madison to the august status of primus inter pares among the "founders." According to Van Buren, the "character and political career of James Madison was *sui generis*. . . . [P]ossessed of intellectual powers inferior to none, and taking an unsurpassed interest in the course of public affairs, he seemed invariably to bring to the discussion of public questions a thoroughly unprejudiced mind."[26] Even though Van Buren admitted that Madison "supported, ably and perseveringly, many, if not most of the propositions for the adoption of which the Federal party was particularly solicitous," he nevertheless concluded, "there was no time when Mr. Madison can, with truth and fairness, be said to have belonged to the Federal party."[27] This is striking revisionism. This was the same wily Madison who arrived in Philadelphia twelve days ahead of the start of business and requested the same of his fellow delegates from Virginia in order to draft the Virginia Plan and frame the agenda for the convention.

Today, American democracy is "unthinkable" without parties; that the party is formally outside of the Constitution raises no eyebrows.[28] Harvey Mansfield observed, for example, that "[p]arty alignment is an informal structure of choice, dependent on the formal structure but specifying what it cannot specify, the actual content of choice."[29] But there was no fudging between formal and informal, static and living constitutionalism, back in the day. It was Van Buren who helped make it the case that democratic choice was to be one structured specifically by parties rather than by a variety of other potential contenders in the nineteenth century, such as personal factions or other organizations such as churches, professional guilds, or fraternal societies. Van Buren's success in grafting an extraconstitutional institution into the constitutional fabric is all the more impressive because of the highly partisan means by which he effected what has come to be seen as a nonpartisan constitutional development. He was able to do so, and effectively erased the name of Anti-Federalism from the political lexicon, by capturing the Anti-Federalists' reservations and objections to the Constitution so completely and supplying an organization that would carry their political values deep into the nineteenth century.

## *The "Living" Constitution, States' Rights, and Democracy*

Modern scholars see "living constitutionalism" and "originalism" as opposite interpretations of the Constitution. Proponents of the former accept that in the course of time and in response to evolving circumstances, new practices and norms are padded around the original text, forming an informal constitution. Defenders of the latter are usually formalists who understand the constitutional text to be sufficient unto itself for all time, and do not see meaning or legitimacy to norms or practices beyond the original text.[30] Today, most living constitutionalists are Democrats and most originalists, Republican. It is a great testimony to Van Buren's creative synthesis of the party to the Constitution that we cannot easily place him on one or the other side of this modern debate, for he found a way to occupy both.

Arguably, Van Buren was the first major theorist and implementer of "living" constitutionalism. Unlike the Federalists who believed that the Constitution was a self-regulating machine "that would go of itself," Van Buren believed that the Constitution's inadequate provision for states-centered democratic self-government should and could be remedied, in particular, by the political party.[31] According to him, "political parties are inseparable from free governments . . . [t]he disposition to abuse power, so deeply planted in the human heart, can by no other means be more effectually checked."[32] This was an important departure from the Federalists' reliance on the separation of powers to check power as well as to orchestrate a fair balance between different estates or interests. Van Buren was saying, as the Anti-Federalists had predicted a generation earlier, that the separation of powers so confidently championed by the Federalists had failed to check and limit government. The political party was, for him, the "extraneous means to secure harmony" among those not privileged to belong to the patrician class.[33] The choice of the word "extraneous" is important, for it indicates that he understood the party to be an extraconstitutional invention. It shows that "he viewed the party system as a corrective to what he understood to be the Constitution's inadequate regard for self-government."[34] Van Buren presided over an extraconstitutional invention, the party, in order to, ostensibly, affirm an original, constitutional end. So successful was this enterprise that we now think it entirely unremarkable that the person who defended the first major artifact of the "living" constitution was also a fierce defender of "strict constructionism."

Van Buren was able to do this because there remained widespread and persisting reservations about the Constitution, and he wrapped his heresy in this strong and relatively coherent tradition of dissent.[35] Insofar as he jettisoned the separation of powers in favor of party competition, Van Buren was a heretic as regards Federalist constitutionalism. It is a tribute to his success in embedding the Democratic Party into the "living" Constitution that scholars no longer acknowledge the irony that his creation helped to reinforce a set of views held by those who originally opposed the Constitution and its centralizing impulse and who lost the ratification debates. This can be seen most clearly in Van Buren's and the Anti-Federalists' commitment to states' rights and democracy.

### States' Rights

Van Buren and nineteenth-century Democrats extolled the Bill of Rights and the Tenth Amendment. As he had made much of Madison's contributions at the Philadelphia Convention, Van Buren also applauded Madison as a congressman because he had "availed himself of the diversities in opinion and feeling between the federal and anti-federal members to secure the adoption of amendments, otherwise unattainable, which gave to that Invaluable Instrument a vitality without which it must long since have perished."[36] For Van Buren, the Constitution lived and thrived only because of the reaffirmation of local democracy jointly delivered by the Bill of Rights and the political party. The idea of local democracy, at the heart of the Democratic Party, harkened of course back to the old Confederation. This is probably why Democrats highlighted the *vertical* checking and balancing of powers in the Constitution when the Federalists, arguably, had argued for an equal portion of regulating work to be done by the separation of powers at the *horizontal* interface of the Constitution. And so, as Milkis notes, "[j]ust as Jeffersonian democracy gave rise to a party that established a wall of separation between the national government and the states, so Jacksonian democracy fortified this barrier."[37] When Andrew Jackson called the Congress the "Federal Legislature of 24 sovereign States," or the United States a "Confederacy" whose "strength and true glory . . . is founded on the prosperity and power of the several independent sovereignties," he was expressing a vision that the Federalists had gone out of the way in 1787 to mollify, in part by redirecting the checking and balancing impulse to a less centrifugalizing mechanism, the separation of powers.[38] Not so for nineteenth-century Democrats. Van Buren believed that the Democratic Party organized at the grassroots level was the only legitimate way of divining the will of the people, and therefore the last word on constitutional interpretation. He would help to graft partisan political organizations, committed to local democracy and states' rights, onto a Constitution that was, at least according to Hamilton's interpretation, written to overcome those jealousies. Though we are now used to thinking of parties as national organizations, the organization Van Buren built was essentially local, thoroughly grounded on the Anti-Federalists' first principle of states' rights. As Milkis and Rhodes observed, "the Jacksonian ambition to make partisanship part of the 'living Constitution' was embodied by the Democratic Party which organized voters on the basis of principles that were militantly decentralizing, as was the very process of party politics they established."[39]

Van Buren assumed that democracy was ineluctably local because he believed that majority rule would reliably displace the rule of elites only in a system that entrenched the maximal dispersal of power. He was not, therefore, thinking of majorities and minorities in the way that Tocqueville did or the way we do today; for him, the challenge of party organization was to give voice to and execute the will of the majority of the people, not to provide safeguards against it. As Milkis notes,

> [t]he persistent, confederate form of political parties stemmed from their creation as agents of constitutional reform. Political parties, in fact, were founded as part of a program to modify the original Constitution so that it would conform in practice to many of the principles of Anti-Federalism. These political associations served the purposes of those who shared the Anti-Federalist commitment to local self-government but joined Jefferson in accepting the Constitution as a working document, hoping to shape it by amendment, interpretation, and practice.[40]

The clash between Federalists and Anti-Federalists would be reinvented in the Jacksonian era in the form of party politics between those who advocated government centralization and those who defended states' rights. Local government now had an advocate and structural embodiment in the "living" Constitution. Loyalty to the party therefore meant a continued affirmation of Van Buren's interpretation of the Constitution; disloyalty meant constitutional apostasy.

One major implication of this commitment to states' rights was that Van Buren, like most of his contemporaries, even John Quincy Adams, as the Waldstreicher chapter of this volume attests, was overridingly concerned with preserving the Union, and not addressing or "politicizing slavery" in the early decades of the nineteenth century. This meant relative neutrality and silence on slavery for both Adams and Van Buren up until the 1830s, and the latter adopted an aggressive stance on states' rights as the best way he knew, at the time, to quell the sectional divide over slavery, and permanently graft the Democratic Party onto the Constitution in a mutually reinforcing relationship.[41]

## Democracy

As a result of this commitment to states' rights, Anti-Federalist theories of republicanism and civic virtue would enjoy a rhetorical renaissance and adaptation in the Jacksonian era. Nineteenth-century Democrats, like the Anti-Federalists, rejected the Federalist vision of a large commercial republic representing the "money power" and preferred instead the promotion of a political economy that would produce virtuous, self-reliant citizens capable of self-government. In this vein, they saw the farmer as the ideal citizen and the fount of the highest virtues, which was why a good amount of their domestic program was dedicated toward the cultivation of a virtuous squirearchy. As Van Buren observed, "the defense of the principles which the colonists cherished, and for the maintenance of which the Revolution was made, rested on the broad shoulders of the landed interest."[42] Jacksonian Democrats revered the patient cultivators of the soil—men who improved the earth on which they labored, acquiring the virtues of independence, frugality, and endurance as they did so. And since an economy consisting of mostly yeoman farmers was an economy in which every man enjoyed the fruits of his labor and no man was exploited, Jacksonian Democrats preferred a political economy that saw no need to import the Marxian distinction between capital and labor, employer and employee, or the socialist ideas of an interventionist state. To be sure, this romantic ideal conveniently underestimated dramatic inequalities even within the "landed interest,"[43] but that too was probably by design. Jacksonian Democrats defended the farmer big or small so that there would be no need for an aggressive national government to step in to manage an industrial economy. For Jacksonian Democrats as it was for the Anti-Federalists, the role of government was reasoned backward from what an idealized citizen's occupation and virtues would look like, not what national problems existed for which governing solutions had to be found. It was in service of the landed interest and not the "money power" that Democrats held that the federal government's strength lay "not in binding the States more closely to the center, but leaving each unobstructed in its proper orbit."[44]

The central concern of Democratic Republicans and later Democrats was that the "money power" would control the central government and petition it for special privileges, and the only check on them was the people, organized and united by the political party. Though this was a process that had already been initiated a generation earlier, 1828 evinced "the raving howl of Democracy"[45] in unabashed defiance of Madison's observations in *Federalist* 10 that "democracies have ever been spectacles of turbulence and contention."[46] Whereas the word was once associated with civil strife and anarchy, Jackson's supporters now dropped the "Republican" part of their party's name and unashamedly called themselves "The Democracy" and adopted the slogan "Let the People Rule" in 1828.[47] How democratic the Jacksonian era actually was remains a matter of debate, but the Democratic Party offered itself proudly and emphatically as a critique of and a solution to the Constitution's unfinished promise to represent "We the People."[48] With this new institution, Democrats inverted the Federalists' understanding of republicanism with the latter's emphasis on indirect rule and complex schemes of representation, and placed their bet instead on majority rule. Instead of the formal institutions of the Constitution, Democrats placed their faith in the people directly: "where the people are everything, and political forms, establishments, institutions, as opposed to the people, nothing, there, and there only, is liberty; such a state, and such a state only, constitutes republican government."[49] Like the Anti-Federalist Melancton Smith, who believed that "representatives [should] . . . resemble those that they represent," Van Buren and Jackson held a mirroring rather than a trusteeship theory of representation.[50] "Every day," Van Buren wrote, "convinces me more of the perfect reliance that may, under all circumstances, be placed on the intelligence, patriotism, and fortitude of the people."[51] In the name of transparency and democracy, Van Buren and Jackson effected a transfer of power from King Caucus and sent it down to state and local party bosses, where it stayed until the era of primaries. To be sure this was less a republic of men than a republic run by party elites; but it was a dramatic shift from the framers' aspiration to forge a republic of institutions.

When nineteenth-century Democrats talked about the people, they meant self-government by the people of the states, not the whole people of the United States. A commitment to local majorities strung together by partisan alliance not only neutralized the extended republic's ability to control faction; it offered a philosophical defense and upgrade of what had once been known as faction—now a national Democratic coalition—for which the objection of majority tyranny became but a quaint afterthought. For a while a least, an alliance of local majorities across the states allowed Democrats to sustain and legitimate the "mischiefs of faction" in a large republic in defiance of the Federalist plan, while silencing any debate about slavery. Democrats, of course, could boast of constitutional propriety because the Anti-Federalists before them had secured potent guarantees for states' rights, which found expression in every electoral rule found in the Constitution. The U.S. Constitution requires that members of the House and Senate be chosen "by the People" (Article I, Sec. 2) and that the electors from the states "vote by ballot for President and Vice-President" (Article II, Sec. 1). In every case, the qualifications to vote are set by the states.[52] Van Buren's and Jackson's contribution to American democratic theory, however, was to tie democracy even more closely to states' rights and to turn the latter into a majoritarian doctrine by way of a partisan umbrella. With democracy thus defined and defended by partisan collusion across the states, there was little room for alternative interpretations, until this partisan glue started to unravel in the 1840s (with Van Buren himself as a major, pro-abolitionist antagonist). Such an understanding of democracy took out all the oxygen from alternative interpretations. As Richard Hofstadter noted of John Calhoun, one of the most vocal defenders of states' rights in the nineteenth century and Jackson's vice president, "Not in the slightest was he concerned with minority rights as they are chiefly of interest to the modern liberal mind."[53] It may sound ironic to modern ears that the golden age of democracy occurred at a time when the true majority, including women and blacks, could not yet vote; but this only indicates the temporary success of Van Buren in marrying democracy and states' rights.

In unlocking direct democracy and linking it closely to states' rights, Jackson and his supporters would deliver a score for the Anti-Federalists. For the Federalists had believed that separate institutions sharing powers best checked power, which is why they carefully constituted a set of interdependent institutions to create a government of laws rather than a government of men. The Anti-Federalists, on the other hand, believed that government was best checked from without and not from within, which is why they were ultimately for a government of men. And this came fully to pass with Jacksonian democracy, which organized a government of men under the umbrella of the political party. While Madison had proposed, in *Federalist* 10, that the defect of "pure democracy," faction, could be solved with republicanism (a system of indirect rule in an extended republic), Jacksonian Democrats countered that the antidote to a corrupted republic was more democracy, organized by a network of parties. As Lawrence Kohl argued of the Democrats, "that the nation was held together primarily by the artificial bonds of constitutional prescription was inadmissible to them."[54] This was a stark repudiation of the Federalists' ambitious "new science"; it was Anti-Federalism in sharp and sweet revenge, because with the surge in democracy, Jacksonian Democrats could sit in offices created by the Federalists' Constitution and at the same time aver that no longer was the Constitution the sole source of political ordering and legitimacy in the United States. Now, the people, as least as they understood it, were as well.

Indeed, as party not only became the engine of politics and the Constitution, it in some respects even became government itself. If the Anti-Federalists believed that rotation in office prevented corruption, and Jefferson introduced the idea of a purge of the Federalists after the Revolution of 1800, Van Buren combined the Anti-Federalists' idea with the Jeffersonian practice to validate another new extraconstitutional development—the spoils system of distributing government jobs as an incentive to reward partisan loyalists. He would enforce strict party discipline with an army of officeholders and the aid of the *Albany Argus*.[55] Within a generation, the Anti-Federalist principle of rotation in office would fuse with the routinization of partisan competition to generate the Machiavellian truth of the Democratic creed, as Senator William Marcy put it, "to the victor belong the spoils." By this system, the very thing that delivered planned disruptions in officialdom, elections and their aftermath, would also cultivate loyalty in the party. Through the party convention system, Van Buren and his followers "replaced constitutional elections with extra-constitutional 'regular nominations.' Through spoils, Van Buren abdicated his constitutional duty to take care that the laws be faithfully executed through his officers. Instead, he took care only that those officers' livelihoods depend on their toeing the party line."[56] The party would enjoy a continual existence even if governments and officials come and go; the health and longevity of the political system would now be guaranteed by something outside of the formal constitutional structure—the party system.

## *"The State of Courts and Parties"*

When Van Buren and Jackson introduced the spoils system to tie party with government, they halted whatever momentum was left from the Hamiltonian effort to create a national bureaucracy independent from politics. In spite of the success of the Jeffersonian-Republican Party, the balance of institutions as well as Supreme Court decisions such as *McCulloch v. Maryland,* (1819) and *Dartmouth v. Woodward* (1819) still leaned Federalist and nationalist in the Era of Good Feelings. The durable retrenchment of federal authority in the Jacksonian era could come about only because a parallel constitution, consisting of state-level political parties that formed a "state of courts and parties," emerged to execute a more decentralized federalism than was envisioned by Hamilton and Washington.[57] Van Buren's and Jackson's defense and cultivation of party and spoils brought on the golden age of states' rights, which but for the interregnum of Reconstruction, would persist for the rest of the century. By supplying the "state of courts and parties" in place of the earliest shell of a national administrative state that emerged during the Washington and Adams administrations as well as in the aftermath of the War of 1812, the Democratic Party was an Anti-Federalist godsend that delayed the onset of the modern, bureaucratic state.

In *Federalist* 17, Hamilton had predicted that "the people of each State would be apt to feel a stronger byass [*sic*] towards their local governments than towards the government of the Union; unless the force of that principle should be destroyed by a much better administration of the latter."[58] Jackson and Van Buren (who persisted, even after the Panic of 1837, in his resistance to "internal improvements," the nineteenth-century term for government-sponsored infrastructural projects to boost the economy) made sure that during their administrations, citizens were afforded few opportunities to experience the benefits of federal largesse. Whereas Hamilton believed that "[a] NATION, without a NATIONAL GOVERNMENT, is . . . an awful spectacle" (*Federalist* 85), Van Buren and the Democrats held fast to "the just and abstemious precepts that the world is governed too much."[59] The Federalists and Whigs believed that the federal government would be venerated the more it showed that it could deliver on what the states had failed to deliver on, whereas at the heart of the Democrats' commitment to states' rights was the static and uncompromising Anti-Federalist starting point that the more limited the central government, the more it could be tolerated. In this regard, Jackson and Van Buren, like the Anti-Federalists, were "men of little faith."[60] They believed, in Jackson's words, that "the successful operation of the federal system can only be preserved by confining it to the few and simple, but yet important, objects for which it was designed"—hardly a whole-hearted endorsement of "a more perfect Union."[61] According to the historian Richard McCormick, "Jackson sought to persuade his fellow citizens that the ineffectuality of the government was a virtue."[62] We are so used to hearing this refrain that we associated it with the "founders"; but this is only because Van Buren and Jackson did so well in recrudescing Anti-Federalism by another name.

With the ratification of the Constitution and the Federalists' victory over the Anti-Federalists complete in that one regard, the losers of that battle have relied on more surreptitious ways to wage an ongoing war to thwart Publius's goal of "a more perfect Union." If the Federalists had used similarly crafty means to capture the term "Federalist" from the original defenders of federalism, so too Van Buren and his cohort were able to reinterpret the Constitution in ways that incorporated the Anti-Federalists' reservations. Van Buren was the counterrevolutionary who helped to inaugurate the "living" constitution, but covered his tracks by affirming the Democratic Party as the truest defender of the formal text. Van Buren and the Democrats reworked American constitutionalism while also creating a system for the peaceful transition of power between parties in American politics. So it was fitting that while he was the third sitting vice president to be elected directly to the presidency, he would also be the last until George H. W. Bush was elected. If the Federalists and their statist disciples dominated the eighteenth and twentieth centuries, most of the nineteenth century was triumphantly Anti-Federalist, and this had much to do with Van Buren's partial but durable restoration of some of the major principles of the Articles of Confederation. The Anti-Federalists may have lost the initial battle over ratification of the Constitution; but with help from Martin Van Buren, the long nineteenth century demonstrated that they had far from lost the ideological war about the proper role of the federal government and its relationship to the people of the states.

## *Notes*

1. Richard Hofstadter, *The Idea of a Party System* (Berkeley: University of California Press, 1966), 226.

2. James Ceaser, *Presidential Selection: Theory and Development* (Princeton, NJ: Princeton University Press, 1979), 136.

3. Saul Cornell, *The Other Founders: Anti-Federalism and the Dissent Tradition in America, 1788–1828* (Chapel Hill: University of North Carolina Press, 1999).

4. Edward Countryman, "The Empire State and the Albany Regency," in Milton M. Klein, ed., *The Empire State: A History of New York* (Ithaca, NY: Cornell University Press, 2001), 295–306, 300.

5. John L. Brooke, *Columbia Rising: Civil Life on the Upper Hudson from the Revolution to the Age of Jackson* (Chapel Hill: University of North Carolina Press, 2010).

6. Martin Van Buren, *The Autobiography of Martin Van Buren,* ed. John C. Fitzpatrick (Washington, DC: Government Printing Office, 1920), 125.

7. Ted Widmer, *Martin Van Buren* (New York: Henry Holt, 2005), 56.

8. David J. Siemers, *The Anti-Federalists: Men of Great Faith and Forbearance* (Lanham, MD: Rowman & Littlefield), 34.

9. William H. Riker, *The Strategy of Rhetoric: Campaigning for the American Constitution* (New Haven, CT: Yale University Press, 1996).

10. A rare exception was Abraham Lincoln in his Cooper Union Address, as the Earle chapter in this volume recounts.

11. Martin Van Buren to Charles Dudley, Jan. 10, 1822, cited in Robert V. Remini, *Martin Van Buren and the Making of the Democratic Party* (New York: Columbia University Press, 1959), 23,

12. Hofstadter, *Idea of a Party System,* 228.

13. Thomas Jefferson to Albert Gallatin, Oct. 29, 1822, in Paul L. Ford, ed., *The Writings of Thomas Jefferson* (New York: G. P. Putnam's Sons, 1905), 12:252.

14. The first parties, which emerged after the Glorious Revolution, were temporary movements created to save the British constitution from corrupt ministers. In the early eighteenth century, the Tory opposition, also known as the "Country" party or persuasion, would emerge behind the leadership of Viscount Bolingbroke to challenge the alleged capture of the House of Commons by Robert Walpole and his ministers. Though Bolingbroke might have hoped his movement would become a permanent opposition, this did not come to be because republican thought at the time tolerated internal strife only insofar as it could help restore constitutional balance; so parties or movements stood accused of becoming the very thing they set out to vanquish if they persisted in existence past a certain point.

15. Alexander Hamilton, John Jay, and James Madison, *The Federalist Papers* (New York: Bantam, 1982), 4.

16. Gerald Leonard, "'Party as a 'Political Safeguard of Federalism': Martin Van Buren and the Constitutional Theory of Party Politics," *Rutgers Law Review* 54 (2001): 221–81, 234.

17. Robert Eden, "The New Deal Revaluation of Partisanship," in Peter W. Schramm and Bradford P. Wilson, eds., *American Political Parties and Constitutional Politics* (Lanham, MD: Roman & Littlefield, 1993), 187.

18. Van Buren, *Autobiography,* 108.

19. Martin Van Buren, *Inquiry into the Origins and Course of Political Parties in the United States* (New York: Hurd and Houghton, 1867), 423.

20. Ibid., 5.

21. Gerald Leonard, *The Invention of Party Politics: Federalism, Popular Sovereignty, and Constitutional Development in Jacksonian Illinois* (Chapel Hill: University of North Carolina Press, 2002), 239.

22. John Q. Adams, *The Jubilee of the Constitution: A Discourse* (New York: Samuel Colman, 1839), 94, 114.

23. Van Buren, *Inquiry,* 61–62.

24. Ibid., 58.

25. Mary S. Bilder, *Madison's Hand: Revising the Constitutional Convention* (Cambridge, MA: Harvard University Press, 2015), 152.

26. Van Buren, *Inquiry,* 59.

27. Ibid., 61.

28. E. E. Schattschenider, *Party Government* (New York: Holt, Rinehart and Winston, 1942), 1.

29. Harvey Mansfield Jr., "Political Parties and American Constitutionalism," in Schramm and Wilson, *American Political Parties and Constitutional Politics,* 1–16, 13.

30. See, for example, Jack M. Balkin, *Living Originalism* (Cambridge, MA: Belknap Press of Harvard University Press, 2011); Antonin Scalia, *A Matter of Interpretation: Federal Courts and the Law* (Princeton, NJ: Princeton University Press, 1998).

31. Michael Kammen, *A Machine That Would Go of Itself: The Constitution in American Culture* (New York: Alfred A. Knopf, 1986).

32. Van Buren, *Autobiography,* 125.

33. Van Buren, *Inquiry,* 5.

34. Sidney Milkis, "Localism, Political Parties, and Civic Virtue," in Martha Derthick. ed., *Dilemmas of Scale in America's Federal Democracy* (New York: Cambridge University Press. 1999), 89–124, 102.

35. Elvin T. Lim, *The Lovers' Quarrel: The Two Foundings & American Political Development* (New York: Oxford University Press, 2014).

36. Van Buren, *Autobiography,* 468n.

37. Sidney Milkis, "Political Parties, the Constitution, and Popular Sovereignty," in Peter D. Bathory and Nancy L. Schwartz, eds., *Friends and Citizens: Essays in Honor of Wilson Carey McWilliams* (Lanham, MD: Roman & Littlefield, 2001), 171–92, 179.

38. Andrew Jackson, First Annual Message, Dec. 8, 1829, http://www.presidency.ucsb.edu/ws/?pid=29471; Andrew Jackson, Second Annual Message, Dec. 6, 1830, http://www.presidency.ucsb.edu/ws/index.php?pid=29472.

39. Sidney Milkis and Jesse Rhodes, "The President, Party Politics, and Constitutional Development," in L. Sandy Maisel and Jeffrey M. Berry, eds., *The Oxford Handbook of American Political Parties and Interest Groups* (New York: Oxford University Press, 2010), 378–401, 382.

40. Milkis, "Localism," 94.

41. Jonathan H. Earle, *Jacksonian Antislavery & the Politics of Free Soil, 1824–1854* (Chapel Hill: University of North Carolina Press, 2004), 6.

42. Van Buren, *Inquiry,* 230.

43. Glenn C. Altschuler and Stuart M. Blumin, *Rude Republic: Americans and Their Politics in the Nineteenth Century* (Princeton, NJ: Princeton University Press, 2000).

44. Andrew Jackson, Veto Message, July 10, 1832, http://www.presidency.ucsb.edu/ws/?pid=67043.

45. Donald Ratcliffe, "The Right to Vote and the Rise of Democracy, 1787–1828," *Journal of the Early Republic* (2013): 219–54; Robert V. Remini, *The Legacy of Andrew Jackson: Essays on Democracy, Indian Removal, and Slavery* (Baton Rouge: Louisiana State University Press, 1988), 8.

46. Hamilton *et al., Federalist Papers,* 46.

47. Jack R. Pole, "Historians and the Problem of Early American Democracy," *American Historical Review* 67 (1962): 626–46.

48. Jeffrey L. Pasley, "Minnows, Spies, and Aristocrats: The Social Crisis of Congress in the Age of Martin Van Buren," *Journal of the Early Republic* (2007): 599–693.

49. George S. Camp, *Democracy* (New York: Harper & Brothers, 1841), 9.

50. Speech of Melancton Smith, New York Ratification Convention, June 21, 1788, in Herbert Storing and Murray Dry, eds., *The Complete Anti-Federalist* (Chicago: University of Chicago Press, 1981), 6:157.

51. Martin Van Buren to Andrew Jackson, October 17, 1837, in John S. Bassett, ed., *Correspondence of Andrew Jackson,* 7 vols. (Washington, DC: Carnegie Institution of Washington, 1926–1937), 5, 516.

52. House: "[T]he Electors in each State shall have the Qualifications requisite for Electors of the most numerous Branch of the State Legislature" (Article I, Sec. 2). Senate: "The Senate . . . shall be . . . chosen by the legislature thereof" (Article I, Sec. 3) / "The electors in each State shall have the qualifications requisite for electors of the most numerous branch of the State legislatures" (Article I, Sec. 3, Seventeenth Amendment). President: "Each State shall appoint, in such Manner as the Legislature thereof may direct" (Article II, Sec. 1).

53. Richard Hofstadter, *The American Political Tradition and the Men Who Made it* (New York: Alfred Knopf, 1948), 90–91.

54. Lawrence F. Kohl, *The Politics of Individualism: Parties and the American Character in the Jacksonian Era* (New York: Oxford University Press, 1989), 178.

55. This was an important instrument for the "Little Magician," who preferred to let others do the talking so that he could keep his opinions to himself. He was also the only president for whom English was a second language.

56. Leonard, *Invention of Party Politics,* 29.

57. Stephen Skowronek, *Building a New Administrative State: The Expansion of National Administrative Capacities, 1877–1920* (New York: Cambridge University Press, 1982).

58. Hamilton *et al., Federalist Papers,* 82.

59. Ibid., 449; Van Buren, *Autobiography,* 363.

60. Cecilia Kenyon, "Men of Little Faith: Antifederalists on the Nature of Representative Government," *William and Mary Quarterly* 12 (1955): 3–43.

61. Jackson, Second Annual Message.

62. Richard McCormick, "The Jacksonian Strategy," *Journal of the Early Republic* 10 (1990): 12.

# 4 Abraham Lincoln Goes to the Archives

## *Slavery, the Cooper Union Address, and the Election of 1860*

Jonathan Earle

Each of the individuals to occupy the office of president of the United States has turned to the past as a way to understand the nation's present and communicate this understanding to both friend and foe. Yet Abraham Lincoln is without presidential peer in the use of history to bind our nation together in memory (from the first inaugural's "mystic chords . . . stretching from every battlefield and patriot grave to every living heart and hearthstone," to the "we cannot escape history" exhortation in his annual message to Congress in 1862, to the famous "Four-score and twenty years ago" of the Gettysburg Address).[1] And he reached his zenith of presidential eloquence, to borrow a phrase from biographer Ron White, at times when he spoke directly to the American people.[2] This ability, as this essay shows, extended to the time before his presidency even began—to the electrifying campaign that took him to the White House at one of our nation's great turning points. During the earliest stages of his first campaign for president, Lincoln was able, through diligent research and some good fortune, to deploy modern historical techniques to support his positions in the debate over whether slavery should be allowed to expand into the West.

Lincoln was hardly the first politician to enlist history to buttress a political stance, or even the first in the campaign of 1860. In fact, Lincoln's historical journey was essentially forced on him by his political rival Stephen A. Douglas, after the Illinois senator published a long and detailed historical defense of his idea of "popular sovereignty" in the fall of 1859. In response, Lincoln chose to visit an unusual destination for an office-seeker—the law library at the state capitol in Springfield, Illinois—to make a serious study of early congressional debates over slavery. The speech that his primary and secondary research yielded was, of course, the famous Cooper Union Address, and it displayed the candidate's new ability, honed over the last months of 1859 and before the speech in February 1860, to compose "historically educated, logical counterarguments to Democratic [proslavery] positions."[3] With intensive research into the words and, more important, *actions* of the earliest Congresses, Lincoln drove home the point that containing slavery (the cornerstone of the Republican ideology) was perfectly in line with the framers' own views. This was a direct rebuttal to Democrats like Douglas who had long claimed to be closely hewing to the Founding Fathers' own views on slavery. Whether or not Lincoln's argument was good history, it turned out to be extremely good politics, expanding the spread of the antislavery tent to cover millions of northerners and westerners who would never call themselves abolitionists.

Abraham Lincoln's historical apprenticeship followed a five-year period of introspection, melancholy, and intellectual growth for Lincoln—a time his biographer Michael Burlingame characterized as his "mid-life crisis."[4] After two years in the U.S. Congress, a term in which he did not distinguish himself in any significant way, Lincoln tried to break an 1846 promise that, if elected, he would not seek reelection. The Whig Party of central Illinois was only too happy to accept this self-imposed term limit, and did not even renominate the dejected incumbent. Over the next five years Lincoln read widely, traveled the length and breadth of the state on the legal circuit, and redefined himself as a top-notch appellate and corporate lawyer. He experienced personal hardship as well. In 1851, his second son, three-year-old Eddie, died after a short illness. At an age where many people experience a heightened sense of mortality and wariness, the forty-two-year-old Lincoln worried to friends about his legacy. "How hard—oh how more than hard," he told his law partner William Herndon, "it is to die and leave one's Country no better for the life of him that lived and died her child."[5]

## *Kansas-Nebraska, Peoria, and Lincoln's First (Tentative) Historical Steps*

Stephen Douglas's introduction of a bill to organize the territory of Nebraska in early 1854 changed Lincoln's political and historical trajectory in profound ways, offering him a new path to national prominence as both a leader of the antislavery movement and a prime mover of the nation's historical memory. Douglas's bill proposed to set up a government in vast parts of the old Louisiana Purchase north of present-day Oklahoma all the way up to the Canadian border, at a time when the United States was restlessly composed of sixteen free and fifteen slave states. While slavery was to be forever excluded from parts of the purchase north of 36° 30′ by the twenty-three-year-old Missouri Compromise, Southern leaders were determined to salvage some slave soil out of this gigantic new territory. Douglas, as a leading aspirant for the Democratic presidential nomination, was all too happy to oblige: in a move intended to make his bill more palatable to powerful Southerners, Douglas divided the territory in two, and the Kansas-Nebraska Act was born.

To a growing number of Northerners growing weary of domination by slaveholders in all three branches of government, Douglas's move looked suspiciously like a scheme to mark out Kansas for slavery and Nebraska as free soil. Douglas, a believer in popular sovereignty, famously declared he could "care not" whether the settlers in new territories chose slavery or freedom—as long as "the tide of immigration and civilization" was permitted to roll onward.[6]

Yet thousands of Americans *did* care. They regarded the expansion of slavery as a national question, and a moral one. "Anti-Nebraska" meetings exploded across the North, unifying Old Whigs, Free Soilers, and antislavery Democrats wary of expanding the peculiar institution west. Douglas's law also provided the spark that catapulted Lincoln the Illinois circuit lawyer back into the national political spotlight. As a private citizen in 1854—neither holding nor seeking public office—Lincoln at first claimed to feel no compelling reason to make a public statement on the Kansas-Nebraska bill. But once he decided to take part in the "anti-Nebraska" movement, he did not hold back.

As soon as Congress adjourned in August 1854, Douglas decided to return home to defend his legislation (he joked that he could have journeyed back to Illinois by the light of the burning effigies of himself). Waiting for him was his old rival—for Mary Todd Lincoln's hand in marriage, for supremacy in the Illinois statehouse, and for high political offices to come. Lincoln was eager to display some of the new fruits of his first serious foray into intensive historical research on the slavery question, and he practically stalked Douglas across the Illinois prairie. When Douglas declined a formal face-to-face debate with Lincoln, the lanky lawyer employed a novel strategy of addressing political crowds soon after Douglas had concluded his own speeches. In his retorts, Lincoln struck hard at Douglas's previous stance as a great champion of the "sacred" Missouri Compromise, even displaying clippings from Douglas's older addresses on the subject and denying that climate and geography would do little to keep slavery out of Kansas and Nebraska, pointing out that five slave states (Delaware, Maryland, Virginia, Kentucky, and Missouri) had similar climates.

Yet in an important departure in Peoria on October 16, Lincoln focused more squarely than he ever had on the morality of slavery itself, grounding his opposition to its extension in the Declaration of Independence. For the first time he made the case that the founders had fought to contain the institution (an argument he would later return to in greater detail in the Cooper Union Address), and stated unequivocally that slaves were humans who possessed natural rights, including the right to self-government. "If the negro is a man," Lincoln said, "then my ancient faith teaches me that 'all men are created equal;' and that there can be no moral right in connection with one man's making a slave of another." Later in the address, which lasted more than three hours, Lincoln admitted he saw no way fully to rid the nation entirely of the "monstrous injustice" of slavery, but "[l]et us return [slavery] to the position our fathers gave it; and there let it rest in peace."[7]

Lincoln's new moral—and *historically grounded*—attacks on Douglas and the Kansas-Nebraska Act were far more compelling than his earlier critiques of Democratic policies like the tariff or the war with Mexico. The abrogation of the Missouri Compromise and the founders' attempts to contain the expansion of slavery gave the committed Whig the political push it took for him to become Lincoln the Republican.

## *Stephen Douglas's Historical Seminar*

The year 1854 was hardly the end of Lincoln and Douglas's political rivalry, or the debates over the issue of slavery and its expansion. The fight over Kansas Territory became a proxy war for every possible side of the slavery issue, from proslavery "Border Ruffians" from Missouri to the abolitionist followers of John Brown, and violence spread easily from "Bleeding Kansas" to the halls of the U.S. Congress.[8] Douglas, meanwhile, continued to hold firm both to his idea of popular sovereignty as well as his determination to secure the 1860 presidential nomination of the Democratic Party, one of the last remaining national institutions.

Yet when Douglas broke with the administration of President James Buchanan in 1858 over the fraudulent and proslavery Lecompton Constitution for Kansas, the dramatic fracture of the Northern Democratic Party gave Lincoln another opening to challenge Douglas and slavery's march to the west.[9] Despite the controversy over the Kansas constitution, Douglas remained the obvious and leading choice to succeed Buchanan in the White House. A Democrat with a national reputation who had long cultivated relationships with Southerners, Douglas charged headlong into the 1860 campaign. But he knew he had work to do mending fences with his colleagues from below the Mason-Dixon Line. Specifically, he had to elaborate more fully on his views of popular sovereignty, Douglas's clever (yet intentionally vague) solution for the slavery question in the West. Essentially, popular sovereignty meant that settlers of a territory should be able to decide for themselves whether it would enter the Union as a slave or free state. As often with seemingly simple solutions to complex problems, the devil was in the details: when (and how) would settlers decide? During the territorial stage, or after statehood was granted? And who would count as a bona fide "settler"—especially after the massively (and obviously) fraudulent votes of Missouri's Border Ruffians came to light in successive elections in Kansas Territory?[10]

Douglas decided he would attempt to square the popular sovereignty circle in one fell swoop: with a carefully argued "manifesto" in an influential new publication. He also chose to capitalize on the methodology and innovations of "scientific history" associated with figures like Leopold von Ranke in Germany and George Bancroft in the United States. In an April 1859 letter Douglas actively sought Bancroft's assistance in preparing an address "upon the right of the people of the Territories to govern themselves in all their domestic relations, without the interference of the federal government." A partisan Democrat as well as the nation's preeminent historian (he was already the author of the multivolume *History of the United States of America, From the Discovery of the American Continent,* with a doctorate from the University of Göttingen), Bancroft agreed.

The historian also assisted Douglas in his endeavor to make the publication of his manifesto more significant than a speech or guest editorial in a newspaper. In an arrangement that represented innovations in magazine publishing as well as the research and writing of American political history, Douglas made a deal with the editors of *Harper's Magazine* to publish his completed essay, with exclusive copyright (in other words, it would not be reprinted extensively in the political press for free).[11] William A. Seaver, who helped broker the deal, believed the subject was of "paramount interest" and that the reading public would welcome "the carefully elaborated views of a statesman whose public experience had necessarily familiarized him with territorial jurisprudence." Seaver, Douglas, Bancroft, and the editors at *Harper's* each worked to keep the arrangements secret, so as to achieve maximum effect upon publication.[12]

In search of arguments to defend his signature policy, Douglas retrieved important works of colonial history and political economy from the Library of Congress, including Henry C. Carey's *Slave Trade, Blackstone's Commentaries,* and Bancroft's recent *History.* The senator, presidential candidate, and newly minted amateur historian also assembled an impressive *équipe de recherche,* including a full-time private assistant to pore over colonial records. Bancroft helpfully offered primary documents he had encountered in his own research, as well as works from his own library, in a Washington, D.C., version of the famous seminar led by the pioneer of modern source-based history Leopold von Ranke. Douglas specifically asked Bancroft to track down examples of enactments by the colonies of British North America that either excluded or prohibited slavery, in an effort to draw direct connections between the experiences of the colonies and contemporary western territories like Kansas. "The Dividing Line Between Federal and Local Authority: Popular Sovereignty in the Territories" appeared in the September 1859 issue of *Harper's New Monthly Magazine,* and immediately commanded the attention of the national political establishment.[13]

Douglas's essay was clearly influenced by modern and even Romantic views of the historian's craft, and strived for both originality and a deliberate use of primary sources and historical documents. As Bancroft wrote in the preface to his *History,* the modern scholar makes the strongest argument "by deriving it entirely from writings and sources, which were the contemporaries of the events that are described." He also proclaimed himself to be an adherent of "the principles of historical skepticism, and, not allowing myself to grow weary in comparing witnesses or consulting codes of laws."[14] In Stephen Douglas, George Bancroft found a willing student of the historical seminar.

Bancroft's method and conclusions might not pass the rigorous and critical scrutiny of today's American Historical Association—he was certainly guilty of inventing and selectively editing quotations and remaining oppressively filiopietistic about the actions of Revolutionary leaders. But he was also, in the words of one recent scholar, "a more sophisticated historian than many scholars have acknowledged." One can see in Douglas's attempt at his own history a strategy to achieve both Bancroftian originality and political vindication over his adversaries and opponents—in this case including both Republicans like Lincoln as well as Southern nationalists who wanted nothing to do with popular sovereignty.[15] Like it or not, Douglas argued, Republicans must accept that the "fathers of the Revolution" themselves had decided that slavery was to be a matter of domestic and internal concern, and created the Union and "divided [it] into free and slave states, with the right on the part of each to retain slavery so long as it chooses, and to abolish it whenever it pleases." Moreover, when the founders used the word "states," they meant both "states" and "territories." In other words, according to Douglas, the federal government had no authority to ban slavery in federal territories, a right that belonged solely to local governments.[16]

Interestingly, Douglas claimed to have discovered some of the antecedents to popular sovereignty in Jefferson's own 1784 plan for western government, to which he liberally referred (while intentionally overlooking the overt prohibition of slavery originally included in Jefferson's plan). Douglas also failed to mention Jefferson's Ordinance of 1787, which prohibited outright the institution of slavery in future states carved out of territories north and west of the Ohio River, and would appear at the center of Lincoln's rebuttal to Douglas's ideas.[17]

Yet Douglas did not stop with the founders and the eighteenth century in his *Harper's* essay. In addition to his detailed discussion of the colonial and territorial periods, Douglas referred even more frequently to the recent (and already much loathed, at least in the North) Supreme Court decision *Dred Scott v. Sandford,* and to the legal arguments set forth by Chief Justice Roger Taney. Compared to earlier sections, the quotations from *Dred Scott* are used far more selectively and misleadingly; they are full of ellipses and cite only the sections that most directly supported his territorial positions. Douglas also transposed sentences in order to heighten this effect, contorting his main arguments (which, according to his leading biographer, led to them becoming "more involved and complicated").[18] In a typical paragraph, for example, Douglas wrote:

> [I]n as much as the Constitution has conferred on the Federal Government no right to interfere with the property, domestic relations, police regulations, or internal polity of the people of the Territories, it necessarily follows, under the authority of the Court, that Congress can rightfully exercise no such power over the people of the Territories. For this reason alone the Supreme Court were [*sic*] authorized and compelled to pronounce the eighth section of the Act approved March 6, 1820 (commonly called the Missouri Compromise), inoperative and void—there being no power delegated to Congress in the Constitution authorizing Congress to prohibit slavery in the Territories.[19]

This resulted in Douglas's *Harper's* article becoming, in the words of Robert Johannsen, "repetitious, contrived, long and tedious . . . [and] written in a turgid style that lacked the vibrancy of his speeches." Politically, the piece was a failure: it won few converts, and alienated moderate (and potentially persuadable) voters in both sections. Antislavery voters in the North, for example, were put off by Douglas's acceptance of the *Dred Scott* decision's rendering of the Missouri Compromise as meaningless. Southerners, on the other hand, seethed that Douglas conceded that there were, in fact, limits to where slavery should be allowed to spread. To a growing number of them this view placed him "outside the pale of the party," according to one Alabama congressman, who declared that the *Harper's* essay dealt the senator's political future "a death blow in the South." A politician's attempt to enlist history to his cause clearly carried risks as well as potential rewards.[20]

## *Lincoln's Archival Response*

The publication of Douglas's "Dividing Line" essay provided his old rival Abraham Lincoln with a straightforward, if risky, avenue for rebuttal: proving that, contrary to the Democrat's assertion, the founders had no intention of leaving the future of slavery entirely up to the states as localities. Douglas's failure to quiet the waters with his own manifesto made Lincoln's decision to answer with his own history lesson perilous. Yet to Lincoln, the potential reward was worth the risk, and he aggressively made preparations to contest Douglas on the new political battleground "scientific history" provided him.

Lincoln also had two advantages over his adversary. First, he had the luxury of following Douglas's own publication. Second, he was provided with an ideal occasion and venue for his response when he received an invitation to speak in New York City, at the brand-new Cooper Union of Science and Art, also known as the Cooper Institute. Lincoln fully seized the opportunity provided by this invitation, and prepared for his debut in front of the national press corps by writing a speech that bore no resemblance to his able and well-known stump speeches. Instead, Lincoln opted to borrow a page from Douglas's book and don the metaphorical robes of the scholar, in hopes it might vault him to the top tier of contenders for national office.[21]

In order to counter Douglas's historical arguments, however, Lincoln understood that he would have to find his own evidence, especially regarding the founders' attitudes and beliefs about slavery and its spread south and west in the years after the Revolution. In other words, he knew he would fail in New York if he simply chose to rehash his two-year-old Illinois debate points, especially since Douglas had ventured deep into the historical record to defend his positions with direct quotations from the Republic's architects. Like a student in Ranke's seminar, Lincoln began to ponder some open-ended historical questions: What did the framers *really* think about slavery and its future? Did they publish their views? And, perhaps most important, did they ever have occasion to cast a *public vote*—to *act* rather than just opine—on the matter? Each of these were research questions that Douglas had failed to ask, preferring instead to assume a fairly standard conclusion (that the founders were entirely comfortable with slavery, and that only states and localities could affect its spread to new states in the West). Lincoln the lawyer decided instead to venture into the basement of the Illinois State Library in the fall of 1859 to conduct some archival research. He did so alone, without the benefit of a staff or famous historian in tow.[22]

Lincoln's research began with a detailed analysis of the intense debates over the U.S. Constitution and votes in the Congress of the Confederation—especially on the Ordinance of 1787, which created the Northwest Territory out of lands north and west of the Ohio River, and prohibited slavery there.[23] Lincoln reported out the results of his research in the first section of his long, detailed, and well-received Cooper Union Address. Unlike most political speeches, this one began with few stories, jokes, or Lincolnian lead-ins. In fact, in just his third sentence he directly quoted Douglas's claim that the founders "understood this (slavery) question just as well, and even better than we do now," an idea he returned to no fewer than thirty times over the course of the address. For the next thirty minutes of the address Lincoln methodically sought to "prove" (as much as one could in a single speech) that the founders *did* understand the issue, and that contrary to Douglas's claims, they inherently and repeatedly acted to support the Republican Party's contention that the federal government had every right to "control" slavery by barring its extension into federal territories.[24]

Interestingly, Lincoln pivoted from the usual definition of the founders as almost-perfect "great men" (that adopted by Douglas in his essay), redefining them as republican delegates and legislators. Just who were "the founders" in Lincoln's Cooper Union analysis? Not the architects and signers of the Declaration of Independence, who later figured so strongly in Lincoln's presidential speeches. Instead, he zeroed in on the men who debated and voted on the Constitution, the twelve amendments so far added to it, and the debates over the Northwest Ordinance. The first portion of the speech concerned the thirty-nine men Lincoln identified as signers of the Constitution in Philadelphia and the seventy-six legislators who subsequently debated and passed the Bill of Rights.

After defining exactly who he meant by "our [nation's] founders," Lincoln re-posed the question Douglas engaged with in the *Harper's* essay: could the federal government legally ban slavery from the federal territories? This new frame allowed Lincoln to engage with Douglas's most recent defense of popular sovereignty as well as the *Dred Scott* decision, which was as popular in the hall as traffic on Broadway. Since the Democratic position was clearly stated by Douglas in *Harper's* and countless speeches ("we maintain that the federal government has no right to interfere with the question, either to establish, to protect, to abolish or prohibit slavery; but that the people in each State and each Territory, shall be left entirely free to decide it for themselves"), Lincoln decided to counter with votes and numbers in addition to quotations. His thesis was that a majority of the "fathers" who debated and signed the U.S. Constitution and the Bill of Rights fully supported the Republican side of the debate, that the federal government could prevent slavery's spread into the territories. What's more, Lincoln intended to "prove" this assertion by leading his audience methodically through the separate votes on the formation of the "free" Northwest Territory in 1784,

1787, and 1789; an 1804 congressional vote on the territorial organization of small part of the Louisiana Purchase without slavery; and the debates over the Missouri Compromise (which barred slavery north of the line of 36° 30′). This required some serious empirical explaining, but Lincoln's straightforward style and the seriousness of the topic brought him some leeway with his listeners.[25]

By the numbers, Lincoln reported that fully twenty-eight of the original signers were "yes" votes to prohibit slavery from the territories north and west of the Ohio River. "This shows that," he argued, "in their understanding, no line dividing local from federal authority, nor anything in the Constitution, properly forbade Congress to prohibit slavery in the federal territory." Additionally, "George Washington, another of the 'thirty-nine' . . . approved and signed the bill; thus completing its validity as a law."[26] The figure of Washington, the undisputed "father of our country," was extremely important to Lincoln's historical argument at Cooper Union. The owner of more than 300 slaves at his death, Washington was at the same time deeply conflicted about the institution, and made numerous previous statements about his willingness to see it pass from the scene. "There is no man living who wishes more sincerely than I do to see a plan adopted for the abolition of it," he wrote to Robert Morris the year before the Constitutional Convention.[27] Washington also wrote that he hoped that the institution could be actively controlled "by legislative authority," just as Lincoln was arguing seventy-five years later. In his *Harper's* essay, Douglas vehemently denied the existence of any federal legislative authority to "control" slavery.

Lincoln then went into some detail regarding instances where early Congresses organized territorial governments that, in one way or another, limited slavery in Mississippi, Louisiana, and, later, Missouri. He again explained that, of the original "thirty-nine," several (including John Langdon, Roger Sherman, William Few, Rufus King, George Read, and Abraham Baldwin) cast two—or, in the case of Baldwin, three—separate votes prohibiting slavery's spread and thus "interfering" with the institution. Careful to subtract the multiple votes left, in Lincoln's enumeration, "twenty-three out of thirty-nine fathers 'who framed the Government under which we live,' who have, upon their official responsibility and their corporal oaths, acted upon the very question which [Douglas's] text affirms they 'understood just as well, and even better than we do now.'" Of these twenty-three, only two voted "nay"—and their reasons for doing so were impossible to know. That meant that twenty-one of those constitutional "fathers"—"a clear majority of the whole 'thirty-nine'"—subsequently voted to forbid slavery's spread into territories owned by the very government they had established. Here Lincoln drove home his main point: "Thus the twenty-one acted; and as actions speak louder than words, so actions, under such responsibility, speak still louder." In just the first third of the Cooper Union Address, Lincoln cited the actions of those he counted as the nation's founders—not simply their words—to undermine the arguments of Douglas's *Harper's* essay. Importantly, his argument also threatened the very heart of Roger Taney's *Dred Scott* decision, which, after all, claimed that once a citizen entered a federal territory the government could exercise no power whatsoever over his or her "person or property."[28]

After establishing his "majority" of actors, Lincoln turned to those founders (including some of the nation's most well known) who left no demonstrable historical record on the slavery prohibition issue. Admitting that while we can't really *know* how these sixteen "silent fathers" would have voted, if given the opportunity, fifteen of them left significant clues for future historians to conclude that they would *likely* have sympathized with Lincoln's side of the argument. These included, among the others, famous slavery antagonists Alexander Hamilton, Benjamin Franklin, and Gouverneur Morris. In fact, only one of the sixteen—the South Carolinian John Rutledge—was a confirmed, dyed-in-the-wool proslavery advocate. Adding these fifteen to the "twenty-one," Lincoln, with extreme satisfaction, proclaimed that fully thirty-six of the original "thirty-nine" stood (or would have) firmly with those favoring curtailing slavery's expansion. It's doubtful a twenty-first-century historian would venture too far with this latter argument, but Lincoln stuck with it nonetheless.

Inside the hall, Lincoln's "scientific history" scored well. According to the young Bostonian theologian Lyman Abbott, used to the "dramatic and impassioned oratory of Henry Ward Beecher," Lincoln's historical arguments were "as passionless, but also as convincing, as a demonstration of Euclid's Geometry, as clear and cogent, but also as absolutely without oratorical ornament of any description." Another attendee, more skeptical than Abbott, reported finding himself coming into agreement with Lincoln under the "merciless logic which no listener could escape, as he unfolded link after link in the iron chain of his argument."[29] Any historian would be proud to have the logic of her or his arguments compared to iron chains or Euclid;

Lincoln had clearly convinced at least some of those in attendance of the validity of his argument.

The response to the Cooper Union Address in the daily press was also more than any aspiring national politician—or historian—could hope for. The entire speech was reprinted the following day in full in four daily papers, including the pro-Douglas *New York Herald.* The *New York Times* devoted three columns to the speech on page 1, but failed to add any meaningful observations besides a generous description of the raucous reception it received. The most conclusive evidence that Lincoln's history section had been compelling was to be found in William Cullen Bryant's *New York Evening Post,* which devoted all of page 6 to the text and headlined the piece: "The Framers of the Constitution in Favor of Slavery Prohibition." One line down the subheadline read: "The Republican Party Vindicated." An editorial also focused on the fruits of Lincoln's archival research: "[t]hat part of it in which the speaker places the Republican party on the very ground occupied by the framers of our constitution," the unsigned column read, "and fathers of our republic, strikes us as particularly forcible. . . . All this may not be new, but it is most logically and convincingly stated in the speech—and it is wonderful how much a truth gains by a certain mastery of clear and impressive statement."[30]

Horace Greeley's *New York Tribune,* whose offices Lincoln visited "to look at the proof slips" before retiring to the Astor Place Hotel on the evening of the speech, contained the most hyperbolic praise, though little of the analysis present in the *Evening Post*'s columns. "No man ever before made such an impression on his first appeal to a New-York audience," the editorial gushed. "The Speech . . . was one of the happiest and most convincing political arguments ever made in this City."[31]

## *Who Was the Better Historian?*

Judging by the evidence offered by Lincoln's and Douglas's competing historical texts from 1859–60, the two men practiced different types of history and sought to achieve different goals. Douglas, chiefly concerned with defending his 1850s policy of popular sovereignty, adopted a variety of "great man" history associated with the Scot Thomas Carlyle. His cherry-picked quotations from the letters, speeches, and documents of colonial and Revolutionary-era leaders bordered on scriptural, and his addition to them of Justice Taney's more recent (and controversial) *Dred Scott* decision was intended to link the two eras together in a single, strict-constructionist manner.[32]

Lincoln's focus, however, was more on the contingency of events, the contextual politics of historical actors, and the words, votes, deeds, and *actions* they took in the real world to illustrate their beliefs. Lincoln was, first and foremost, a talented lawyer and politician, but here he also displayed considerable nuance as a historian. He, too, relies heavily on the founders—but urges his listeners to avoid logic like Douglas's, which placed men like George Washington on the side of popular sovereignty and disunion. "Could Washington himself speak," he asked Southerners who accused Republicans of ignoring the first president's warnings against sectional parties in his Farewell Address, "would he cast the blame of that sectionalism upon us who sustain his policy, or upon you, who repudiate it?" In his conclusion Lincoln went still farther, urging his listeners to pay attention not only to the words of "great men" like Washington but to their deeds as well:

> Let us be diverted by none of these sophistical contrivances . . . such as Union appeals beseeching true Union men to yield to Disunionists, reversing the divine rule, and calling, not the sinners, but the righteous to repentance—such as invocations to Washington, imploring men to unsay what Washington said, and undo what Washington did.

Lincoln here was urging a revision of the "great man" view of history, and suggesting replacing it with a more "scientific" version that relied on putting founders' views, debates, and votes in the changing contexts of their time. In this he was anticipating the critiques the Victorian philosopher and political theorist Herbert Spencer applied to the "great man" history, which he regarded as naive and primitive. Regarding the founders and slavery, Lincoln implored, "speak as they spoke, and act as they acted upon it. This is all Republicans ask—all Republicans desire—in relation to slavery. As those fathers marked it, so let it be again marked, as an evil not to be extended, but to be tolerated and protected only because of and so far as its actual presence among us makes that toleration and protection a necessity." This was not merely a rhetorical point. Instead of the strictly scriptural approach of Douglas's *Harper's* piece ("the founders sayeth"), Lincoln insisted it mattered what they did, and the context in which they did it. In doing so, he demonstrated how this new, modern, "scientific history" might be used as a tool for politics and persuasion.[33]

In this era just at the cusp of the "professionalization" of the historical discipline, it is not surprising that the politicians digging into historical sources were trained as lawyers. They were not, as professional historians of the twentieth and twenty-first centuries were and are, trained to use only the best primary sources available to reach, "objectively," for the closest thing to the truth. Instead, able lawyers like Lincoln and Douglas utilized past heroes to give and lend credence to the policies they wanted to enact in the late-antebellum present, the way a prosecutor constructs a closing argument based on the best argument he or she can muster. It is interesting, then, that Lincoln's argument ventures farther than he was used to as a criminal defense attorney. "Beyond a reasonable doubt" would not have won Lincoln the praise he received as a logician and historical narrator. He needed to reach for more.

These same themes can be seen, as well, in the politics of our own time, including recent strains of populist conservatism associated with the Tea Party. These "patriots"—adorned in tricorn hats and other Revolutionary garb—are also notorious for cherry-picking scriptural antecedents among the writings of the founders, in what the historian Jill Lepore has called "historical fundamentalism." The net effect of this, and the related syndrome of "founders chic" that fills the pages of so many hagiographic biographies published by nonprofessional historians, is the complete collapse of past and present and the embrace of the past as just like the present. What Abraham Lincoln accomplished first in Peoria, but in a more sustained way in the Cooper Union Address, was different, and more impressive: by examining and interpreting how a particular generation reacted, in the political context of the early Republic, he made a convincing case that at least *his* founders favored placing the power of the federal government on the side of freedom rather than slavery. Few historical arguments have proven more powerful or more enduring.

## *Notes*

1. David Zarefsky, the leading scholar of rhetoric and speech communications, makes a strong case for "rhetorical leadership" being among a president's greatest tools and ways to wield power, and that it stems from his personal powers of persuasion (as

opposed to those enumerated in the Constitution). See David Zarefsky, "Lincoln's 1862 Annual Message: A Paradigm of Rhetorical Leadership," *Rhetoric and Public Affairs* 3, no. 1 (Spring 2000): 5.

2. Ronald C. White Jr., *The Eloquent President: A Portrait of Lincoln through His Words* (New York: Random House, 2005), 171.

3. Gary Ecelbarger, *The Great Comeback: How Abraham Lincoln Beat the Odds to Win the 1860 Republican Nomination* (New York: Thomas Dunne, 2008), 106; Harold Holzer's *Lincoln at Cooper Union* (New York: Simon and Schuster, 2004) goes into rich and fine-grained detail on the speech and its significance.

4. Michael Burlingame, *Abraham Lincoln: A Life* (Baltimore: Johns Hopkins University Press, 2008), 1:357–62.

5. Ibid., 1:358.

6. On Lincoln during the aftermath of the Kansas-Nebraska Act, see Jonathan Earle, "'If I Went West, I Think I Would Go to Kansas': Abraham Lincoln, the Sunflower State, and the Election of 1860," in Jonathan Earle and Diane Mutti Burke, eds., *Bleeding Kansas, Bleeding Missouri: The Long Civil War on the Border* (Lawrence: University Press of Kansas, 2013), 119–30.

7. Speech at Peoria, Ill., Oct. 16, 1854, in Roy P. Basler, *The Collected Works of Abraham Lincoln* (New Brunswick, NJ: Rutgers University Press, 1953), 2:247–83, quotations on 266, 276.

8. During one ferocious week in May 1856, proslavery terrorists sacked the free-state town of Lawrence, John Brown retaliated with a massacre of proslavery settlers on Pottawatomie Creek, and South Carolina congressman Preston Brooks caned Massachusetts senator Charles Sumner in the U.S. Capitol. See Joanne B. Freeman, *The Field of Blood: Violence in Congress and the Road to Civil War* (New York: Farrar, Straus and Giroux, 2018).

9. On Lecompton, see Nicole Etcheson, *Bleeding Kansas: Contested Liberty in the Civil War Era* (Lawrence: University Press of Kansas, 2004), 185, 197; Pearl Ponce, "'The Noise of Democracy': The Lecompton Constitution in Congress and Kansas," in Earle and Mutti Burke, *Bleeding Kansas, Bleeding Missouri,* 81–96.

10. Etcheson, *Bleeding Kansas,* 96, 113.

11. Douglas to Bancroft, April 11, 1859, in Robert W. Johannsen, ed., *The Letters of Stephen A. Douglass* (Champaign: University of Illinois Press, 1961), 442; Douglas to Seaver, July 17, 1859, in Johannsen, *Letters,* 449. See also Robert W. Johannsen, *Stephen A. Douglas* (New York: Oxford University Press, 1973), 706–8. On Bancroft, see Russell B. Nye, *George Bancroft, Brahmin Rebel* (New York: Knopf, 1944).

12. Johannsen, *Stephen A. Douglas,* 708.

13. One innovative feature of the essay was its copyright, prohibiting newspaper editors from simply reprinting it without permission, in what one paper called "a revolution in modern systems of Presidential campaigning." See *New York Herald,* Aug. 29, 1859; Johannsen, *Stephen A. Douglas,* 707–8. On the origins and practices of "scientific history," see Bonnie G. Smith, "Gender and the Practices of Scientific History: The Seminar and Archival Research in the Nineteenth Century," *American*

*Historical Review* 100, no. 4 (Oct. 1995): 1150–76; Peter Novick, *That Noble Dream: The "Objectivity Question" and the American Historical Profession* (New York: Cambridge University Press, 1988).

14. George Bancroft, *A History of the United States* (Boston: Charles Bowen, 1834), 1:v. See also Anthony Grafton, *The Footnote: A Curious History* (Cambridge, MA: Harvard University Press 1997), 55–60, on the German university's emphasis on primary sources and eighteenth-century commitment to originality.

15. Eileen Ka-May Cheng's *The Plain and Noble Garb of Truth: Nationalism & Impartiality in American Historical Writing, 1784–1860* (Athens: University of Georgia Press, 2008) deals in impressive depth with the historiography of the post-Revolutionary and antebellum years. Quotation on 144.

16. Stephen A. Douglas, "The Dividing Line between Federal and Local Authority," *Harper's* (Sept. 1859), 519, http://harpers.org/sponsor/balvenie/wp-content/uploads/Popular%20Sovereignty%20in%20the%20Territories-Douglas.pdf.

17. Ibid., 521–26.

18. Johannsen, *Stephen A. Douglas,* 709; Douglas, "Dividing Line," 529–33.

19. Douglas, "Dividing Line," 529–30.

20. Eli Shorter to Franklin Pierce, Sept. 7, 1859, Franklin Pierce Papers, Library of Congress.

21. Lincoln's Cooper Union Address is easily compared to then state senator Barack Obama's keynote address at the 2004 Democratic National Convention in Boston (another national speech delivered by a little-known Illinois lawyer with lofty political aspirations).

22. Holzer, *Lincoln at Cooper Union,* 10–11; telegram in the Lincoln Papers, Library of Congress.

23. Reginald Horsman, "The Northwest Ordinance and the Shaping of an Expanding Republic," Wisconsin Magazine of History (1989): 21–32. See also Harold M. Hyman, *American Singularity: The 1787 Northwest Ordinance, the 1862 Homestead and Morrill Acts, and the 1944 GI Bill* (Athens: University of Georgia Press, 2008); Peter S. Onuf, *Statehood and Union: A History of the Northwest Ordinance* (Bloomington: Indiana University Press, 1987).

24. "Address at Cooper Union," in Basler, *Collected Works,* 3:523. Lincoln's arguments about the Founders also inform Sean Wilentz's just-published *No Property in Man: Slavery and Antislavery at the Nation's Founding* (Cambridge: Harvard University Press, 2018).

25. Holzer, *Lincoln at Cooper Union,* 52. Lincoln's "go-to" source appears to have been *Elliott's Debates in the Several State Conventions on the Adoption of the Federal Constitution as Recommended by the General Constitution at Philadelphia,* 3:534, 590. Twenty-three of the thirty-nine signers Lincoln identified spoke out against slavery's expansion.

26. *Elliott's Debates,* 523.

27. Washington to Robert Morris, Apr. 12, 1786, http://founders.archives.gov/documents/Washington/04-04-02-0019.

28. *Elliott's Debates,* 523–32. See also Ecelbarger, *Great Comeback,* 138–39.

29. Lyman Abbott quoted in "Lincoln as a Labor Leader," in Nathan William MacChesney, *Abraham Lincoln: The Tribute of a Century, 1809–1909* (Chicago:

University of Chicago Press, 1910), 281; Henry M. Field quoted in Henry M. Field, *The Life of David Dudley Field* (New York: Charles Scribner's Sons, 1898), 123. See also Holzer, *Lincoln at Cooper Union,* 28.

30. *New York Evening Post,* Feb. 28, 1860.

31. *New York Tribune,* Feb. 28, 1860.

32. In *Heroes and Hero-Worship* (1840) Carlyle famously wrote that "the history of the world is but the biography of great men," reflecting the belief that so-called heroes shape history through both their personal qualities and divine inspiration. Gutenberg Project: http://www.gutenberg.org/files/1091/1091-h/1091-h.htm.

33. Basler, *Collected Works,* 5:550.

# II Reimagining American Power and Responsibility

# 5 Theodore Roosevelt's Historical Consciousness and Lincoln's Generous Nationalism

Kathleen Dalton

In the autumn of 1901, after an assassin killed President William McKinley, his forty-one-year-old successor, Theodore Roosevelt, hurried to Washington to take the reins of office. Few wondered what effect Roosevelt's previous career as a historian might have on his presidential decision-making. But TR left clues aplenty in his writings and his previous political career about his well-formed historical consciousness and his view that his nation needed strong leaders. He had praised the advance of civilization and the dominance of developed nations over weaker ones, and as a student of history he believed that making the United States a mighty and respected nation-state would promote progress and stability in world history. His study of history provided him with a benchmark of presidential greatness; he longed to become a great president like Abraham Lincoln. His own historical writings showed that TR brought to the presidency a romantic nationalist and even imperialist consciousness. Would Roosevelt's brash eagerness to become a strong leader and make America a world power be tempered by his attachment to the model provided by the wise and patient Lincoln?

## *Roots of TR's Historical Consciousness*

TR's historical outlook developed first from his boyhood adoration of the military heroes of the Civil War. He watched parades not far from his boyhood home in Manhattan, and he heard his father's letters from the battlefield read aloud. Theodore Roosevelt Sr. worked with his friend President

Lincoln on an allotment system to send soldiers' pay home, and he also dispensed patriotic propaganda during the war. Following Lincoln's lead, TR Sr. opposed the centrifugal political forces that threatened the nation-state and instructed his son in nationalism. TR confessed that "from reading of the people I admired—ranging from the soldiers of Valley Forge, and Morgan's riflemen, to the heroes of my favorite stories—and from hearing of the feats performed by my Southern forefathers and kinsfolk, and from knowing my father, I felt a great admiration for men who were fearless and who could hold their own in the world, and I had a great desire to be like them."[1] Reverence for a strong national government and the heroic impulse figured large in TR's life story and his writing of history.

Intense nationalism also permeated TR's hero worship, and reading Thomas Babington Macaulay, Thomas Carlyle, and Mungo Park convinced him that the romance of rising nation-states conquering the weak and advancing the course of civilization was a worthy story to be told. Although TR Sr. did not plan to turn his favorite son into a historian, he organized Grand Tours of Europe and the Mediterranean by requiring his son to read the histories of the places they visited. TR Sr. encouraged the boy to learn several languages and even placed TR in a German family so he could study German language and history. Because the Roosevelts were wealthy New Yorkers, the boy could buy almost any history book he wanted, and the library he amassed by the end of his life ranged widely in world history. TR Sr. brought his son to visit his uncle James Bulloch, who had been one of the founders of the hurriedly-constructed Confederate navy. Long before Alfred Thayer Mahan touted naval power as the route to world power, TR had been converted to his uncle's view that naval preparedness was a requirement for a nation-state's survival in a competitive world. Harvard and Columbia Law School followed, and TR made himself a historian at an early age.

Hints that he would become a loud advocate of military preparedness appeared early on. TR began his career as a professional historian when he was a student at Harvard, and, in his book about American naval warfare in the War of 1812, he slammed President Thomas Jefferson for his "criminal folly" in failing to prepare for war.[2] In a similar vein, he berated James Madison as a weak president who failed to protect his nation from British armies burning the capital. TR's heroes were fighting men like Captain Macdonough, who triumphed at the Battle of Plattsburg, praiseworthy for their "indomitable pluck" and tactical skill.[3] Though his characterizations were often overblown, TR used primary research effectively to detail battles and praise heroism. "Embrace preparedness or suffer defeat" emerged as the lesson he taught his readers, and he took this historical precept with him to the White House.

TR viewed history as inevitable struggle. He had studied the rise and fall of great powers and worldwide paths of migration and conquest, and when he wrote his own history he honored manly leaders and dominant peoples (usually defined in racialized terms). He read many books with themes of conflict and military conquest, including those by Edward Gibbon, Francis Parkman, John Lothrop Motley, and William Prescott. Given what he read, it is no surprise that he embraced the great man theory of history. He chose to chronicle the Daniel Boone and Davy Crockett phase of settlement of Kentucky and Tennessee, and he did not spend much time regretting the slaughter of Native Americans whose land the western settlers took. TR celebrated the westward movement of English-speaking peoples in his four volumes of *The Winning of the West,* primarily because he believed English-speaking people were inherently prone to bring democracy with them. Progress, race, great men, and democracy went hand in hand.

TR was not, however, a defender of every example of expansion in history. In his biography of Thomas Hart Benton he criticized the Mexican War as an unjust slaveholders' war. Presidents John Tyler and James Polk were to him no more than "apologists for slavery" and General Winfield Scott a "flatulent personage."[4] Nevertheless, the America that emerged from Atlantic to Pacific after the Mexican War was a nation-state he loved, and his romantic nationalism echoed the writings of other late nineteenth-century historians. TR also believed that the frontier experience shaped American character and had schooled Washington, Jackson, and Lincoln to become strong leaders. For TR, the expansion of the nation-state deserved to be the great subject of history: progress, he believed, required civilized conquerors to defeat weaker, less-developed people.

TR brought his own worries about moral decadence and feebleness in Gilded Age men to his writing of history, and he often wrote history as a form of advice literature. In *Hero Tales from American History,* a textbook intended to inspire boys, TR and his friend Henry Cabot Lodge warned that "America will cease to be a great nation whenever her young men cease to possess energy, daring, and endurance, as well as the wish and the power to fight the nation's foes."[5] Extolling military heroes for their manliness and courage in particular, TR hoped to alert Gilded Age Americans to the fighting qualities he believed they were losing. In his famous 1899 "Strenuous Life" speech he interpreted his own moment of history by complaining that America's Gilded Age bourgeoisie loved "ignoble ease" and lived "sunk in scrambling commercialism." He used history to urge his peers to redirect their own lives, calling upon them to seek a "higher life . . . of strenuous endeavor" and to pursue the "goal of true national greatness." As he redefined his vision of "the strenuous life" in the coming years, he always came back to the idea that the nation needed strong leadership to achieve greatness.[6] TR asked the same question on the campaign trail: "Is America a weakling, to shrink from the world work of great world-powers?"[7] His advice to his audiences was grounded in his understanding of history, and he meant to energize them to abandon sloth and materialism in order to serve their nation and to think bigger about America's destiny on the world stage. He had studied what happened to weak powers, and he did not want the United States to follow the path of defeat suffered by nineteenth-century China.

As a historian TR often displayed ambivalence and a divided heart, especially when his scholarly self struggled with the practicing politician in him, most notably when he wrote about *Oliver Cromwell.* TR was mulling over his difficult term as governor of New York when he began his work on Cromwell. As a frustrated politician-reformer he identified with the reform-minded Cromwell in his most thwarted moments, but TR the historian also knew that Cromwell's excesses made him one of the architects of his own tragic end. At the beginning of the book TR expounded vociferously against previous accounts of Cromwell written by "pedants" and the "cloistered type" who failed to appreciate Cromwell the constitutionalist and defender of popular government. In TR's sympathetic telling Cromwell led a "moral awakening" against the "the political and ecclesiastical tyranny of the previous century."[8] TR blamed the Stuart kings, zealots defending the divine right of kings, for leading the English so badly that they caused a "gradual rotting of the national fibre."[9] In fact, TR judged it understandable (and possibly commendable) that Cromwell and his parliamentary forces fought the English Civil War to punish the excesses of King Charles I. Roosevelt admired Cromwell's "energy, fervid zeal, [and] great resourcefulness" as a cavalry leader, but found him "too impatient to found the kind of legal and constitutional system which could alone prevent the recurrence of" monarchical absolutism.[10] TR the historian admitted that Cromwell had been a moralistic and vindictive leader who lost his role as the leader of the Puritan Revolution by despotically grasping excess power. Nevertheless, TR forgave Cromwell as a fellow politician-reformer worthy of excuses. He came down on Cromwell's side in language that anticipated his "Man in the Arena" speech:

> Sooner or later, justice will be done him; sooner or later, he will be recognized, not only as one of the greatest of all Englishmen, and by far the greatest ruler of England itself, but as a man who, in times that tried men's souls, dealt with vast questions and solved tremendous problems; a man who erred, who was guilty of many shortcomings, but who strove mightily toward the light, as it was given him to see the light; a man who had the welfare of his countrymen and the greatness of his country very close to his heart, and who sought to make the great laws of righteousness living forces in the government of the world.[11]

Never mind that Cromwell committed near genocide in Ireland; never mind the rest of Cromwell's bloody record.

TR the historian could also be self-serving, especially in his book about his regiment in the Spanish-American War. His book *The Rough Riders* glorified his own leadership and military courage at the expense of other, braver men. He settled his old score with the army and its arrogant "game-cock" leaders like General Wheeler and chronicled chaotic army transportation of his troops and the lack of medical planning in the Cuban campaign.[12] Because writing history to buck up the feeble young men of his era was always on his agenda, TR characteristically noted "the value of a display of courage among the officers in hardening their soldiers." Then he recorded at length how bravely he led his men up Kettle Hill.[13] Like Winston Churchill, TR found that writing history allowed him to make sure his version of events got told.

TR's career as a historian allowed him to promulgate his particular type of nationalism and defense of strong leaders, but it also helped him explore his own views about what democracy should mean in America. When he wrote a biography of Gouverneur Morris, a little-known figure in the American Revolution and the Constitutional Convention, he revealed considerable sympathies with Federalist thought. TR praised Morris for his loyalty to George Washington even during the low points of the American Revolution, and his advocacy of stronger executive power during the writing of the Constitution, a moment when defenders of a more centralized government were, in TR's view, on the right side of history. But Federalists sometimes went too far even for TR. He roundly criticized Morris for his antidemocratic disdain for the common man during the debates at the Constitutional Convention. TR also lambasted Morris's and other Federalists' "treason" when they talked secession during the War of 1812. At the time he wrote this book TR revealed that he shared some of Alexander Hamilton's and Gouverneur Morris's views that the poorest and least-educated voters might best be weeded out of democracy by imposing a property qualification for voting.[14] Over time he would reconsider the antidemocratic positions he had taken as a young historian.

## *TR Emerges during the Age of Nationalism*

Born in 1858 and a precocious early reader of history, TR would be steeped in the ideological currents of the nineteenth century, including its nationalisms. Parts of Europe once dominated by Napoleon became ripe after his defeat for the idea of organic nationhood founded upon common language, ethnicity, and culture. The new national spirit and mission celebrated by historians such as Johann von Herder encouraged the unification of Germany and Italy, nation-building pushing aside localism. From the 1860s on, TR traveled in Europe and studied in Germany, and he read widely about romantic nationalism, including the works of the German historian Heinrich von Treitschke. Von Treitschke preached that the nation-state was a "moral community" that shapes "national character" and teaches men to defend the honor of their country as well as their own honor as men. Von Treitschke argued that war could be an antidote to national "feebleness" and decadence, and "elevating because the individual disappears before the great conception of the state." War, in this German historian's view, could unite as well as purify a nation of its crass materialism as it inspired its young men to embrace "political idealism" by sacrificing their lives for the good of the nation-state. War could also provide the nation with heroes to worship and thereby elevate the national character. Von Treitschke saw Aryans as the natural leaders of Germany and Jews as unwelcome outsiders, and later Germans used his writings to justify racialist ideologies, including National Socialism, or

Nazism.[15] Though many versions of nineteenth-century nationalism encouraged love for the land and people, German nationalism evolved into a volatile and dangerous nationalist brew, within which George Mosse and others have seen the exaltation of irrationality, primitivism, male virility, and violence.[16] Though TR read and understood von Treitschke and agreed that war was necessary and central to history (and that war built character and manliness in men and could purify the nation's soul), he deplored the German's extreme racism, anti-Semitism, and monarchism.

But racialism of a different form did appear as part of TR's historical and political consciousness. TR's romantic nationalism was certainly tinged by a defense of the Anglo-Saxons' capacity for democracy. He also pointed out in his early historical writings that "priest-ridden peoples" and "half savage" Negroid Haitians were unready for self-government.[17] He continued to believe with cultural evolutionary thinkers that "[t]he peoples of the world have advanced unequally along the road that leads to justice and fair dealing," and that some races were bogged down "in the childhood stage of race development," while others slowly moved toward civilization. But he insisted that strong "civilized" nations needed to keep order among the weaker powers, a racialist justification of imperialism. A Lamarckian, TR understood that races could learn and grow, so he did not agree with von Treitschke that race was destiny or that the nation-state existed for the advancement of one race alone.[18] TR looked away from German nationalisms and embraced Lincoln's version instead.

The depth of TR's attachment to Lincolnian nationalism and its centrality to his later work as president came from deep roots. Roosevelt had witnessed a season of heightened nationalism as a boy. The intensified nationalism of the Civil War North permeated his boyhood home, where Sanitary Commission volunteers, Lincoln Republicans, and Union generals visited. His Lincoln Republican father raised TR to believe that the nation that Lincoln and his followers saved was sacred. TR learned from his father that world civilization advanced when a benign nation-state crushed divisive local forces. In addition to his strong support of Lincoln and the Union cause, TR Sr. applauded Italian unification by raising funds for a statue in New York City to honor Garibaldi, its military hero. TR judged his father to be "the best man I ever knew," and imbibed his romantic nationalism.[19] TR's view of the world was molded by the nationalist atmosphere of his home during that Civil War moment when "[t]he nation became an object of more passionate attachment and self-conscious reflection."[20] Today historians such as Melinda Lawson interpret Lincoln (and his allies like TR Sr.) as Civil War "nation-builders" who invented a new version of American nationalism tied to the average citizen's "right to rise." In the middle of wartime sacrifice Lincoln and his supporters "enveloped the nation-state in a mystical" and sacred "aura." They argue further that Lincoln also "redefined the relationship between the individual and the national state, presenting the state as benefactor, not a threat, to individual Americans."[21] The Roosevelt family helped orchestrate many of the Lincolnian rituals of revived, transcendent nationalism. They planned Union League parades to honor black Union recruits, and gave money to the Loyal Publication Society, which distributed patriotic pamphlets. TR Sr. also donated to Sanitary Fairs to fund medical care on the battlefront. These and other Roosevelt family participations in spreading a benevolent Lincolnian nationalism became a source of pride for TR and his siblings later in life.[22] As he grew up, Roosevelt viewed the American nation as the repository of his father's and Lincoln's deepest hopes that all of mankind could be inspired by America's Civil War struggle to unite behind renewed devotion to liberty and equality.

TR's Civil War education in nationalism launched his ongoing struggle to come to terms with democracy as a political process and as an ideal that respected rich and poor alike as citizens and decision makers. Hearing his father talk about Abraham Lincoln and reading about Lincoln's hardscrabble early life and his empathy for the suffering of others helped TR see people at the bottom of the economic ladder as potential political equals. Lincoln had been dirt poor, and yet he had educated himself to become a thoughtful voter and a humane leader. Furthermore, Lincoln's deep attachment to bettering the lives of the plain people he represented as president fascinated Roosevelt.

Coming from one of New York's richest families, TR initially accepted elitist views of classes below his own. He gradually educated himself about less-privileged people through reading and personal experience. TR Sr. took TR to work with poor newsboys and immigrants as a child, but none of those relationships became equal friendships. In college he camped with Bill Sewall, a sturdy Maine guide who taught him how to survive in the woods and became his friend. Later in his ranching days in the Dakotas he lived among cowboys and farmhands as near equals. When he worked as one of New York's police commissioners he walked the poorest districts of New York with Jacob Riis, a new immigrant; there TR saw for the first time the depths of poverty and the ways the poor were vulnerable to criminals. Lincoln and Theodore Roosevelt Sr.'s concerns for the poor had helped TR understand history and politics outside of his own class cocoon.

Lincoln also provided TR with an example of a strong nationalist leader who advanced the progress of all humanity toward the spread of democracy by using government to serve the interests of the public. An heir of Hamiltonian and Whig traditions of using the federal government to guide the economy and to make internal improvements that would encourage economic development, Lincoln had supported canal, road, and homestead projects as well as veterans' and widows' benefits.[23] He also left his own reform legacy in his support of measures designed to enable citizens to rise up economically via land redistribution, economic advancement by gaining an education in a land grant college, and other forms of government-sponsored opportunities designed to promote greater economic equality.[24] Lincoln had strengthened the reach of the federal government to shape the economy in order to care for veterans and widows; he wanted to encourage citizens to view the state as a benign collective enterprise that their ancestors gave their lives to create and which promised high ideals, justice, opportunity, and democracy. Lincoln's generous nationalism stood in TR's mind as the best model of leadership that American history had to offer.

Lincolnian generous nationalism remained at the core of TR's historical worldview, but by the 1880s and 1890s he was increasingly swayed by the ideology of imperialism. He became convinced that civilized people needed to lift uncivilized people up using colonial rule as a form of tutelage and philanthropy. As a young assistant secretary of the navy TR vociferously lobbied for intervention in the Cuban War for Independence against Spain, which then became the Spanish-American War. Later he endorsed the suppression of the Filipino independence movement. TR became a loud defender of American expansion and the rise of America to world power status, and he went to war as a Rough Rider in Cuba, which pushed his political career forward. In TR's developing historical thinking, imperialism, racialism, and nationalism mixed freely at first. By the time President McKinley chose him to be his vice presidential running mate in the election of 1900, TR's self-publicized wartime heroism and his youthful aggressive spirit had made him a national hero. Then McKinley was shot.

As he entered the White House, Roosevelt realized his own occasional hot-headed, vindictive, and combative tendencies might not measure up to the best presidential standards of statesmanship. His understanding of history would be helpful to him as president, but it was not clear to outside observers when he took office if he would govern as an imperialistic war lover or a judicious mediator and true leader. TR wanted to become a great president like Lincoln, but he understood that "if there is not a great occasion you don't get the great statesman; if Lincoln had lived in times of peace no one would have known his name now. The great crisis must come, or no man has the chance to develop great qualities."[25] Would Theodore Roosevelt be equal to the crises that could make a president great, and would his knowledge as a historian help him make his mark on history?

## *TR's Historical Vision in the Arena of Politics: Living with the Ghost of Lincoln*

As soon as he became president, TR sought out the spirit and memory of Lincoln for guidance. He especially liked to remind himself of his family's historic connection with presidential greatness. At a family dinner on his first night in the White House he spoke with his sisters about their father, and they understood TR had a "romantic attachment" to the White House because "it had sheltered the hero of his boyhood and manhood, Abraham Lincoln."[26] He did not use Ouija boards or mediums to ask advice of the president he admired above all others. Instead, after church on Sunday President Roosevelt often stopped at the nearby home of Lincoln's former private secretary and biographer, John Hay, who had been like a son to President Lincoln and still felt watched over by him. Hay had often dined in the Roosevelts' Manhattan home when TR was a youth, and the new president considered Hay a trusted family friend of long-standing. Hay's connection with Lincoln made Roosevelt's Sunday visits a way of communing with Lincoln through Hay.

Roosevelt often asked Hay to tell him stories about Lincoln, and the question "What would Lincoln do?" came up in their conversations. Hay had also served as President McKinley's secretary of state, and TR decided to keep Hay in office. Lincoln had been a great president with Hay by his side, and it was TR's fondest wish to keep Hay nearby in the hope that he might become a great president, too.

Not only did TR learn to exercise presidential power by studying Lincoln, but he also used his hero as a model of indomitable determination.

Given what he had written as a historian, it came as no surprise that TR set out to make the United States a world power almost as soon as he took office. To promote commerce and enhance U.S. naval power, TR and Hay had long wanted to build a canal to link the Atlantic and Pacific. When an arrangement with Colombia to use its territory in Panama fell through, TR was tormented by the possibility of failure. He wrote to his son Kermit: "It is a great comfort to me to read the life and letters of Abraham Lincoln. I am more and more impressed every day, not only with the man's wonderful power and sagacity, but with his literally endless patience, and at the same time his unflinching resolution."[27] Buoyed up by Lincoln's "unflinching resolution," Roosevelt, with Hay's advice, supported a Panamanian revolution against Colombia and then launched the construction of the Panama Canal. In the end, TR considered uniting the Atlantic and Pacific Oceans via the canal his biggest accomplishment as president.

In foreign policy, Roosevelt had other lessons to learn from Lincoln as commander in chief. Lincoln had understood from the start of the Civil War that he acted each day tethered by public opinion. It was a galling lesson to learn for TR, but as he and Hay proceeded with their plans to enhance America's world power, they realized that public opinion was balking. To retain a foothold far across the Pacific, TR had supported the forceful U.S. suppression of the independence movement in the Philippines, but when a scandal over harsh U.S. wartime tactics, including water torture, provoked public outrage, TR had to respond to public opinion by adjusting his course. He disciplined the general who had ordered the water torture and declared the war over. Though he extended U.S. naval power with new bases and battleships, TR realized that an expansive foreign policy disturbed many isolationists. It was safe to extend humanitarian aid to the victims of the Messina earthquake in Italy but more controversial to govern Cuba in colonial fashion. As president of all the people he had to hold back his own imperial beliefs because he was obliged to respect public opinion, as Lincoln had been. He started no new wars and made sure he advanced with caution. He emulated Lincoln's talents as a mediator and brought peace in the Russo-Japanese War and the Moroccan Crisis, thereby increasing American diplomatic standing among the major world powers using peaceful means.

Similarly, though he intended to act like Lincoln to assert himself as a strong president, TR often was stymied by Congress, especially when it came to conservation of natural resources. TR had studied the history of nations like China, where the cutting down of too many trees had caused erosion, dust storms, flooding, and famine. Though Roosevelt did not predict the Dust Bowl of the 1930s, he tried hard to awaken Congress and the public about the dangers that might come if lumber and mining companies were allowed to devastate forests. Congress resisted when TR asked for federal protection of forests and game preserves. Though begrudgingly allowing him to create the Forest Service, Congress also passed a law blocking TR from adding any more reserves to protected land. The night before the law went into effect TR ordered 16 million acres of forests added to reserves, thus defying Congress. By the end of his term he quadrupled federal forestland.[28]

Though no Civil War arose to provide the crisis that could make TR a great president in the eyes of history, he took as his blueprint for presidential achievement Lincoln's belief that the president had broad responsibility and powers to protect the public welfare. Lincoln served as the model and precedent for TR's own stewardship theory of the presidency. TR said he had insisted "upon the theory that the executive power was limited only by specific restrictions and prohibitions appearing in the Constitution or imposed by the Congress under its Constitutional powers." He added that it was not just the president's "right but his duty to do anything that the needs of the Nation demanded unless such action was forbidden by the Constitution or by the laws." TR knew that Lincoln had used "more arbitrary power than perhaps any other President," and so Roosevelt felt justified in using the power of proclamation, executive order, and prosecution vigorously.[29]

In office TR followed Lincoln and the Civil War Republicans by accepting responsibility for overseeing certain nationwide economic relations.[30] TR said he did it because the public welfare required presidential action to curb the monopolies. The rising merger movement further increased the concentration of economic power in the hands of a few, and President Roosevelt decided to prosecute the Northern Securities Company for attempting to monopolize a regional railroad system. TR's precedent-setting assertion of presidential power to trust bust survived Supreme Court scrutiny, though his critics accused him of Caesarism for continuing thereafter with antitrust action and then new regulatory laws like the Hepburn Act. By 1906, TR further attacked growing economic inequality and called for legislation such as the graduated income and inheritance taxes and the regulation of corporations to curb "swollen fortunes" and to "try to preserve a measurable equality of opportunity."[31] He again made himself the steward of the economy during the

Panic of 1907 when he arranged for failing banks to be recapitalized. In his speeches he acted as historian in chief by arguing for his policies as the next logical step in Lincoln's presidential leadership. In a speech called "Lincoln's Attitude Toward Evil-doers" Roosevelt argued that, like Lincoln, he needed to use the people's will acting through the national government to stop "evil-doers," in this case monopolistic corporations.[32] Eager to associate his efforts to gain "proper control of capitalistic wealth" with Lincoln's democratic "spirit," TR justified the establishment of the Department of Labor and Commerce, food and drug safety regulation, his calls for employers' liability, guarantees for labor unions to gain the right to collective bargaining, limitations of workers' hours, and curbing child labor as logical extensions of Lincoln's concerns about the well-being of the plain people.[33] In speech after speech TR reminded his audiences that the "principles which Lincoln applied to the solution of the problems of his day are those which we must apply if we expect successfully to solve the different problems of our own day."[34] His Lincolnian strategy was successful in shifting public opinion to accept expanded federal regulation of food and drug safety and railroad rates, but Congress still blocked him. Wrapping himself up in the mantle of the beloved Lincoln worked some political magic for TR, but it did not win all his battles for him. Lincoln's voice was especially effective in making TR more compassionate.

Lincoln had a notably positive effect in broadening TR's class attitudes and his sympathy with laborers. In 1902, the writings of Lincoln again helped President Roosevelt understand the plight of plain people (in this case, coal miners). The nation faced a serious labor-management crisis when anthracite coal miners in Pennsylvania went out on strike and representatives of the mine owners refused to negotiate. President Roosevelt felt pulled in many directions as he pondered how to proceed as the Anthracite Coal Strike of 1902 worsened. He could see that the dangers of a humanitarian tragedy and social unrest loomed if he took no action: frozen children, unheated hospitals, stalled transportation, and starving families could spark possible riots. In the past, Gilded Age presidents, Democrats and Republicans alike, had sided with management in labor disputes, calling in federal troops to break strikes. Violent clashes between Pinkerton guards and strikers had marred the Gilded Age, and workers' anger over low pay and harsh working conditions fueled a growing Socialist Party and other groups that threatened the absolute power of factory owners and other employers. TR was bombarded by advice from many quarters, and the mine owners refused to speak with the union.

Not really a patient person, during the Anthracite Coal Strike Roosevelt came close to losing his temper with the recalcitrant workers and mine owners. But TR looked back upon the equanimity Lincoln brought to moments of crisis when it seemed as if he were surrounded by screaming partisans from a hundred factions. TR endured long meetings in which he listened to irreconcilable, contradictory, and unrealistic advice, and he reminded himself that a true leader like Lincoln could find a decisive path forward. He took time out to read all of Hay and Nicolay's multivolume biography of Lincoln, including Lincoln's many letters, and he noted crises in which Lincoln stood up to fierce advisers and critics and showed remarkable empathy too. TR knew his old habits of rough-and-tumble political infighting (including name-calling) did not fit with the dignity of the presidency, and he struggled to copy Lincoln's patience for listening to all parties in the dispute. As TR cajoled the recalcitrant mine owners to compromise, he said in private that he felt like throwing their leader down the stairs. Yet he admitted that Lincoln's example taught him to "try to be good-natured and forbearing and to free myself from vindictiveness."[35] He resolved the crisis by threatening federal intervention to take over the mines; TR forced both sides to accept mediation and settled the historic strike. It was the first time a president had intervened to aid workers in gaining bargaining power and better working conditions, and many critics said it exceeded the presidential prerogatives outlined in Article I of the Constitution. TR didn't care: he had Lincoln on his side. He attributed his success to Lincoln's example of deft mediation of conflicting factions. President Roosevelt said he especially wanted to learn to "be as resolute as Abraham Lincoln had been in seeking to achieve decent ends."[36]

## *TR Uses Lincoln as His Bridge to the New Nationalism*

Roosevelt sincerely admired Lincoln and sought his guidance and his help in justifying new policies, but Lincoln also created a problem of high expectations for him. Lincoln could make politics go his way at the same time he used eloquence to win over hearts—and he could speak to the ages. After all, besides saving the Union and winning the Civil War, when he gave the Gettysburg Address Lincoln had looked beyond the immediate grief of the moment. He painted a bigger picture for his audience by linking their loss to the lives sacrificed in the making of a nation at the time of the American Revolution. Lincoln had placed the Civil War generation in a chain of historical connections, making them beneficiaries of and receptacles for the courage and vision of past generations. He also cast Civil War Americans as guardians of the future and "the last best hope of mankind"; thus Lincoln had made the preservation of democracy an international mission and a fulfillment of America's national destiny. In addition, Lincoln had used his persuasive eloquence as historian in chief to elevate the meaning of the Civil War by issuing the Emancipation Proclamation to redefine the abolition of slavery as the redemption of the nation's founding principles of liberty and equality.

The bar may have been set too high when TR embraced Lincoln as his model of eloquent presidential leadership, but he nevertheless tried in Lincolnesque fashion to use the "bully pulpit" to reiterate Lincoln's commitment to democratic government and the equality of all citizens. He echoed Lincoln's principles in a 1903 speech at the New York State Fair when he declared, "We must treat each man on his worth and merits as a man. We must see that each is given a square deal, because he is entitled to no more and should receive no less."[37] Roosevelt's Square Deal, the name he gave his domestic policies, came to symbolize an equality of opportunity that many Americans still opposed. How could TR emulate Lincoln and use his example in order to persuade his own generation that they had a patriotic duty to strengthen their nation-state as a tool to achieve the goal of equality? TR left the White House in 1909 a popular president, a man who had modernized the army, navy, State Department, and the relationship between the federal government and corporations, but he knew he was still not Lincoln.

TR became a restless spirit as an ex-president, hunting, traveling, writing, and then slowly reentering the world of politics. Still haunted by inequality and growing corporate wealth and power, Roosevelt visited European nations where industrial workers had won unemployment insurance and elderly workers were saved from poverty by government pensions. Compared to comparable industrial nations such as Germany, Denmark, and Great Britain, the powers of the U.S. central government were too weak to address the inequality and human distress created by industrialization. By then these issues mattered more to Roosevelt than the fact that he had not equaled Lincoln as a great president. But he brought Lincoln into this last battle as an ally and fellow nationalist.

Lincoln's nationalism had inspired TR's Square Deal, his "bully pulpit," his conservation and foreign policy gains, and his expansion of presidential power, but labor problems still troubled TR in 1910. In his famous "New Nationalism" speech, former president Roosevelt invoked Lincoln as his guiding spirit as he called for a "new birth of freedom" for workers. Because Lincoln had sought "human betterment," his rightful heirs, TR insisted, had to grapple with the next national humanitarian crisis, which in his mind was still the question of inequality and the growing number of citizens who lived in poverty. TR and many others feared that workers were being radicalized by the harsh conditions of their workplaces, frequent bouts of unemployment, and recalcitrant employers. He expected a civil war between labor and capital to break out because factory and mine owners and railroad and corporate heads would not budge. Gaining a larger share of the nation's wealth for the worker would require bargaining power, so TR spoke out for the eight-hour day and labor's right to organize. He defended his position by invoking Lincoln's words: "Labor is the superior of capital and deserves much the higher consideration." TR believed that the spirit of Lincoln required him to campaign to save the nation's average people from corporate greed. Privately TR promised himself "to *eliminate* privilege, and to work for a more genuine equality of opportunity and for the betterment of the conditions of those who are not well off."[38]

To accomplish this, TR launched his candidacy for the Republican nomination for president in 1912, and then, after losing the nomination to President Taft, he founded the National Progressive (or Bull Moose) Party in which he supported what today we would call the welfare state or social safety net. He promised to make the government serve the needs of average people, not just the wealthy few. In exchange for loyalty to the nation-state, citizens would receive government help in managing the risks of old age, sickness, poverty, and unemployment. TR pronounced the Progressive Party "The Heirs of Abraham Lincoln" because Lincoln had said that the purpose of government was "to elevate the condition of man, to lift artificial weights from all shoulders, to clear the paths of laudable pursuit for all, to afford all an unfettered start and a fair chance in the race of life."[39] The platform of the Progressive Party called for unemployment insurance, old age pensions, an end to child labor, the regulation of corporations, national health insurance, the right to collective bargaining, and woman suffrage, and in TR's mind it enlarged the scope of the nation-state to create a larger compact with the

American people, a new set of protections from the government for its citizens. Though TR lost in 1912, for the rest of his life he continued to support labor's right to collective bargaining and welfare state proposals as his generation's program of generous nationalism. His niece Eleanor Roosevelt sat in the Bull Moose audience applauding. Later, with the politically shrewd man she married, Eleanor Roosevelt took her uncle's ideas and made them part of the New Deal.

Historians have ranked Theodore Roosevelt in recent times among the top five great presidents.[40] Nevertheless, many historians remain focused on his dark side: his Brownsville racism, the near-genocide committed by the U.S. army in the war in the Philippines, his preachings about race suicide and the full baby carriage for whites, his willingness to stand pat on Jim Crow, and his ugly tirades against the Huns within our gates during World War I. No assessment of TR should neglect his complex and contradictory nature. He spoke out against lynching and white race rioters in East St. Louis, and he stood next to W. E. B. DuBois during World War I calling for better race relations. Despite those antiracist gestures, he let segregation creep into his federal government and took no risks to achieve better race relations in his Bull Moose campaign. He called for an international organization to prevent war before President Wilson advocated a League of Nations, but he had no good word to say for President Wilson's bold attempts to change the nature of world diplomacy. Being a historian and a devotee of Lincoln probably made TR a better president, and his advocacy of diplomatic solutions to international conflict and his defense of benevolent nationalism and the welfare state modernized and elevated Lincoln's ideas. With all of his concerns about the nation-state's obligation to guarantee a decent chance to succeed for every class of people TR speaks to our times. Despite the fact that competing ideas of imperialism, racialism, and warrior-style patriotism popped up too often throughout TR's political career, Lincoln's generous nationalism encouraged the "better angel" of Theodore Roosevelt's political career.

## *Notes*

1. Theodore Roosevelt, *An Autobiography* (New York: Charles Scribner's Sons, 1920), 27.

2. Theodore Roosevelt quoted in Kathleen Dalton, *Theodore Roosevelt: A Strenuous Life* (New York: Alfred A. Knopf, 2002), 84.

3. Theodore Roosevelt, *The Naval War of 1812 Or The History of the United States Navy during the Last War with Great Britain to Which Is Appended an Account of the Battle of New Orleans,* (New York: 1882), 492.

4. Dalton, *Theodore Roosevelt,* 103.

5. Theodore Roosevelt and Henry Cabot Lodge, *Hero Tales from American History* (New York: Century, 1908), ix–x.

6. Theodore Roosevelt, "The Strenuous Life," in Gordon Hutner, ed., *Selected Speeches and Writings of Theodore Roosevelt* (New York: Vintage Books, 2013), 11–22.

7. Theodore Roosevelt, *American Ideals,* vol. 15, *Memorial Edition of the Works of Theodore Roosevelt* (New York: Scribner's, 1919–1926), 10, 57.

8. Theodore Roosevelt, *Oliver Cromwell,* National Edition of the Works of Theodore Roosevelt, vol. 10 (New York: Charles Scribner's Sons, 1926), 187–88, 193.

9. Ibid., 198.

10. Ibid., 235, 219.

11. Arthur Lee, "Cromwell and Roosevelt," in *ibid.,* 183.

12. Theodore Roosevelt, *The Rough Riders* (New York: G. P. Putnam's Sons, 1900), 96.

13. Theodore Roosevelt, *The Rough Riders,* excerpt, in Hutner, *Selected Speeches and Writings of Theodore Roosevelt,* 264.

14. Theodore Roosevelt, *Gouverneur Morris* (Boston: Houghton, Mifflin, 1899).

15. Extracts from *History of Germany in the Nineteenth Century and Historical and Political Writings,* in Alfred J. Andrea and James H. Overfield, eds., *The Human Record: Sources of Global History, vol. 2, Since 1500,* 5th ed. (Boston: Houghton Mifflin, 2005), 295–96.

16. George L. Mosse, *Nationalism and Sexuality: Respectability and Abnormal Sexuality in Modern Europe* (New York: H. Fertig, 1985), 57.

17. Roosevelt, *Gouverneur Morris,* 260; Dalton, *Theodore Roosevelt,* 118.

18. Jeffrey A. Engel, "The Democratic Language of American Imperialism: Race, Order, and Theodore Roosevelt's Personifications of Foreign Policy Evil," *Diplomacy and Statecraft* 19, no. 4 (2008): 678; Thomas G. Dyer, *Theodore Roosevelt and the Idea of Race* (Baton Rouge: Louisiana State University Press, 1980).

19. Theodore Roosevelt, *An Autobiography* (New York: Charles Scribner's Sons, 1920), 7.

20. Dorothy Ross, "Lincoln and the Ethics of Emancipation: Universalism, Nationalism, Exceptionalism," *Journal of American History* 96, no. 2 (2009): 394.

21. Melinda Lawson, *Patriot Fires: Forging a New American Nationalism in the Civil War North* (Lawrence: University Press of Kansas, 2002), 161, 11. For the economic content of Lincoln's nationalism, see Gabor S. Borit, *Lincoln and the Economics of the American Dream* (Memphis, TN: Memphis State University Press, 1978).

22. Corinne Roosevelt Robinson, *My Brother Theodore Roosevelt* (New York: Charles Scribner's Sons, 1921), 19–33; Union League Club of New York, *Theodore Roosevelt, Senior: A Tribute, the Proceedings at a Meeting, Feb. 14, 1878* (New York: The Union League, 1902); Dalton, *Theodore Roosevelt,* 27–35; Anna Roosevelt Cowles's memoirs

of family life, "The Story of the Roosevelt Family," in Theodore Roosevelt Collection, Houghton Library, Harvard College Library.

23. James Macpherson, *Abraham Lincoln and the Second American Revolution* (New York: Oxford University Press, 1991), 39–40.

24. Heather Cox Richardson, "Abraham Lincoln and the Politics of Principle," *Marquette Law Review* 13 (2009–2010): 1383–98.

25. Theodore Roosevelt, "The Conditions of Success: A Speech Delivered at the Cambridge Union, May 26, 1910," in *African and European Addresses* (New York: G. P. Putnam's Sons, 1910).

26. Robinson, *My Brother,* 206.

27. Theodore Roosevelt to Kermit Roosevelt, Oct. 2, 1903, in *Letters to Kermit from Theodore Roosevelt, 1902–1908* (New York: Charles Scribner's Sons, 1946), 43.

28. Michael McCarthy, "The First Sagebrush Rebellion: Forest Reserves and States Rights in Colorado and the West, 1891–1907," in Harold K. Steen, ed., *Origins of the National Forests: A Centennial Symposium* (Durham, NC: Forest History Society, 1992), 190–92; Dalton, *Roosevelt,* 239–48.

29. Carl N. Degler, "One Among Many: The United States and National Unification," quoting James Randall in Carl Guarneri, *America Compared: American History in International Perspective* (Boston: Houghton Mifflin, 2005), 1:355.

30. Richardson, "Abraham Lincoln," 13:1383–98, 2009–10.

31. Theodore Roosevelt, "Graduated Inheritance and Income Tax," and "There Will Be No Change in Policy," in *The Roosevelt Policy: Speeches, Letters and State Papers, Relating to Corporate Wealth and Closely Allied Topics* (New York: Current Literature Publishing, 1919), 2:465–68, 560.

32. Theodore Roosevelt, "Lincoln's Attitude Toward Evil-doers," in *Roosevelt Policy,* 2:91–397.

33. Theodore Roosevelt, "Record of Fifty-Ninth Congress," in *Roosevelt Policy,* 2:401–3.

34. Theodore Roosevelt, "Federal Regulation of the Interstate Railways," in *Roosevelt Policy,* 1:240.

35. Morison, *Letters,* 3:300, 615.

36. Theodore Roosevelt, *Theodore Roosevelt's Letters to His Children* (New York: Charles Scribner's Sons, 1919), 63.

37. Theodore Roosevelt, "Class Government," in *Roosevelt Policy,* 1:158.

38. William Leuchtenburg, ed., *Theodore Roosevelt: The New Nationalism* (Englewood Cliffs, NJ: Prentice-Hall, 1961); Theodore Roosevelt to Jack Greenway, Dec. 19, 1910, Subject File, Theodore Roosevelt Collection, Houghton Library, Harvard College Library.

39. Abraham Lincoln, First Message to Congress, at the Special Session, July 4, 1861, in *Letters and Addresses of Abraham Lincoln* (New York: H. W. Bell, 1903), 203.

40. "Introduction: An All-time Historian's Favorite," in Serge Ricard, ed., *A Companion to Theodore Roosevelt* (Malden, MA: Wiley-Blackwell, 2011), 1. TR ranked fourth in each of the 2000, 2009, and 2017 C-SPAN polls of historians.

# 6 A Scholar and His Ghosts

## *Woodrow Wilson as Historian in the White House*

John Milton Cooper Jr.

Riding up in the White House elevator on the night of April 2, 1917, after he gave his address to Congress asking for a declaration of war, Woodrow Wilson reportedly remarked to his young cousin Fitz Woodrow, "Fitz, thank God for Abraham Lincoln. I won't make the mistakes that he did." Nothing Wilson ever said better demonstrated how much his study and writing of history guided his thought and action.[1]

Likening himself to Lincoln came inescapably to Wilson. He had just asked Congress to plunge the nation into the biggest and bloodiest conflict since the Civil War. His war address was Lincolnesque in its somber beauty, and near the close he had practically lifted a sentence from Lincoln when he said, "There are, it may be, many months of fiery trial and sacrifice ahead of us."[2] More than circumstance linked Wilson to Lincoln. He admired Lincoln more than any of his predecessors in the White House. Although he was a Democrat, he repeatedly invoked the words, deeds, and example of Lincoln in his speeches, especially in his presidential campaigns. Indeed, his race against Theodore Roosevelt in 1912 often became a tug-of-war over the mantle of Lincoln. Whereas Roosevelt lauded Lincoln as the savior of the Union, Wilson exalted him as the apotheosis of the common man. Neither said anything about the Great Emancipator.

It is easy to see why Wilson said, "Thank God for Abraham Lincoln." It is not so easy to see why he said, "I won't make the mistakes that he did." In his writings and speeches, he never said much about Lincoln as a war leader. In his book that covered Lincoln's presidency, *Division and Reunion, 1829–1889,* published in 1893, Wilson had contented himself with a recitation of Lincoln's actions with little analysis, much less criticism, of his military policies. The same was true of his sweeping and grandiloquent production *A History of the American People,* published in 1902. In both works, Lincoln emerges as a heroic, thoroughly admirable figure, with plenty of attention paid to his politics but not much to him as commander in chief. The best explanation of Wilson's remark comes from the son of the man to whom he made it. Fitz Woodrow Jr. has said that his father told him the president meant that he would pick one commanding general and stick with him, not switch them around, the way Lincoln had done. The younger Woodrow, who became a career officer himself, added that Wilson's resolve was never tested because the war was so short and the American forces did not fight the Germans all that long.[3] This explanation sounds right. For the duration of American belligerency in World War I, Wilson took a largely hands-off stance toward strictly military matters. He left the ground war to the generals, to their gratitude and relief. Naval matters and war aims were a different story.

Wilson's allusion to Lincoln was not the first time during World War I that he compared himself to one of his predecessors. At the end of September 1914, just two months into the war, he pondered Great Britain's newly instituted blockade of maritime trade with Germany and the other Central Powers, and he worried that frictions from this blockade could lead to escalating controversies with the British like the ones a century earlier that had eventually led to the War of 1812. Like most historians then and later, Wilson thought that war had been needless and mistaken. His adviser Colonel Edward M. House recorded in his diary that when they discussed the situation, the president read a page from his *History of the American People,* "telling how during Madison's Administration, the War of 1812 was started in exactly the same way as this controversy is opening up." Wilson called Madison "a peace-loving man, . . . [who] desired to do everything to prevent" going to war, "but popular feeling made it impossible." Wilson added, "Madison and I are the only two Princeton men that have become President. The circumstances of the war of 1812 and now run parallel. I sincerely hope they will not go further."[4]

The desire to avoid Madison's fate offers an example of one of the most important ways in which Wilson drew upon his knowledge of history to guide his policies and actions. Even before he made those remarks to House, he had striven to dampen popular feeling toward the nations at war. On August 18, 1914, shortly after its outbreak, he had issued an appeal to the public. The president recognized that, given many Americans' origins in the countries now fighting, they might sympathize with one side or the other, but he admonished them to resist such impulses and not become divided against each other. "It will be easy to excite passion," Wilson warned, "and difficult to allay it." Instead, he admonished, "[t]he United States must be neutral in fact as well as in name during these times that are to try men's souls. We must be impartial in thought as well as in action, must put a curb upon our sentiments . . . that might be construed as a preference of one party to the struggle before another."[5]

Wilson employed more than rhetoric in his effort to avoid the kind of controversies that he believed had forced the reluctant Madison to go to war. With the concurrence of his advisers, including his secretary of state, William Jennings Bryan, he decided not to issue a broad legal challenge to the British blockade, which the United States could easily have done. Rather, he would wait and see what transpired and contest restrictions on American trade, where necessary, on a case-by-case basis.

Without question, Wilson was going easy on the British, and later critics would charge that he was biased in their favor. Those charges had some basis in fact. All of the president's grandparents had been born in the British Isles, and his mother had been born in England. Like most educated Americans of that era, he was a cultural Anglophile, and he loved to travel to England and Scotland. A month into the war, the British ambassador reported the president telling him, "Every thing that I love most in the world is at stake. . . . If they [the Germans] succeed, we shall be forced to take such measures of defence here which would be fatal to our form of Government and American ideals." The ambassador also noted that the president "spoke of the long trial of the Civil War, and said with deep emotion that he was sure our country [Britain] would show its powers of endurance for a high cause." Officially, Wilson would maintain "absolute neutrality, and would bear in mind that a dispute between our two nations would be a crowning calamity."[6]

Wilson's expression of sympathy for Britain was noteworthy but not unusual. In the current atmosphere of international outrage at the Germans' callous violation of Belgian neutrality and destructive invasion of that country, the president's private statement was fairly typical of what many others were saying publicly. The operative words in this statement were the last ones—about avoiding a dispute between the United States and Britain. That was what he believed had ultimately forced Madison into war, and he wanted to nip in the bud any chances for a recurrence of such disputes.

As Wilson and his advisers viewed the situation, this was strictly a bilateral affair, involving the United States and Britain alone. Germany was not a party to the matter and would not be, even collaterally, until the opening of submarine warfare four months later. Appropriately, all of Wilson's advisers agreed on the policy of going easy on Britain. They included Secretary of State Bryan, who, unlike Colonel House and the number-two man in the State Department, Robert Lansing, harbored no biases in favor of Britain and the Allies. Mounting a legal challenge to the British blockade looked like buying unnecessary trouble, and no one wanted to do that. Madison's ghost, not Wilson's or his advisers' sympathies, played the decisive role in this decision.

Coincidental with the outbreak of the world war and not long before those remarks to Colonel House and the British ambassador, the president said something else that revealed how his reading of history shaped his approach to world affairs. On August 8, 1914, he told his belligerent-minded secretary of war, Lindley M. Garrison, to forswear any notions about intervening in Mexico. "We shall have no right at any time to intervene in Mexico to determine the way in which Mexicans are to settle their own affairs," he admonished. Many things might happen in Mexico that Americans would not like, but that was the Mexicans' business. "There are in my judgment no conceivable circumstances which would make it right for us to direct by force or by threat of force the internal processes of what is a profound revolution, a revolution as profound as that which occurred in France. All the world has been shocked ever since the time of the revolution in France that Europe should have undertaken to nullify what was done there, no matter what the excesses committed."[7]

That statement was deeply revealing. Events of the next several years, especially Pancho Villa's March 1916 raid on Columbus, New Mexico, would test Wilson's resolve to stay out of Mexico. Although he dispatched the Punitive Expedition under Brigadier General John J. Pershing in a futile attempt to catch Villa, he resisted demands to widen the scope of the mission. In May 1916, he told the journalist Ray Stannard Baker that he was basing his Mexican policy upon one of "the most deeply seated convictions of his life: . . . his shame as an American over the first Mexican war, & his resolution that while he was president there should be no such predatory war."[8] Guilt over the Mexican-American War of the 1840s had grown upon Wilson fairly recently. He had not expressed such views in his historical writings, but, though late blooming, this conviction was heartfelt. In his reelection campaign in 1916, the famous slogan "He Kept Us Out of War" and Republican attacks on his foreign policy would fixate far more on Mexico than on Europe.

More revealing still in Wilson's admonition to Garrison was his comparison between the events in Mexico and the French Revolution. Like most educated people in the English-speaking world, he was no admirer of the events in France following 1789. Charles Dickens's *A Tale of Two Cities* and the bloody siege of the Paris Commune in 1871 had left indelible images of violence, vengeance, and anarchy. Many American conservatives of the time used those images in forming their responses to unrest in their country in the 1880s and 1890s among industrial workers, as well as embryonic socialist and radical movements and the agrarian protests manifested in the Populist Party and the Bryanite takeover of the Democrats. A scattering of them, most notably Theodore Roosevelt, came to espouse progressive reform as a means to fend off potential revolution, while others, such as Roosevelt's close friend Henry Cabot Lodge, remained steadfastly resistant to any unbending.

Wilson, who did not get involved in politics until after 1900, did not warm to the Populists or Bryanites, but he never shared the alarmist bent of such men as Roosevelt, Lodge, and their friends and fellow historians Henry and Brooks Adams. For his part, Wilson befriended the historian Frederick Jackson Turner in the early 1890s and eagerly embraced not only Turner's "frontier thesis" but also his general emphasis on the importance of common white folk, particularly pioneer farmers, in shaping American politics and society. With that background of historical study, it was not surprising that, as president, Wilson could view the French Revolution with an understanding of its causes, if not sympathy for its methods. Willingness to give revolution a chance became a guiding principle of his foreign policy, not just in Mexico but later toward the Bolshevik Revolution in Russia. Of all the leaders during World War I, Wilson took the most circumspect stance toward that revolution and the conflicts it spawned, and he resisted large-scale Allied intervention in Russia at the end of the war.

What made Wilson's tolerant view of the French Revolution surprising was that he was a disciple of Edmund Burke. In the United States during his youth, Burke had enjoyed broad admiration as a sympathizer toward the American Revolution, and in conservative circles he elicited high esteem for his condemnation of the French Revolution. The young Wilson shared those attitudes to some extent, but in his thirties he came to a different and deeper understanding of Burke. He grasped Burke's essential vision of anti-ideological politics, praising him in 1893 as espousing a politics that "has never been speculative; it has been profoundly practical and utilitarian. Speculative politics treats men and situations as they are supposed to be; practical politics treats them (upon no general plan but in detail) as they are found to be at the moment of actual contact." Five years later Wilson further lauded Burke's thought for clinging "to the slow pace of inevitable change and invent[ing] nothing" but still having "the power of life in it—the power of growth."[9]

Such an understanding of Burke might appear to make Wilson's tolerance of revolution look truly remarkable. He was anticipating by half a century the "end of ideology" position taken by Daniel Bell and others in rejecting twentieth-century totalitarianism. Yet Wilson's Burkean views did not make him a conservative in his politics. His stress on "the power of growth" led him to exalt adaptability and "expediency"—which he used in a positive, nonpejorative sense. As president, he applied these thoughts to his policies at home and abroad. In an interview dealing mainly with domestic affairs that was published in a magazine at the beginning of 1915, a reporter noted, "He [Wilson] showed me why a writer was wrong who said he could not be a progressive Democrat if he admired Edmund Burke."[10] Unfortunately, the reporter let the matter drop there and did not record how Wilson blended Burke with his progressivism.

Three years later, after the United States entered the war, the president explained to visiting foreign journalists—off the record—what he meant by fighting for democracy. He cited Burke by name and paraphrased his definition of a free government as a "government which those under it will guard." Then he asserted, "Now, there isn't any one kind of government under which all nations ought to live. There isn't any one kind of government which we have the right to impose on any nation. So that I am not fighting for democracy except for the peoples who want democracy."[11] Those words would not be published for nearly six decades after Wilson uttered them—which was a pity. If he had made those convictions widely known at the time, he could have shielded himself from barrages of denigration of himself as a utopian visionary and closeted imperialist who sought to foist his own hypocritical notions of democracy on the world. Being a good Burkean inoculated him against any such delusions.

Those revelations speak to Wilson as an intellectual and as a political thinker, but they do not necessarily speak to how his reading of history shaped his thought and action. In some ways, it can be asked whether he ever was much of a historian. His large output of published work includes only a scattering of articles and three books that were primarily historical. Besides *Division and Reunion* and the four-volume *History of the American People,* there was a biography of George Washington. That was a quick knock-off, based on no original research, and it showed Wilson uncharacteristically as a saccharine stylist. One Princeton faculty colleague scoffed at *History* as "a gilt-edged pot boiler."[12] He was right. "I had no particular intention of being a historian," Wilson later claimed, but he found that he did not know enough history to write his long-planned but never executed magnum opus, "Philosophy of Politics," a projected grand synthesis from the Burkean, nonideological perspective. "So, in order to learn the history I needed, I wrote a history." That was probably true, but only in part. Wilson also earned what he admitted was "an immense sum" of money from the *History*'s magazine serialization and book royalties.[13]

Of Wilson's three historical works, only *Division and Reunion* stands up to much scrutiny on scholarly grounds. The book presents a nicely written narrative and synthesis that covered the years nearly up to the time of its publication. Wilson had done next to no primary research. In graduate school at Johns Hopkins, exposure to burrowing in archives and manuscripts had repelled him, as had the "scientific" method of accumulating facts to speak for themselves without literary art and interpretation—an approach he later deplored in a magazine article.

In its author's estimation, the main strength of *Division and Reunion* lay in its viewpoint, which he believed transcended sectional biases. In 1889, he told the editor of the prestigious series in which it appeared, *The Epochs of American History,* that he could treat the Civil War impartially because, despite his birth and upbringing in the South, he did not have deep roots there. Moreover, he declared, "Ever since I have had independent judgments of my own I have been a Federalist(!)"[14] By that he meant that he had rejected the states' rights, limited-government credo that prevailed in the former Confederacy and believed instead in strong, centralized government. In addition, Wilson sympathized with Andrew Jackson and the political rise of the West, and he expressed ideas about the influence of the frontier partly picked up from Turner. In his sympathies for the South and West and Turnerian overtones, Wilson was joining a vanguard of scholars who sought to redeem their nation's history from the dominance and biases of New Englanders.

Unfortunately, he also echoed those historians' disdainful attitudes toward African Americans and shared their dismissal of Reconstruction as a corrupt, misbegotten enterprise.

When Wilson proclaimed himself a Federalist at the age of thirty-two, he offered a key to his political thinking and to the influence on him of his reading and reflecting on history. When he referred a bit redundantly to having "independent political judgments of my own," he was looking back as early as his undergraduate years at Princeton. Never a model student, the young Wilson had rendered just enough attention to his courses and grades to squeak into the top quarter of his class, but he had read widely and deeply on his own. Encountering the work of the English writer Walter Bagehot had imparted an epiphany that led him to study politics, not through laws and formal institutions, as was the fashion of the day, but by looking at how politics really worked. Wilson also read a good bit of American, English, and European history. That reading abetted his own restless temperament in enabling him to reject states' rights and limited government, which marked a break with his Civil War–era southern upbringing and his family's views. Soon after his graduation from Princeton in 1879 he published essays in which he welcomed the defeat of the Confederacy and the demise of slavery.

Wilson took a bit longer to give full voice to his espousal of strong central government. Shortly after *Division and Reunion* appeared in print in 1893, he published a magazine article entitled "A Calendar of Great Americans," in which he revealed both his immersion in writings by and about major figures in the nation's history and his preferences among them. Lincoln ranked first—"the supreme American of our history." Washington stood almost as high, despite the colorless way his biographers depicted him. He was "the most suitable instrument of the national life at every moment of crisis." Others, including Andrew Jackson, Daniel Webster, Henry Clay, and John C. Calhoun, fell short in different ways. Among the founders, Madison came off as too cautious. Thomas Jefferson suffered from "the strain of French philosophy that permeated and weakened all his thought"—in other words, he was a non-Burkean led astray by the ideological cast of mind. Although he did not say so outright in this article, Alexander Hamilton was and always would be his favorite founder, and here he asserted that without Hamilton and men like him, "our national life would have miscarried at the very first."[15]

Wilson did not say much more about Hamilton in public, except when, in 1910, he praised F. S. Oliver's recent laudatory study of that founder as "[o]ne of the most interesting books of recent years" and its subject as one of the few leaders of his time who "had a constructive program."[16] His relative silence about Hamilton stemmed in part from his shift in 1902 from writing about politics and history to educational administration as president of Princeton. It also stemmed from his budding involvement in Democratic Party politics, which he believed required him to reorient himself toward Jefferson. For Democrats, Jefferson's aegis overshadowed all other past party leaders, including Jackson—much the same way Lincoln's aegis did with Republicans. From the time of Bryan's nomination for president in 1896 until Wilson's nomination in 1912, Democrats waged a civil war over the Jefferson aegis. The waning conservative, or "Bourbon," wing of the party, which was still devoted to ex-president Grover Cleveland, exalted Jefferson as the apostle of states' rights and limited government. The rising Bryanite-populist wing of the party bowed to Jefferson as the champion of the common white people, particularly farmers and more generally sectional outlanders from the South and West.

Ironically, Wilson's first small foray into Democratic politics came when some conservatives suggested that this dynamic, well-publicized college president might become a potential savior of the party from the Bryanite heresy. Wilson tried to please his newfound patrons by criticizing economic reform measures being advanced by Bryan Democrats, together with a little but growing band of midwestern and western insurgent Republicans and, ever so gingerly, President Roosevelt. But Wilson could not bring himself to embrace the conservatives' limited government absolutism. In 1908, in his last scholarly book, *Constitutional Government in the United States,* he invoked Burke to reject such notions, declaring, "Government is part of life, and with it must change, alike in its objects and practices." The only absolute was the "principle of liberty, that there must be the freest right and opportunity of adjustment."[17] This was how Wilson could remain faithful to his Burkean perspectives and yet become a progressive reformer, as he was already quietly doing.

Jefferson played a critical part in the political reinvention of this admirer of Hamilton. Once Wilson got seriously involved in politics by winning the governorship of New Jersey and emerging almost at once as a presidential prospect, he spurned his erstwhile conservative patrons and began to court Bryan for support or at least benevolent neutrality. In the process, he repeatedly proclaimed himself a "Jeffersonian," professed his "ever renewed admiration" for Jefferson, and pledged fidelity to Jefferson's vision of restoring the hinterlands to national leadership and utilizing their "great unexhausted reserves of unused thought and unemployed power."[18] In another ironic twist, this newfound devotion to Jefferson allowed him to vie with Roosevelt in 1912 for the mantle of Lincoln, in this case as the prime example of how high someone so humble and disadvantaged could rise, given a fair and level playing field.

Wilson did not mention Hamilton as he made this political reorientation, but he did not forget him. While campaigning for president in 1912, he stated that "there is one principle of Jefferson's which no longer can obtain in the practical politics of America"—namely, the dictum "that the best government is that which exerts its power as little as possible." He averred that he did not fear "the utmost exercise of the powers of the government . . . provided that they are exercised with patriotism and intelligence and really in the interest of the people."[19] He was doing what other progressive thinkers, most notably Herbert Croly, were calling for. He wanted to pursue Jeffersonian ends through Hamiltonian means.

Wilson's combining of those means and ends was not original, but it was deeply significant. Ever since Bryan and his followers had gained ascendancy among the Democrats, that wing of the party had sloughed off any vestigial fondness for states' rights and limited government in favor of far-reaching measures of government intervention in the economy, such as railroad regulation, aid to farmers, currency management, antitrust legislation, and a tilt in favor of organized labor. In his third and final run as the party's presidential nominee in 1908, Bryan called for government ownership of railroads and telegraph lines. In one sense, then, Wilson was only ratifying the main thrust of his party's policies.

In another sense, however, he was making that policy thrust more potent and more lasting. Wilson's academic standing as both a renowned scholar and president of one of the most prestigious universities lent much intellectual and social respectability to these views—so much so that such leading progressive writers as Croly and Walter Lippmann would forsake their earlier devotion to Roosevelt in favor of Wilson when he ran for reelection in 1916. His vision of using strong, activist government to better the lives of disadvantaged groups would remain the hallmark of the Democratic Party for the next century.

Wilson was also advancing the party toward assembling the coalition that would attract popular and electoral majorities in coming decades. When he won his second term in 1916, he added farmers and organized labor to the Democrats' traditional white southern base. Not until later would they add an augmented and energized urban base that embraced non-Protestant white ethnics and African Americans. The attraction of white ethnics was gradually developing apart from Wilson. The attraction of African Americans would come a generation later and in spite of his administration's record in race relations. During his first months in office, Wilson allowed several cabinet secretaries who came from the South to attempt to introduce formal racial segregation into the workplace in their departments. Protests by the newly founded National Association for the Advancement of Colored People (NAACP), joined by some Republicans, brought that effort to a halt, but informal segregation persisted, and the number and status of black federal workers plummeted. Wilson also permitted the cinematically brilliant but scurrilously racist film *Birth of a Nation* to be shown at the White House in 1915. Contrary to later legend, he did not endorse the movie, and he discouraged its re-release. In all, Wilson was not an actively committed racist, like most southern whites of the time. Rather, he was indifferent to racial injustice and impatient when the mater came up, as it seldom did. In those attitudes, he resembled most whites in the North, where he lived almost his entire adult life.

What Wilson did achieve with the Democratic Party owed in largest measure to his spectacular success in enacting a monumental program of domestic legislation. Behind those feats of presidential leadership lay the ways in which he drew upon his academic work to guide him, especially the way he used history to inform his study of politics. In disciplinary terms, he was first and foremost what was then already being called a political scientist. "I do not like the term political science," he once declared. "Human relationships, whether in the family or in the state, . . . are not in any proper sense the subject-matter of science. They are the stuff of insight and sympathy and spiritual comprehension."[20] Ironically, that declaration came in a speech to a gathering of people who liked and embraced the term "political science." Wilson was delivering the presidential address to the American Political Science Association (APSA), the discipline's national organization. He is the only president of the United States to have headed that organization.

Wilson's presidency of the APSA came two years before he went to the White House, and it came in recognition of his scholarship in the field. Much as he disliked the term, he still ranks as one of the greatest political scientists America has produced. His two books in the field, *Congressional*

*Government* (1885) and *Constitutional Government* (1908), remain in print in the twenty-first century and are still widely read. Part of the continued interest in those books understandably derives from his later political career, and both of them have become hunting grounds for those who want to see how, as president, he either followed or broke the rules he set down in them. Yet the books also retain value in themselves, not only as insightful descriptions of American politics and government at that time but also as broader analyses of its workings, shortcomings, and possible reforms applicable in later times and circumstances.

Wilson was the scholar *of* politics who became the scholar *in* politics. He had the opportunity to take what he had learned from his reading, writing, and teaching into the political arena. Most broadly, he applied his Burkean view of politics as constantly changing and adapting to circumstances and searching for "expediency." The principal specific lessons he took from the academy into the arena involved how to overcome the separation of powers, both as governor in New Jersey and as president. His most celebrated symbolic move in that direction came when, after just a month in the White House, he revived the practice abandoned by Jefferson of the president speaking to Congress in person; he went on to speak to Congress more times than any president before or since. His most important substantive move in Trenton, New Jersey, and in Washington, D.C., was to rely on his party as the bridge between the executive and legislative branches. Earlier, he had been a theorist of party government, and now he became its practitioner. This approach worked better in both places when his party controlled the legislature; it did not work so well when the opposition controlled one or both houses.

When it worked, Wilson's party-government approach reaped rich rewards. During his first term in the White House, he secured passage of tariff revision, the income and inheritance taxes, the Federal Reserve, antitrust laws, the Federal Trade Commission, federal aid to farmers, prohibition of child labor (later struck down by the Supreme Court), an eight-hour day for railroad workers, a tariff commission, a maritime commission to regulate shipping, creation of the National Park Service, and the appointment and confirmation of Louis Brandeis to the Supreme Court. Those actions came to be called the "New Freedom," and they rank Wilson alongside Franklin Roosevelt, with the New Deal, and Lyndon Johnson, with the Great Society, in a triumvirate of greatest legislative presidents of the twentieth century, perhaps in all of American history. Such a ranking for Wilson is all the more remarkable because he lacked the second Roosevelt's national emergency and blank check from Congress and the second Johnson's decades of experience and mastery of Capitol Hill. When Wilson launched his legislative juggernaut, he was only two years removed not just from private life but also from reputedly the worst of all preparations for practical affairs—academic life.

The lessons and insights he brought to politics did not always serve him well. When he ran for reelection in 1916, some prominent Democrats tried to get Wilson to drop his colorless vice president, Thomas R. Marshall, in favor of his widely respected secretary of war, Newton D. Baker. Colonel House argued that having Baker as vice president could elevate the office into something approaching a copresidency. Wilson brushed the suggestion aside, saying he did not want to waste Baker. It is a tantalizing might-have-been to imagine how different things could have been three years later when Wilson suffered his massive stroke, which precipitated the worst crisis of presidential disability in the nation's history. With an able, trusted vice president such as Baker, Wilson might have thought seriously about stepping down or making some arrangement either to stand aside temporarily or cede duties to the vice president.

Likewise, reliance on his party served Wilson badly during World War I. In the fall of 1918, he appealed to voters to return Democratic majorities in Congress as a vote of confidence in his war leadership. This move incensed Republicans, who took it as a slur on their patriotism, and it made a bad situation worse when they won control of both houses of Congress. Wilson did not adjust well to divided government. The term "bipartisanship" would not come into use for another quarter century, but the concept was something that this scholar of politics could grasp. He knew how coalition governments worked in parliamentary systems, and one such coalition was governing Britain at the time. The most conspicuous example of his failure of bipartisanship came when he failed to include any prominent Republican on the American delegation to the peace conference in Paris in 1919. Yet, for all his mistakes, relying on previous scholarly insights and approaches served Wilson well as president. His career remains the most shining justification of the study of politics as preparation for the practice of politics in this, or perhaps any, nation's history.

It would be wrong to separate his engagement with political science from his work in history. In his APSA presidential address, he warned against those who read history only for "facts," meaning numbers and isolated incidents;

"if they miss the deepest facts of all, the spiritual experiences, the visions of the mind, the aspirations of the spirit that are the pulse of life, I do not see how they can understand the facts or know what really moves the world."[21] In other words, political scientists must use history, not as miners of data or cherry-pickers of convenient examples, but as true historians. That attitude suited not only Wilson's views and temperament but also something he had found to his liking in graduate school. He and his fellow students at Johns Hopkins met in the Historical Seminary room, which featured in large letters at the top of one wall a quotation from the English historian Edward Freeman, "History is past Politics and Politics present History."[22]

The current term "political history" is a retronym. It would have been redundant to say it in Wilson's day because it went without saying that all history was political history. Wilson's major professor was a historian, Herbert Baxter Adams, who championed the "scientific," archive-digging approach to history, but Adams made a virtue of his laxness as an adviser by allowing Wilson to pursue his own interest, which was to write his first book, *Congressional Government.* In his three professorships—at Bryn Mawr College, Wesleyan University, and Princeton—Wilson taught many courses in history, ranging from ancient to recent times, and he had graduate students who were historians. As his academic star shot upward, however, he made it a condition for staying at Princeton that he no longer had to teach history, though he did continue to write occasional historical essays and the *History of the American People.* At the end of his life, he would serve as president of the American Historical Association (AHA)—one of two U.S. presidents to hold that office. He would also be one of only two people to serve as president of both the APSA and the AHA.[23] This was possible because the boundaries between the disciplines were fluid and permeable, and, aside from his teaching preferences, it probably never occurred to Wilson to choose between being a historian and a political scientist.

As president, he drew upon his scholarly background in both disciplines to chart his course and make decisions. Of the two disciplines, history ultimately weighed more heavily in his biggest decision of all—to go to war in 1917. Historians are in the business of dealing with ghosts, and three of them haunted Wilson at this moment. He did not mention Madison again by name, but the example of his fellow Princetonian in the White House stayed with him. Wilson likewise saw himself as "a peace-loving man" who had done everything he could to stay out of war. Two weeks before he went before Congress, the president bared his soul off the record to a sympathetic journalist. Wilson feared both the international and domestic consequences of entering the war. Abroad, "there would be dictated a dictated peace, a victorious peace. . . . There won't be any peace standards left to work with. There will be only war standards." At home, "Once lead this great peaceful people into war, and they'll forget there ever was such a thing as tolerance. To fight you must be brutal and ruthless, and the spirit of ruthless brutality will enter into the very fibre of our national life, infecting congress, the courts, the policeman on the beat, the man in the street. . . . If there is any alternative, for God's sake let's take it."[24]

This most eloquent of arguments against going into the war came from the lips of the man who took the country into war. The ghosts of both Lincoln and Madison hovered over him. He had Lincoln on his mind because he knew how similar their circumstances were—except that this war was even more terrible than the Civil War had been. In November 1916, as he was preparing to try to end the war through mediation, he had written in a note to himself describing how this mechanized carnage made war no longer "a sort of national excursion, a necessary holiday to vary the monotony of a lazy, tranquil existence." Now, there were "no brilliant battles such as we thrill to read about . . . and no particular glory. . . . Where is any longer the glory commensurate with the sacrifice of the millions of men required in modern warfare to carry and defend Verdun?"[25]

Madison was on Wilson's mind because he knew that, at bottom, their circumstances were now different. Outraged public and congressional opinion was not forcing Wilson into war. Interventionist sentiment had grown after Germans unleashed their submarines and with the publication of the Zimmermann telegram, in which they offered the Mexicans American territory in return for coming in on their side, but such sentiment had not grown by all that much. Every indicator of public opinion agreed that the great majority of Americans still thought the same way they had ever since the sinking of the *Lusitania* almost two years earlier. They clung to what Wilson had then called "the double wish of our people, to maintain a firm front in respect of what we demand of Germany and yet do nothing that might by any possibility involve us in the war."[26] Moreover, a large minority remained adamantly opposed to entering the war. On Capitol Hill, members of Congress and observers alike found opinion there similarly divided, uncertain, and awaiting the president's lead. Several of them reported that when he came to address Congress on April 2, 1917, he could have carried majorities in both houses for whatever he chose to do.

In the end, the United States entered World War I because Woodrow Wilson decided to take the country in. Why he chose war has remained something of a puzzle, but it should not be. In his war address he outlined strategic considerations that made intervention appear somewhat more desirable than staying out, and he stressed that becoming a belligerent would give America a place at the peace table and a chance to influence the shaping of the postwar settlement. He argued that the brief experiment with armed neutrality had shown that it had most of the hazards and disadvantages of war without any possibilities for decisive action. His reading of the history of Jefferson's and Madison's frustrations with their measures short of war may have entered into his judgment, and, although he could not say so, he nearly always favored bold action over sitting tight.

Still, the heart of Wilson's choice lay elsewhere and involved yet another ghost. It was not an American or someone from the recent past. Rather, it was a German who had lived four centuries earlier—Martin Luther. Many have written about the role of religion in Wilson's life and thought, and he remains one of the most conspicuously religious of presidents. For him, no conflict pitted his strong religious background and deep religious faith against his intellect and scholarship. Just the opposite—he believed they meshed perfectly. As a Presbyterian, he came from the most intellectual and least evangelical of Protestant denominations, and he had grown up in a highly sophisticated ministerial family, spending part of his youth on the campus of a theological seminary. He did not believe in mixing religion in politics, and he opposed the leading "moral" reform of his time, prohibition. He had no truck with fundamentalism, and he was disgusted when his uncle James Woodrow, who was a seminary professor and father of Fitz Woodrow, became an early casualty in the fight over Darwin's theory of evolution. For Wilson, his religion was like his idealism, supremely important and deeply felt but also largely in the background and taken for granted when he made his way in the world.

At first, he had confronted intervention in the world war the same way. Three days after the sinking of the *Lusitania,* he had responded to a telegram imploring him to declare war in the name of God by remarking to his stenographer, "War is not declared in the name of God; it is a human affair altogether."[27] That was true for Wilson, but it was not so simple. Now he faced a choice that was agonizing and unavoidable and where there was no truly good or innocent answer.

Wilson was too much of an orthodox Christian to believe that he would hear God telling him what to do. As a good Protestant, he must pray, read Scripture, and think hard in trying to perceive what God's will might be. He knew that, as a human being and a sinner, he could never be sure he was carrying out God's will. How then to act? This is where Luther came to his aid. For Luther, the Christian must act on faith and Scripture and do her or his imperfect best to follow in God's way. What she or he could not do was avoid sin. Any course chosen would involve sin. Luther's answer was, "Sin boldly."

Wilson cast his nation in the same role as Luther's Christian. This war was the greatest collective sin in human history. One way or another, America could not avoid being a party to that sin. Wilson was asking his fellow citizens to join him in choosing the bolder and—he hoped—more promising sin of fighting and winning this war in order to try to build a better world in the future. Likening Wilson to Luther is no fanciful conjecture. At the end of his war address, following soon after the near quotation from Lincoln and another from the Declaration of Independence, he apostrophized America spending her blood for her deepest values. Then came his final words: "God helping her, she can do no other."[28] Changing only two words, it repeated Luther's declaration to the Diet of Worms: "God helping me, I can do no other." In the end, it was a ghost from history that guided him to make the decision that did more than anything else to shape history from that time onward.

## *Notes*

1. Fitz W. Woodrow to Arthur C. Walworth, Apr. 12, 1948, quoted in Arthur C. Walworth, *Woodrow Wilson* (New York: Norton, 1948), 2:102. Walworth states that Woodrow confirmed this statement later in an interview and over the telephone. Arthur C. Walworth Papers, Yale University Library, folder 61. The original of the letter is not among these papers.

2. Woodrow Wilson address to Congress, Apr. 2, 1917, in Arthur S. Link, ed., *The Papers of Woodrow Wilson* (Princeton, NJ: Princeton University Press, 1983), 41:526 (hereafter cited as *PWW*).

3. Author's telephone conversation with Fitz W. Woodrow Jr., Aug. 2, 2016.

4. Edward M. House Diary, entry Sept. 30, 1914, *PWW,* 31:109.

5. Wilson statement, Aug. 18, 1914, *PWW,* 30:393–94.

6. Sir Cecil Spring Rice to Sir Edward Grey, Sept. 3, 1914, *PWW,* 30:472.

7. Wilson to Lindley M. Garrison, Aug. 8, 1914, *PWW,* 30:362.

8. Ray Stannard Baker memorandum of interview with Wilson, [May 12, 1916], *PWW,* 37:36.

9. Woodrow Wilson, "Edmund Burke: The Man and His Times," [ca. Aug. 31, 1893], *PWW,* 8:342; Woodrow Wilson, "Edmund Burke: A Lecture," Feb. 23, 1898, *PWW,* 10:421.

10. Samuel G. Blythe, "A Talk with the President," [Dec. 5, 1914], *PWW,* 31:402–3. The interview with Blythe was published in the *Saturday Evening Post,* Jan. 9, 1915.

11. Woodrow Wilson, Remarks to Foreign Correspondents, Apr. 8, 1918, *PWW,* 47:288.

12. Edward S. Corwin interview with Henry S. Bragdon, June 6, 1939, Henry W. Bragdon Collection, Princeton University Library.

13. Blythe, "Talk with the President," *PWW,* 31:398; Wilson to Robert Bridges, Jan. 12, 1900, *PWW,* 11:368. The magazine serialization brought him $12,000, and the book's royalties brought $30,000. In 2016 dollars, those sums would be $290,400 and $726,000, respectively, for a total of $1,016,400.

14. Wilson to Albert Bushnell Hart, June 3, 1889, *PWW,* 6:243. The essay deploring "scientific history" is Woodrow Wilson, "On the Writing of History: With a Glance at the Methods of Macaulay, Gibbon, Carlyle, and Green," *Century Magazine* (Sept. 1895), *PWW,* 9:287–305. Wilson later said he regretted having expounded on how to write history before he had done much of it himself.

15. Woodrow Wilson, "A Calendar of Great Americans," *Forum* (Feb. 1894), *PWW,* 8:368–80.

16. Wilson speech, Apr. 7, 1910, *PWW,* 20:339–40. Privately, Wilson had further praise for Oliver's book. His brother-in-law later recalled that he said he had liked it more than any other recent book he had read, and a Princeton faculty colleague remembered him calling it "one of the greatest books sent me by a friend." See Ray Stannard Baker interview with Stockton Axson, Feb. 8–11, 1925, Ray Stannard Baker Papers, Library of Congress, Box 99; William Starr Myers, "Woodrow Wilson in My Diary," in William Starr Myers, ed., *Woodrow Wilson: Some Princeton Memories* (Princeton, NJ: Princeton University Press, 1946), 42.

17. Woodrow Wilson, *Constitutional Government in the United States,* in *PWW,* 18:71.

18. Wilson speeches, May 12, 1911, Apr. 17, 1912, *PWW,* 23:33, 24:402.

19. Wilson speech, Sept. 23, 1912, *PWW,* 25:222, 224–25. Wilson came close to but did not make the common error of ascribing to Jefferson the dictum "That government is best which governs least." It comes from Henry David Thoreau.

20. Wilson speech, Dec. 27, 1910, *PWW,* 22:271.

21. Ibid., *PWW,* 22:264.

22. For photographs of the Historical Seminary showing that motto, see *PWW,* 3:296ff; Henry W. Bragdon, *Woodrow Wilson: The Academic Years* (Cambridge, MA: Belknap Press of Harvard University Press, 1967), 98ff.

23. The other U.S. president to head the AHA was Theodore Roosevelt in 1912. The other person to head both the organizations was Charles A. Beard, who was president of the APSA in 1926 and the AHA in 1933.

24. Frank Irving Cobb, *Cobb of "The World,"* ed. John L. Heaton (New York: E. P. Dutton, 1924), 368–70. Wilson said many of the same things, although probably with less anguish, to Representative William C. Adamson of Georgia. See Adamson memorandum, Ray Stannard Baker Papers, Library of Congress, Box 99.

25. Wilson, unpublished prolegomenon to peace note, [ca. Nov. 25, 1916], *PWW,* 40:67–68, 70.

26. Wilson to William Jennings Bryan, June 7, 1915, *PWW,* 33:349.

27. Entry, May 10, 1915, Charles L. Swem diary, *PWW,* 33:38.

28. Wilson speech, Apr. 2, 1917, *PWW,* 41:527.

# 7 The Ordeal of Paris

## *Herbert Hoover, Woodrow Wilson, and the Search for Peace*

Charlie Laderman

In April 1958, a unique book was published. This work was both a personal memoir of the Paris Peace Conference and a study of President Woodrow Wilson's attempt to realize his diplomatic ideals at Versailles and secure endorsement for his peacemaking at home. However, it was not the book's subject that made its publication unprecedented; many of the conference's attendees had already published their own accounts, and there had been plenty of other works on Wilson's presidency and his diplomacy. What made this a study of singular importance was the identity of its author: Herbert Hoover, the twenty-eighth president of the United States. Hoover's study, *The Ordeal of Woodrow Wilson,* marked the first time that a former U.S. president had published a book about another ex-president whose political life intersected so closely with his own. It soon became a best seller, reaching number 14 on the *New York Times* list and selling almost 30,000 copies.[1] It even spawned a television program, featuring an interview with the then eighty-eight-year-old Hoover, that was broadcast on NBC in September 1962 and was watched by 10 million viewers across the country.

*The Ordeal of Woodrow Wilson* was not Hoover's first book, nor would it be his last. The former president was a prolific writer, publishing more than forty books over his lifetime. A number of these books are historical in nature, and many explore Hoover's own role in the significant national and international events of his day. This chapter does not attempt to explore all of these studies, Hoover's broader historical philosophy, or the various ways in which he sought to use the past to shape current affairs. Instead, it focuses exclusively on his remarkable study of Wilson and what it tells us about both presidents. This chapter explores Hoover's interpretation of Wilson's statecraft, how he depicted his own role in the drama that surrounded Wilson's "ordeal," and how he used this study to outline his vision of America's national destiny and its place in the world.

Hoover stressed to his readers that the book was neither a traditional work of history nor biography but a personal reflection on Wilson's leadership during the First World War, the peace conference, and its aftermath. He was well placed to analyze Wilson's experience, having served the president as head of the Belgian relief agency during the years of American neutrality, then, after American entry into the conflict, as food administrator and a member of Wilson's War Council, and finally as a member of the president's Economic Advisory Council in Paris and the director of relief and reconstruction of Europe. During this period, Hoover had amassed over one million documents relating to the First World War. He had already drawn on these items, and thousands from other collections, to prepare his extensive memoirs on the conflict. For this study of Wilson, Hoover and his research assistants supplemented these personal records with thousands of pages of diaries, diplomatic records, and memoirs from libraries and archives across the United States. Many of Hoover's other books are also characterized by prodigious research, but the inclusion of so many documents means that they often resemble legal briefs and make for heavy reading. In contrast, *The Ordeal of Woodrow Wilson,* while still incorporating many verbatim extracts from primary sources, is a coherent and colorful narrative that captures Wilson's idealistic crusade to reform international politics, the constraints on his diplomacy, and the ultimate catastrophe that befell him.

The book also illustrates Hoover's own pivotal role in the "second intervention" to "save life and prevent anarchy" in Europe through the provision of economic assistance after the turmoil of total war.[2] Hoover was extremely proud of the relief operation that he directed, emphasizing that through this initiative the United States had "saved civilization" and salvaged 100 million lives.[3] Nor was he alone in this estimation. As the British economist John Maynard Keynes would later remark, Europe "should never forget the extraordinary assistance afforded her during the first six months of 1919 through the agency of Mr. Hoover and the American commission of relief. Never was a nobler work of disinterested goodwill carried through with more tenacity and sincerity and skill, and with less thanks either asked or given." According to Keynes, "Hoover was the only man who emerged from the ordeal of Paris with an enhanced reputation," and the economist suggested his American colleague's work was characterized by "reality, knowledge, magnanimity and disinterestedness which, if they had been found in other quarters also, would have given us the good peace."[4]

The failure to achieve a "good peace" at Paris would continue to haunt Hoover over the succeeding decades. He would blame mistakes made at the Paris Peace Conference for the global economic crisis that wrecked his own presidency and for the breakdown in international order in the 1930s. When discussing the role that the United States should play in establishing peace after the Second World War, Hoover would constantly refer to the Paris Peace Conference and urge Americans not to make the same mistakes again. Nevertheless, although Hoover believed that Wilson had made too many compromises at Versailles and too few at home, he would laud his former commander in chief as the clearest example of America's moral force in international diplomacy and lay responsibility for his failure to reform global politics at the feet of the perfidious European and Asian powers. All these are present in Hoover's account of Wilson's "ordeal." For Hoover, Wilson's experience served as an example to Americans of their nation's high ideals and an enduring lesson of its separateness from the "Old World."

The First World War brought Hoover and Wilson together. In the eighteen years prior to the conflict, Hoover had spent much of that time living outside of the United States, establishing himself as an internationally successful mining engineer. He was living in London when war broke out in the summer of 1914. As Europe descended into carnage, 120,000 Americans were caught on the Continent. It was Hoover, at the head of a committee of Americans based in London, who assumed responsibility for assisting his fellow compatriots and helped ensure their safe passage back to the United States. This was just the start of Hoover's wartime service. As his biographer David Burner has illustrated, Hoover had long expressed his desire to undertake a "great public service for America."[5] An opportunity arose to do just that when, with the backing of the U.S. ambassador to London, Walter Hines Page, and Belgian banker Emile Franqui, Hoover took on the task of organizing relief for German-occupied Belgium. Before the war, Belgium had imported the majority of its food supplies. With the Allies' blockade of the Continent restricting Germany's own imports, its rulers were unwilling to supply much food to the Belgians. With their supplies running low, the Belgians appealed to the world for sustenance, and their plight evoked widespread sympathy.

Under Hoover's direction, an unprecedented relief operation was established, and around a billion dollars–worth of aid was ultimately supplied to Belgium. Hoover would later describe it as "the greatest job Americans have undertaken in the cause of humanity."[6] Not everyone agreed. A number of British leaders resented Hoover's work, as it removed German responsibility for providing Belgian relief. In his study of Wilson, Hoover recalled that Senator Henry Cabot Lodge was also suspicious of his activities and had charged him with violating the Logan Act, which forbade private U.S. citizens from interfering in diplomatic relations between the United States and foreign governments. Hoover was concerned that Lodge's opposition to his relief commission could undermine American public confidence in his work if it became public. As a result, he returned to the United States to rebut the charges, and, soon after his arrival, he met Wilson for the first time.

*The Ordeal of Woodrow Wilson* records that Hoover sailed for the United States on May 7, 1915, and met the president later that month. However, a number of scholars, including Mark Hatfield in his introduction to the reissued volume of *Ordeal,* suggest that Hoover's recollection of the date of his meeting with Wilson is off by several months and that he did not meet Wilson until November 3.[7] It was not uncommon for Hoover to incorrectly recall dates. As Burner notes, despite the exacting standards that Hoover usually held himself to in his research, he could be careless in recording details. For example, Hoover's own *Memoirs* has his mother dying in the wrong year and even has him being born on the wrong day![8] Hoover might have incorrectly recalled the date of his first meeting with Wilson, but he was certainly correct in his belief that the president fully appreciated the significance of his work. As Wilson wrote to his future wife, Edith, after this meeting, Hoover was a "real man . . . one of the very ablest men we have sent over there . . . a great international figure. Such men stir me deeply and make me in love with duty!"[9]

Hoover and Wilson had much in common. They were both political progressives at this time, although Wilson's rhetoric emphasized collaborative democracy while Hoover espoused, in the words of Burner, "an engineer's progressivism, stressing efficient organization, sensible ways to progress and a morality centred on workmanship."[10] For both men, their political philosophy was informed by their religious faith. As Hoover noted about Wilson, "his mind ran to moral principles," and this derived from his Presbyterian faith; "he often referred with pride to his ancestral inheritance from the Scottish

Covenanters of 1638."[11] Hoover's own commitment to peace and his belief that the world required, and could attain, redemption stemmed from his Quaker upbringing.[12] Furthermore, both Wilson and Hoover shared the conviction that U.S. neutrality in the war must serve a broader international goal. Wilson's concept of neutrality was intended to "preserve the foundations on which peace may be rebuilt."[13] In 1914, he had urged Americans to be "impartial in thought as well as in action" so that when the time came, the United States could fulfill its "duty as the one great nation at peace, the one people holding itself ready to play a part of impartial mediation and speak the counsels of peace and accommodation, not as a partisan, but as a friend."[14] Hoover viewed his relief work in Belgium as "turning barren neutrality into something positive, a thing which has never been before." It would serve as "a monument in American history" and "the greatest charity the world has ever seen."[15]

While both Hoover and Wilson were committed to establishing a more peaceful international order, neither man was a pacifist. In 1913, Wilson had confided to his closest friend and adviser, Colonel House, that "he did not share the views of so many of our present day statesmen that war was so much to be deprecated" and that "he thought there was no more glorious way to die than in battle."[16] During the period of American neutrality, Hoover noted that the Germans had a "Roman empire 'Masters of the World' sentiment," and consequently the United States would need to build up its armaments as someday "the civilized world has got to fight these people to a finish." Although he does not mention it in his book on Wilson, Hoover had also objected to Wilson's response to the sinking of the *Lusitania,* privately remarking that "Americans in England are humiliated with the interpretation put on [Wilson's] Philadelphia speech that we are too proud to fight."[17] Nevertheless, both men retained hope up until 1917 that the United States could avoid being drawn into the conflict, although Hoover felt that the president's efforts to secure a negotiated peace were futile and that Wilson did not fully appreciate that "Europe would not recoil from the abyss on the edge of which civilization hung."[18] Ultimately, however, both reluctantly came to accept that the German declaration of unrestricted submarine warfare and the sinking of American ships in the Atlantic meant U.S. intervention in the war was unavoidable.

With the outbreak of war between the United States and Germany in April 1917, Hoover notes that he was appointed to the position of U.S. Food Administrator, reporting directly to the president. He describes this in *Ordeal,* although he does not divulge that he had been hinting at his desire to obtain the position, if the United States entered the war, since late 1916.[19] Hoover would also help initiate the establishment of Wilson's war cabinet and served on it from its first meeting in March 1918. It was in assisting the president in the prosecution of the war that Hoover came to appreciate Wilson's administrative talents. Hoover rejects House's suggestion, issued in his unpublished diaries, that Wilson did not "have the kind of ability necessary to organize the country for war."[20] Instead, Hoover contends that Wilson's wartime record compared favorably with all other administrations from the Civil War to the 1950s, high praise from a figure so renowned for his own administrative abilities. Hoover only devotes one chapter in the book to the conduct of the war itself. What is most notable about this section is Hoover's emphasis on Wilson's attitude to the Allied nations alongside whom the United States was fighting the war. He reprints a letter that he had received from Wilson in December 1917, urging Hoover to avoid the use of the words "Our Allies" in the posters of the Food Administration, and instead use the term "Our Associates in the War." Wilson states that this was due to the American public's jealousy "of any intimation that there are formal alliances."[21] However, Wilson's request also reflected his belief that the United States did not share the same objectives in the conflict as the Allies. And it reflected Hoover's views, too. Hoover had already revealed to his readers that he had advised House in February 1917 that the United States should "enter into no political alliance with Allied Governments" and his belief that "our terms of peace will probably run counter to most of the European proposals."[22] Throughout *The Ordeal of Woodrow Wilson,* the stark contrast between U.S. war aims and ideals and those of the Allies is a consistent refrain.

Hoover lauded Wilson's "Fourteen Points" speech and his subsequent addresses as profound "expressions of the idealism of the American people and the New World," encapsulating "American ideals as old as the Revolution of 1776."[23] He described Wilson's achievement in establishing an armistice with Germany based on these addresses as "one of the most monumental feats of international action of any statesmen of history," which had ensured German "complete surrender" and Allied agreement to his principles.[24] However, even at the time of Wilson's "vast triumph," Hoover claimed to have been "haunted by my knowledge that they were doctrines strange to the Old World."[25] Hoover's international business activities ensured that he was one of the most widely traveled Americans of his day, and his relief work meant that he had associated with many of the leading figures in Europe. Yet it seemed that the more Hoover saw of that continent, the more enamored he became of the United States and the less confident he was that Europe, or at least its governing classes, shared American values.

Hoover declared that "at the Peace Conference the ordeal of Woodrow Wilson began and the forces inherent in the Old World took over the control of human fate."[26] Hoover's own fear that "Wilson's New World idealism would clash seriously with the Old World concepts of the Allied statesmen" had led him, like a number of other advisers, including Secretary of State Robert Lansing, to believe that the president should not risk diminishing his ability to speak on behalf of international public opinion by directly participating in the conference.[27] Hoover acknowledges that Wilson believed that it was his duty to participate in the conference to ensure that American ideals shaped the peace. He also claims that the president confided to him in December, after his arrival in Paris, that he was satisfied that the Allied statesmen would adhere to his ideals. Hoover reported that he had urged Wilson not to "ignore the shapes of evil inherent in the Old World system," but his concerns were "brushed aside with a remark that Europe had a changed spirit as the result of the blood bath through which it had passed."[28] However, he alleged that Wilson had confessed three months later that Hoover's assessment had been correct.

Hoover echoed the observations of others present in Paris that Wilson was greeted by an overwhelming outpouring of public emotion on his arrival in Europe. He went so far as to claim that "Wilson had reached the zenith of intellectual and spiritual leadership of the whole world, never hitherto known in history." Yet Hoover suggested that although the "masses" revered Wilson, seeing him as an "evangel of peace" on a scale not seen since "Christ preached the Sermon on the Mount," European officials received Wilson's pronouncements with disdain.[29] For Hoover, this just confirmed the difference between the United States and European governments, societies, and civilizational values. He proclaimed that Wilson embodied an American nation that "had been implacably anti-imperial, anti-colonial, and generally, anti-the-subjugation-of-one-people-by-another from the day of our Declaration."[30] On the other hand, the Allied statesmen were "dominated by the forces of hate and revenge of their peoples for grievous wrongs; by the economic prostration of their peoples; and by the ancient system of imperial spoils."[31] While Americans believed in "self-determination," the guiding principle of the European leaders was "empire," and the new nations that emerged in eastern Europe were motivated by an "extreme nationalism," leading to exaggerated territorial demands.[32] At times in his narrative, Hoover drew a distinction between the Allied leaders and their bureaucracies, who practiced power politics, and their citizens, who were attracted to Wilson's principles. For the most part, however, Hoover depicted "two worlds [that] were indeed in many ways strangers to each other." He even went so far as to describe the differences between the United States and Europe as a "collision of civilizations."[33] Many leading American policy makers and publicists in the years prior to the war had spoken of the United States and Europe as sharing a common "civilization"; for Hoover, though, there were fundamental, centuries-old differences between them.

The war had brought a new dynamic to European politics with the 1917 Bolshevik Revolution in Russia, and statesmen of all the major nations at Versailles feared the spread of Communism across the continent. Hoover stated that both he and Wilson were opposed to every manifestation of this "murderous tyranny."[34] Yet what is striking about Hoover's account is the nuanced analysis of the reasons for the success of the Bolsheviks and his cautious counsel as to how the United States should respond to the revolution. In a letter to Wilson in 1919, reprinted in *Ordeal,* Hoover declared that "it cannot be denied that that this swing of the social pendulum from the tyranny of the extreme right to the tyranny of the extreme left is based on a foundation of real social grievance."[35] Hoover had conducted mining business in Russia before the First World War and was antagonistic toward the tsar's regime. Before visiting Russia, he had read *Siberia and the Exile System,* written in 1891 by explorer George Kennan, an uncle of the famous diplomat, which left in him a deep feeling of revulsion toward the tsarist autocracy. When the tsar's government fell in 1917, Hoover regarded it as an event of great "spiritual" importance, and even after the Bolsheviks seized power, he had expressed hope that Russian laborers might expand their possession of property.[36] He was staunchly opposed to an intervention in Russia itself, telling Wilson in that March letter that "to attempt to suppress this phenomenon by military intervention was the height of folly" as it would involve the United States in "years of police duty" and make the United States "a party with the Allies to re-establishing the reactionary classes."[37] This chimed with Wilson's own thoughts on the subject. Although he had told his staff while sailing to Europe aboard the *George Washington* that he regarded Bolshevism as a "poison," he would tell Allied leaders in March that he believed that "trying to stop a revolutionary movement by troops in the field is like using a broom to hold back a great ocean."[38] Although he did sanction a limited intervention in Siberia to assist a Czech legion and to block Japanese expansion, his policy to the revolution was summed up by his conviction that the Russians should be allowed to "work out their own salvation even though they wallow in anarchy for a while."[39] Hoover, like Wilson, was suspicious of Allied motivations for intervening in Russia. Nor did he believe that the conditions that had led to the revolution were unique to Russia. In a 1919 speech, he had speculated that more revolution might be required across Europe to rectify the "inequalities and injustices of centuries," which had only been exacerbated by the war.[40] As he told Wilson in his March note, "our people, who enjoy so great liberty and general comfort, cannot fail to sympathize to some degree with these blind gropings for better social conditions."[41] By including this memorandum in his study, Hoover was further emphasizing the disparity between New World ideals and the most reactionary elements of the Old World.

If Hoover was opposed to a military intervention in Russia, he also rejected any suggestion of recognizing the Bolshevik government. Furthermore, he was committed to challenging Communism wherever it spread and to preventing the Bolsheviks from undertaking "large military crusades in an attempt to impose their doctrines on other defenceless people."[42] He believed that the way to achieve this was through the facilitation of relief, which would help the nations of Europe to recover, establish representative institutions, and stave off the threat of revolution. His letter to Wilson called for a "second Belgian Relief Commission for Russia."[43] Hoover suggests that Wilson supported this plan because it would bring stability to Europe and keep the "Allied militarists in Paris busy debating for some time," although Hoover's book does not mention that Wilson himself had conceived of a similar plan for a large-scale relief operation the previous year.[44] At this point, Hoover devotes considerable space to his own role in relief work. He justifies this partly on the basis that previous "chroniclers" of the president's work in Paris, by focusing exclusively on the political scene, had neglected the importance of the relief and reconstruction of Europe, which were under his direction.[45]

Hoover's discussion of his own part in the drama of Paris reflects a curious dichotomy that Burner has identified in Hoover's personality. Hoover regularly shied away from publicity and rejected a number of medals for his relief work after the war, which Burner attributes to his Quaker faith and belief that "good works became tainted if promulgated." At the same time, however, Hoover hated his actions being misinterpreted. Consequently, Burner suggests that "it was as though two forces warred within him: the need of an orphan to show the world he had made good . . . and the Quaker aversion to public tribute."[46] Both traits are evident in Hoover's account of Wilson. He is keen to stress that, in recommending the establishment of the relief operation to Wilson, he had no desire to acquire a position for himself but only took on the responsibility out of a sense of duty. While Hoover only accepted two of the various decorations that he was offered right after the conflict, he also informs his readers that he had "received invitations from scores of countries in Europe to become their guest as a mark of appreciation for services in the First World War."[47] Although he objects that "little expression of consequence" came out of Europe for America's relief work, he informs his readers that he personally "received generous messages of appreciation [from] more than thirty Presidents or Prime Ministers together with all the great religious prelates in Europe."[48]

Part of the reason why Hoover emphasized the gratitude that many Europeans, particularly in eastern Europe, felt for his activities is because he objected to the Allied leaders doubting the "purely humanitarian nature" of American relief work. He notes that the Allies were aware that Wilson could use American economic strength to set the terms of the peace and suggests that, as their officials would have used that power for "political purposes," they were sceptical of the "altruism of American motives."[49] The historian Gary Dean Best has argued that, in fact, "relief was something of a misnomer in Hoover's frantic desire to unload high-priced pork and grain" on to the European market, "except in the sense that almost all American credits advanced for food were never repaid."[50] Other scholars have debated whether Hoover's determination to export American food on credit terms to Europe was motivated more by a desire to contain the spread of Bolshevism or to guard against America's own economic problems. Hoover's humanitarianism blended moral impulse, strategic concerns, and pragmatic business sense, and so discerning his primary motivation is often difficult. What is more important for the purpose of analyzing Hoover's discussion of relief in this study of Wilson is the contrast that he draws between America's determination to rehabilitate and stabilize the European continent and the calculated ways in which the European nations were making use of American foodstuff to undermine their enemies.

Hoover was particularly disgusted by the continuation by the Allies of the food blockade against Germany for four months after the armistice. He described it as "a crime in statesmanship against civilization as a whole" that "sowed dragon's teeth of war which two decades later again enveloped most of mankind." While Wilson bore no responsibility for this "crime," Hoover discussed the subject in detail, as it demonstrated "the wide divergence between the American and Allied points of view."[51] For his own part, Hoover suggests that the United States perhaps should have used its economic power and dominance of the world's food supplies to dictate peace terms to the Allies. However, Hoover maintains that Wilson "was too great a man to bargain in this way," and "American idealism indeed was unfitted to participate in a game played with power as the counters."[52]

In depicting Wilson as the supreme American idealist, Hoover also insinuates that the president underestimated the intransigence of the Allied leaders and failed to appreciate the "dynamism" of their opposition.[53] As a result, Hoover suggests, he too often compromised his ideals. Hoover objected to the separate Anglo-American security guarantee negotiated at Paris, regarding it as a military alliance that violated Wilson's principles. He laments the insertion of the "war guilt" clause into the treaty, the reparations imposed on the Germans, and the maintenance of the Allied blockade, all of which he blames for hampering Germany economically and politically, and paving the way for subsequent turmoil. In addition, he deplores the "mandates compromise," which was "neatly managed so as to comply with many of the secret treaties" and to enable the imperial expansion of the Allied nations at the expense of self-determination.[54] In discussing Wilson's decision, under British and French pressure, to recommend to Congress that the United States should take its own mandates for Armenia and Constantinople, Hoover reveals that he was the designated choice as governor for these potential American protectorates. But Hoover was fundamentally opposed to accepting this responsibility, regarding the assumption of the mandates as a grave strategic error that would enmesh the United States in an unstable region while acting as a cover to allow the Allied powers, particularly the British Empire, to acquire the world's resources. In general, he blames Wilson's naivety and "unfamiliarity with Old World diplomacy" for his concession on the mandates, bluntly stating that the president was "just fooled."[55] While rejecting any suggestion that Wilson's fellow peace commissioners conspired against him at Versailles, Hoover suggests that, on the whole, the men serving Wilson in Paris were "amateurs in the ancient art of diplomacy."[56] This fatally weakened Wilson in his negotiations with the Europeans, who were far more skilled in power politics. In Hoover's portrayal, a collection of American innocents, led by a too credulous president, were no match for the wily Europeans.

Throughout his study, Hoover paints himself as a more practical-minded idealist, whose greater international experience ensured that he was more alive to the tricks of the Allied leaders and more prescient about the ways in which the "seeds of another war" were contained in the terms of the treaty.[57] Moreover, he suggests that, unlike the president whose commission was comprised of "amateurs and college professors," he was supported by a relief organization that "knew every economic and political back alley of Europe better than any one group of the peacemakers."[58] Based on this knowledge, Hoover states that he and his staff were thoroughly disillusioned by the Treaty of Versailles. Like Keynes, Hoover particularly feared the "economic consequences of the peace," which he believed the principal peacemakers had neglected.

As Hoover makes clear in the book, he made his objections clear to Wilson at the time. In a memorandum to the president, sent on June 5, 1919, eleven days before the final version of the treaty was handed to the Germans, Hoover warned that the proposed terms would "take all the economic surplus of Germany for a generation." It risked undermining any hope of a stable democracy in Germany and turning that country to "Communism of Reaction." He urged Wilson not to "sacrifice the United States to the objectives of the European Allies" and instead adhere to his "original contentions" as contained in the Fourteen Points and subsequent addresses, even if it risked breaking up the Peace Conference.[59] Hoover failed to convince Wilson, and the disagreement led to a breach in their relationship and his removal from the president's group of advisers.

Hoover's book does not delve into the full details of the deterioration in their relationship. He does not mention that he subsequently described Wilson as a man on the verge of greatness, until he lost his mind and sought to dominate the world with Hoover's assistance. Nor does he relate Wilson's trenchant critique of him as "one of the most selfish people I have ever known, who would rather see a good cause fail than succeed if he were not the head of it."[60] What Hoover does say in this book is that, although Wilson had engaged in compromises that had "sowed the whole earth with dragon's teeth," he does not blame him. He saw Wilson's compromises as his means to salvage the League of Nations, which "could redeem the world from these evils." In any case, Hoover believed that dwelling on "the 'points' which the President lost at Paris is of little importance to history except as a demonstration of the hostility of Old World concepts to New World ideals."[61] Here again, Hoover was emphasising the central thesis of his book—America's exceptionalism and the antagonism of Europe's leaders to its diplomatic principles.

If anything, Hoover held to a faith in the redemptive power of the League to an even greater degree than Wilson in the subsequent national debate over ratification of the treaty. While he initially supported Wilson in his campaign to have the treaty ratified without reservations, he came to believe that the president's unwillingness to compromise was holding up peace and urged him to placate his domestic opponents. *The Ordeal of Woodrow Wilson* does not necessarily reflect the extent of Hoover's disgust with Wilson and the Senate Democrats during the debate over the treaty. During the treaty fight, Hoover actually accused the Democrats of a "failure in statesmanship" for disregarding "one half of the people of the United States" for partisan reasons and for failing to "make those compromises necessary to secure the League of Nations and the peace of the world."[62] By this time, Hoover had committed himself to the Republican Party, after what he described as "six years of rigorous nonpartisanship."[63] As Hoover truthfully states in his book, however, he had taken his own position in the League fight, working through the Republican Party and William Howard Taft's League to Enforce Peace to push for treaty ratification with reservations, on the principled ground that he believed it was the best means to get the United States into the League of Nations, rather than for political expediency. As Hoover makes clear in his study, he had continued to identify himself with the League even as it became increasingly unpopular with the public. He even challenged the irreconcilable Senator Hiram Johnson in the 1920 Republican Californian primary, claiming in *Ordeal* that he did so as a "sacrifice hit" on behalf of the League.[64] This account is corroborated by the *El Paso Times* at the time, which stated that "in choosing the League of Nations as the chief issue, the former Food Administrator has placed his bet on a dead card."[65]

The reasons that Hoover outlines in the book for why he supported League membership were the same as those he stressed in his speeches and public statements at the time: to bring peace and stability to Europe, to advance the spread of democratic institutions, and to secure America's own commercial and economic interests. Unlike Wilson, he did not believe that the League's success depended on Article 10, the clause that came to be known as the "collective security" provision and that committed member nations "to preserve as against external aggression the territorial integrity and existing political independence of all member nations." Instead, Hoover believed that America's "economic and moral weight, our idealism, and our disinterested sense of justice" were far more important to international stability than military power.[66] Indeed, as Hoover reports telling Wilson in April 1919, the American people were "not prepared for us to undertake the military policing of Europe while it boils out its social wrongs." This reflected Hoover's own belief that the United States was the "one great moral preserve in the world today," but it could not "maintain the independence of action through which this reserve is to be sustained if we allow ourselves to be dragged into detailed European entanglements."[67] Even while urging American membership in the League, Hoover was determined to ensure that it did not become too entwined with Europe. In a speech advocating League membership in September 1919, Hoover stated that his experiences in Paris had convinced him "of the enormous distance that we of America have grown away from Europe in this century and a half of our national existence." At the same time, however, he insisted that the "supreme importance of this Americanism" did not permit Americans "to abandon the moral leadership we have undertaken of restoring order in the world."[68] Both of these themes, the separateness of America's values and ideals from those of Europe and the need for the United States to assume a leadership role in global affairs, are at the core of *The Ordeal of Woodrow Wilson.*

Hoover bemoans that Wilson's physical collapse, his acute illness, and his seclusion from the political scene prevented him making the compromises necessary to bring the United States into the League. In addition, he regrets that the president was willing to accept far more drastic changes to the Treaty in Paris than he was at home. However, Hoover does not dwell long on the battle for ratification of the treaty by the Senate. This is likely explained by his conviction, expressed to the journalist William Allen White soon after Wilson's death in 1924, that Wilson had developed a pathological streak after he suffered an initial stroke in Paris in April 1919; this had made him stubborn and more unbending in his opinions, and led to the "great tragedy—his refusal to accept the reservations of the treaty." Consequently, Hoover believed that the onset of Wilson's illness at the close of the Paris Peace Conference meant "his real history ought to end there." Hoover informed White that he believed "men should be judged by the good they do" and that his own personal differences with Wilson were immaterial when set against his "extra-ordinary service for the American people."[69]

By the time Wilson died, Hoover was serving as a cabinet member in a Republican administration that kept the United States at arms-length to the League. His own attempts to convince President Warren Harding to support American League membership following the Republican victory in the 1920 presidential election had proved fruitless. In *Ordeal,* Hoover defended the Harding administration's (and, implicitly, his own decision to serve in it) by stating that the attitude of the country toward ratification at the time of Harding's inauguration meant it was politically impossible to push for American entrance into the League and that this remained the case for the next eight years of Republican rule.

When Hoover himself entered the White House in 1929, he suggested that the United States was now prepared to assume greater global responsibilities, and, under his presidency, American official engagement with the League of Nations did expand. As he stresses in *Ordeal,* his administration contributed to a Preparatory Commission for a multilateral disarmament conference, engaged extensively with the League in all its nonpolitical functions, and appointed American representatives to the League's commission to investigate Japan's military assault on China's Manchurian province. However, the Wall Street crash of October 1929 and the subsequent worldwide economic depression undermined the fragile framework on which international order rested and dominated Hoover's one, unhappy term in office.

Hoover believed that the origins of the world depression could be found in the neglect of the economic implications of the Paris peace settlements, which not only failed to resolve existing problems but helped unleash new ones. In particular, Hoover suggested that the maintenance of the Allied blockade during the postwar armistice had contributed to a collapse in the German economy from which the nation struggled to recover. Furthermore, the "preposterous method of collective reparations" was a "running sore" in international economic relations for the next two decades. Together with the failure to stabilize currencies, reduce armaments, and eliminate trade barriers, these factors "had much to do with the violence of the hurricane of economic and revolution that came ten to fifteen years later."[70] For Hoover, Wilson's "ordeal" was inextricably linked to the great tragedy of his own presidency, and both stemmed from the reactionary policies of the European powers.

Hoover concludes *The Ordeal of Woodrow Wilson* by arguing that the "seeds planted by the Old World statesmen at Versailles" were responsible for "another, and even more terrible, World War."[71] As the world had descended into that conflict, he had warned Americans against again attempting to solve Europe's problems. In early 1939, he had declared that "all European history is a treadmill of war for power and mastery," and as late as September 1941 he had pointed to "the eternal malign forces of Europe."[72] However, following American entry into the war, he was outspoken in his recommendations for restoring peace to Europe and establishing a new international order. Wilson's experiences in Paris were a constant reference point for Hoover. He was opposed to convening a large-scale postwar international conference, advising Americans that "such assemblies as Versailles, with all its surroundings of emotion, propaganda, high pressure by groups and logrolling of governments can be avoided."[73] He retained his suspicion of European imperialism and regarded the lowering of trade barriers as essential to the reestablishment of independence for the small nations of central and eastern Europe. In general, he urged far more attention be devoted to economic factors than had occurred in Paris. He also favored the establishment of regional councils for ensuring stability on their continents without the need for constant American involvement.

This was in keeping with Hoover's relatively positive attitude to the Concert of Europe, which he praises in *Ordeal* for "keeping the world free from worldwide wars between 1814 and 1914."[74] At Paris, he had urged Wilson to use the Concert as a model for international organization, reminding him that it had prevented large-scale conflicts for "one hundred years without so definite an organization as that proposed for the League." Wilson had dismissed Hoover's suggestion on the grounds that the Concert "had failed, its great test being this war, and that much stronger action was necessary to prevent such a disaster in the future."[75] However, Hoover had retained his belief in the utility of the Concert for maintaining order in Europe. In contrast to the North Atlantic Treaty Organization (NATO), the establishment of which Hoover had opposed, the Concert model had the benefit of being a regional arrangement that did not commit the United States to involvement in all the conflicts and boundary disputes of Europe. In the 1950s, Hoover remained opposed, as he had told Wilson at Versailles, to the United States engaging in "the military policing of Europe while it boils out its social wrongs."[76]

Yet if Versailles served as a cautionary tale, Hoover also channelled Wilson's principles in his recommendations for U.S. foreign policy after World War II. In calling for the abandonment of reparations after the war, Hoover alluded to Wilson's call for a "peace without victory" by declaring, "We can have peace or we can have revenge, but we cannot have both."[77] His emphasis on elective parliamentary government as the basis for the international state system echoed Wilson's argument that "a steadfast concert for peace can never be maintained except by a partnership of democratic nations."[78] He celebrated Wilson's commitment to national self-determination. In particular, he gave the former president "everlasting credit" for securing the independence of the nations of Eastern Europe, all of which were now under Soviet domination. He contrasted Wilson favorably with his Democratic successor, Franklin Roosevelt, whom he blamed for recognizing the Soviet Union and for "appeasing" the Soviets at Yalta. In *Ordeal,* Hoover also argued that the establishment of the United Nations (UN) was a continuation of the "League concept" and ensured "the spirt of Woodrow Wilson came to the world again." However, Hoover also suggested that the League differed from the new organization in one respect: Wilson's original organization was "an association of free nations, not to include men and dictatorships conspiring for its ruin."[79]

During the early 1950s, Hoover was prominent in the "great debate" over U.S. foreign policy, after the nation entered into an alliance to defend Western Europe from Soviet aggression and American troops were sent on a UN mission to aid South Korea. In a series of speeches, a number of which were broadcast nationally, Hoover questioned the wisdom of the American commitment to protect Western Europe, arguing that those nations were taking insufficient measures to provide for their own defense. As a result, they were saddling the "overstrained" American economy with the expense and risking the lives of American soldiers, who would be stationed on the European continent with inadequate military support from their Western European counterparts.[80] Hoover remained a visceral opponent of Soviet Communism, referring to it as a "great malignant force" and the "one enemy of peace in the world," and was adamantly opposed to any suggestion of appeasing the

Soviet Union.[81] However, he argued that the United States could not be expected to assume the burden of combating the Communist forces unaided and should rely on air and sea power for protection, rather than committing its land forces to an unwinnable war in Europe. The Western European nations should primarily be responsible for their own defence. Yet to Hoover's disdain, "in persistence to an old habit, we are taking up the check."[82]

Furthermore, Hoover outlined his disgust with the UN, "our great hope" when it was initially established, which had now been reduced by Moscow "to a propaganda forum for the smearing of free peoples" and "been defeated in its major purpose as a maker of peace and good will."[83] Hoover was convinced that the UN was destined to suffer a similar fate as the League. Whereas the "tragedy of the League" was that it became "an instrument to protect imperial spoils of war," the "tragedy of the United Nations was that it turned into an instrument to protect Red imperialism."[84] Consequently, he called for the Communist nations to be expelled from the UN, and, if that was not possible, then he suggested the establishment of a "New United Front," comprising nations "who disavow Communism, who stand for morals and religion, and who love freedom." Hoover maintained that his proposals offered an alternative foreign policy, one that would avoid either committing the United States to "a military alliance" or forcing it to "crawl into isolation and defend the Western Hemisphere alone."[85]

Hoover's opposition did not prevent the Senate from sanctioning the stationing of four divisions of U.S. ground troops in Europe in 1951. Nor did Hoover's arguments win out within the Republican Party. After securing the presidency in 1952, Dwight D. Eisenhower would entrench his Democratic predecessor Harry Truman's strategy of large-scale military armament; a forwardly deployed presence of U.S. troops overseas; the erection of a system of international alliances, centered on NATO; and the concentration of unprecedented power in the executive. Although the Eisenhower administration did increasingly adopt a defensive posture of "massive retaliation" that echoed Hoover's emphasis on air and sea power, this was not intended as a substitute for the large-scale deployment of ground forces overseas. In addition, despite growing American disenchantment with the UN, neither the Truman nor the Eisenhower administration was willing to entertain Hoover's radical proposals for the organization.

By the time that Hoover embarked on *The Ordeal of Woodrow Wilson,* he had gradually warmed to aspects of Eisenhower's foreign policy, praising him for succeeding in lessening global tensions while simultaneously remaining resolute in countering Soviet advances in areas around the world that were core American interests, such as the Middle East.[86] Yet his disillusionment with America's European allies persisted, and he remained resentful of the European governments for their unwillingness to do more to share the burden of their own defense. As he wrote to an old friend in 1957, the year before its publication, he hoped that they would "illustrate some lessons on the old world."[87] Hoover hoped that Wilson's "ordeal" would remind Americans that they must remain alert to European schemes and guard against attempts by European governments to take advantage of America's idealism to serve their own selfish purposes.

Furthermore, although Hoover had come to accept that it was not feasible for the Soviet nations to be expelled from the UN, he continued to argue that the organization "had failed to give us even a remote hope of lasting peace."[88] He continued to contrast the UN unfavorably with Wilson's creation, and in the 1961 NBC documentary of *Ordeal,* he assured his audience that Wilson would "never have agreed to accept dictators to membership" in an international organization.[89] The following year, on his eighty-eighth birthday, Hoover would issue an appeal "for a new and stronger world-wide organization," which he called "the Council of Free Nations" and which would "include only those nations who are willing to stand up and fight for their freedom and independence."[90]

Hoover's account of Wilson's "ordeal" was therefore not simply intended as a memoir of a bygone era but was designed to influence the contemporary American debate over the nation's role in the world. Hoover sought to summon Wilson, the U.S. president most closely associated with the League, to support his case against the UN and to encourage Americans to work for the eventual establishment of an international organization that subscribed more closely to their national principles. Moreover, Hoover was seeking to illustrate that his conception of America's global role, one that was distinct from, and avoided too close an association with, the "Old World" European powers, was in keeping with American ideals and the spirit of Wilson, the nation's most noted idealist.

The year before *The Ordeal of Woodrow Wilson* was published, the historian Arthur Schlesinger Jr. had claimed that Hoover was someone who "transmuted all adventure into business."[91] In recounting Wilson's "ordeal," however, Hoover had sought to capture the adventure and the drama of the historical moment that surrounded the Paris Peace Conference. He consciously imagines his account as a "Greek tragedy," even going so far as to invoke Pericles's funeral oration in Thucydides's *History of the Peloponnesian War* to capture the essence of Wilson's "crusade." For Hoover, his predecessor's campaign for international peace was essentially "a struggle between the concepts of the New and Old Worlds."[92] And in Hoover's account of this "ordeal," Wilson serves as an emblem of America's exceptionalism, an example of the dangers of becoming too entangled in the affairs of the "Old World," and as the clearest embodiment of the "heritage of idealism of the American people."[93]

## *Notes*

1. Timothy Walch, "The Ordeal of a Biographer: Herbert Hoover Writes about Woodrow Wilson," *Prologue Magazine* 40, no. 3 (Fall 2008).

2. First quote in "Hebert Hoover's Impressions of Socialism in Europe," speech at dinner in Waldorf Astoria, New York, Sept. 16, 1919, *Mining and Metallurgy* (Oct. 1919): 154; second quote in "Stanford University Address, October 2 1919," Box 113, Herbert Hoover Papers, Hoover Institution Archives.

3. Herbert Hoover, *An American Epic, vol. 1, The Relief of Belgium and Northern France, 1914–1930* (Chicago: Harry Regnery, 1959), xv.

4. John Maynard Keynes, *The Economic Consequences of the Peace* (New York: Harcourt, Brace and Howe, 1920), 274.

5. David Burner, *Herbert Hoover: A Public Life* (New York: Knopf Doubleday Publishing Group, 1979), 74.

6. Quoted in Martin L. Fausold, *The Presidency of Herbert Hoover* (Lawrence: University Press of Kansas, 1985), 9.

7. Hebert Hoover (with a new introduction by Mark Hatfield), *The Ordeal of Woodrow Wilson* (Washington, DC: The Woodrow Wilson Center Press, 1992), xiii; David S. Patterson, *The Search for Negotiated Peace: Women's Activism and Citizen Diplomacy in World War I* (New York: Routledge, 2008), 374, n.13.

8. Burner, *Herbert Hoover,* 58.

9. Quoted in William E. Leuchtenburg, *Herbert Hoover: The American Presidents Series: The 31st President, 1929–1933* (New York: Henry Holt, 2009), 32.

10. Burner, *Herbert Hoover,* 19.

11. Hoover, *Ordeal of Woodrow Wilson,* xxvii.

12. Martin L. Fausold, "Quaker President Herbert C. Hoover and American Foreign Policy," in Lee Nash, ed., *Herbert Hoover and World Peace* (Lantham, MD: University Press of America, 2010), 1–27.

13. Address to the Daughters of the American Revolution, Continental Hall, Washington, DC, Oct. 11, 1915, in James Brown Scott, *President Wilson's Foreign Policy: Messages, Addresses and Papers* (New York: Oxford University Press, 1918), 110.

14. "An Appeal to the American People," Aug. 18, 1914, *Wilson Papers,* 30:393–94.

15. All quoted in Burner, *Herbert Hoover,* 74.

16. Quoted in John A. Thompson, *Woodrow Wilson* (London: Longman, 2002), 79.

17. All quotes in Burner, *Herbert Hoover,* 81.

18. Hoover, *Ordeal of Woodrow Wilson,* 3.

19. Burner, *Herbert Hoover,* 96.

20. Colonel Edward M. House Diary, July 4, 1917, *House Papers,* Yale University Library, quoted in Hoover, *Ordeal of Woodrow Wilson,* 13.

21. Wilson to Hoover, Dec. 10, 1917, quoted in Hoover, *Ordeal of Woodrow Wilson,* 12–13.

22. Ibid., 5–6.

23. Ibid., 19.

24. Ibid., 60.

25. Ibid., 27.

26. Ibid., 68.

27. Ibid., 61.

28. Ibid., 68.

29. Ibid., 68. For other accounts that echo Hoover's, see Thompson, *Woodrow Wilson,* chapter 1, "Images of Wilson"; Erez Manela, "Imagining Woodrow Wilson in Asia: Dreams of East-West Harmony and the Revolt against Empire in 1919," *American Historical Review* 111, no. 5 (2006): 1327–51.

30. Hoover, *Ordeal of Woodrow Wilson,* 72.

31. Ibid., 300.

32. Ibid., 94.

33. Ibid., 78.

34. Ibid., 119.

35. Ibid., 118.

36. Burner, *Herbert Hoover,* 57.

37. Hoover, *Ordeal of Woodrow Wilson,* 118.

38. Quoted in John Milton Cooper, *Pivotal Decades: The United States, 1900–1920* (New York: W. W. Norton, 1990), 316.

39. Quoted in John Milton Cooper, *Woodrow Wilson: A Biography* (New York: Vintage Books, 2009), 439.

40. Burner, *Herbert Hoover,* 119.

41. Hoover, *Ordeal of Woodrow Wilson,* 118.

42. Ibid., 118–19.

43. Ibid., 119.

44. Burner, *Herbert Hoover,* 119.

45. Hoover, *Ordeal of Woodrow Wilson,* 87.

46. All quotes in Burner, *Herbert Hoover,* 92.

47. Hoover, *Ordeal of Woodrow Wilson,* 134.

48. Ibid., 296, 269.

49. Ibid., 95.

50. Gary Dean Best, "Food Relief as Price Support: Hoover and American Pork, January–March 1919," *Agricultural History* 45 (Apr. 1971): 79–84.

51. Hoover, *Ordeal of Woodrow Wilson,* 157.

52. Ibid., 76.

53. Ibid., 196.

54. Ibid., 222.

55. Ibid., 224.

56. Ibid., 77.

57. Ibid., 234.

58. Ibid., 77, 235.

59. Ibid., 248.

60. Quoted in Burner, *Herbert Hoover,* 151.

61. Hoover, *Ordeal of Woodrow Wilson,* 264.

62. Burner, *Herbert Hoover,* 155.

63. The one exception was when he urged the election of a Congress supportive of the president's peace plans in 1918, a stance that he later regretted.

64. Hoover, *Ordeal of Woodrow Wilson,* 297.

65. Quoted in Burner, *Herbert Hoover,* 153.

66. Herbert Hoover, Stanford University Address, Oct. 2, 1919, Herbert Hoover Papers, Box 113, Hoover Institution Archives.

67. Hoover, *Ordeal of Woodrow Wilson,* 202.

68. "Hebert Hoover's Impressions of Socialism in Europe," 154.

69. Quotes in Royal J. Schmidt, "Hoover's Reflections on the Versailles Treaty," in Lawrence E. Gelfand, ed., *Herbert Hoover: The Great War and Its Aftermath* (Iowa City: University of Iowa Press, 1979), 81–82.

70. Burner, *Hebert Hoover,* 72.

71. Hoover, *Ordeal of Woodrow Wilson,* 302.

72. Quoted in Justus D. Doenecke, "The Anti-Interventionism of Herbert Hoover," *Journal of Libertarian Studies* 8, no. 2 (Summer 1987): 320.

73. Ibid., 321.

74. Hoover, *Ordeal of Woodrow Wilson,* 179, n.1.

75. Ibid., 184.

76. Ibid., 202.

77. Hoover and Gibson, *Problems,* 248.

78. Hoover, *Ordeal of Woodrow Wilson,* 302.

79. Ibid.

80. Quoted in Gary Dean Best, "Herbert Hoover and the Great Debates Over Foreign Policy, 1940–41 and 1950–51," in Nash, *Herbert Hoover and World Peace,* 159.

81. Herbert Hoover, "The United Nations and World Peace," July 11, 1950, in Herbert Hoover, *Addresses Upon the American Road* (Stanford, CA: Stanford University Press, 1951), 71.

82. Herbert Hoover, "The Voice of World Experience," Apr. 27, 1950, in Hoover, *Addresses Upon the American Road,* 66.

83. Herbert Hoover, "Our National Policies in this Crisis," Dec. 20, 1950, in Hoover, *Addresses Upon the American Road,* 206.

84. Herbert Hoover, "The United Nations and World Peace," July 11, 1950, in Hoover, *Addresses Upon the American Road,* 74.

85. Herbert Hoover, "Speech of April 27, 1950 to American Newspaper Publishers Association," *New York Times,* Apr. 28, 1950, 13.

86. Gary Dean Best, *Herbert Hoover: The Post-Presidential Years, 1933–1964, vol. 2, 1946–1964* (Stanford, CA: Hoover Institution Press, 1983), 397–425.

87. Quoted in ibid., 404.

88. *New York Times,* Aug. 11, 1962.

89. "Herbert Hoover: The Ordeal of Woodrow Wilson," Jan. 31, 1961, C-SPAN, https://www.c-span.org/video/?426121-1/the-ordeal-woodrow-wilson&start=87.

90. *New York Times,* Aug. 11, 1962.

91. Arthur M. Schlesinger Jr., *The Crisis of the Old Order, 1919–1933* (New York: Houghton Mifflin, 2003), 78.

92. Both quoted in Hoover, *Ordeal of Woodrow Wilson,* 300–301.

93. Ibid., xxvii.

# III Reckoning with Liberalism and the New Deal

# 8 Franklin Delano Roosevelt and the Problem of Historical Time

David Sehat

Franklin Delano Roosevelt was the most important president of the first half of the twentieth century. His four terms in office served to establish a liberal consensus that would guide American government for forty years after his death. His policy innovations changed the nature of the presidency, fostered a wider transformation within American constitutionalism, and made all who came after him, whether they agreed with him or not, wrestle with his example. But one of his most important accomplishments, if it can be called that, remains among his least known. Roosevelt had a supreme ability to sell his policies before the public and to justify his actions by making them above all about historical necessity. He was able to shape the historical consciousness of the nation in a way that legitimated his initiatives by offering a series of historical fables that we continue to see today.[1]

His rhetorical mastery was evident from the beginning of his quest for the presidency in 1932. In the midst of the Great Depression, then-president Herbert Hoover had only reluctantly begun to use the powers of government to turn the crisis around. Hoover believed that there was only so much that could be done to fix the economy while staying within the boundaries of the American tradition. The American way relied upon the political, the economic, and the spiritual principles of strictly limited government. Those principles had nurtured what Hoover called the "progressive individualism" at the core of the American project. To use the government in an indiscriminate or too aggressive manner, Hoover thought, would undermine American individualism and betray the legacy handed down from the past.[2]

Then-governor Roosevelt could not have disagreed more. As he looked over the nation, he saw a rupture between the present conditions and the past. In this, Roosevelt's ideas came directly from the progressive thinkers of the prior thirty years. He believed, with Walter Weyl, that a commitment to "ancient political ideas" would only encumber "our modern brains" in addressing contemporary problems. He thought, as Walter Lippmann put it in 1913, that government officials could not hope to meet new challenges "with a few inherited ideas, uncriticised assumptions, a foggy vocabulary, and a machine philosophy." It was only through "a new sense of political values" (Lippmann again) that the burdens of a new time could be met.[3]

The times themselves, Roosevelt thought, had only become more demanding since progressivism's heyday. The need for new ideas was only more pressing. The problem was a historical one. The economic development of the last century had created the crisis of the 1930s. The Industrial Revolution, begun shortly after the American revolt from Great Britain, had yielded a concentration of economic power and the possibility of mass suffering to such a degree that it threatened the economic and the political orders. The problems were "so complex, so widely distributed over our whole society," Roosevelt told an audience in Atlanta in 1932, that tinkering with the old values would not do. "I believe that we are at the threshold of a fundamental change in our popular economic thought," he told the Atlanta crowd. "In the future we are going to think less about the producer and more about the consumer." That change in thought would entail a host of changes in government practices. It would ultimately require a rearrangement of the American political economy, modifying laws, tax structures, and more.[4]

Roosevelt's basic historical posture in 1932 was, in short, that of a progressive modernist. He emphasized that the economic transformations of the previous century and a half had culminated in new social and economic realities on the ground. So fundamental was the transformation that the ideas and governing structures of the past had become dangerously disconnected from existing conditions. Only by recognizing the scale of the transformation, Roosevelt claimed, and only by coming to historical terms with the old social and economic structures, could government adapt itself to meet these new realities.[5]

Roosevelt accordingly set up his entire campaign to broadcast his sense of historical change and to call for a corresponding break with the governing ideas of the past. After he received the Democratic nomination for the presidency, he went against tradition by requesting that party leaders hold the convention in session. He then flew to Chicago in order to accept the nomination in person. When he appeared before the crowd, he acknowledged that his actions were "unprecedented and unusual." But they were justified, he said, because "these are unprecedented and unusual times." He wanted it understood that he broke tradition with a frankly symbolic purpose. "Let it be from now on the task of our party to break foolish traditions," he told the crowd. Only by doing so would they be able to meet "the demands of the new time."[6]

Yet there was some ambiguity in his address. As much as he called for a break in outmoded practices, and as much as he promised "a new deal for the American people," Roosevelt laced his message with a surprising sense of historical continuity beneath his call for change. He invoked "the continuing logic of history" to suggest that the Democratic Party had long been the champion of liberalism and the party most able to conserve American institutions. He claimed that Democrats had made it a habit to disregard obsolete political forms while nevertheless maintaining core political ideals. By recognizing the inner logic of history and by applying old principles in new ways, he said, the party could continue to uphold the best of America.[7]

Put simply, he was not a revolutionary. His break from the past was not total. What Roosevelt had in mind was that principles stood in some sense outside of time or at least were able to be disconnected from time and circumstance, in ways that allowed for a constant generation of new intellectual applications and new political forms. The fact that he was calling for new governmental institutions and practices did not mean that the old principles were gone. In proposing a new deal for the American people, he claimed to be standing with core American principles that had been handed down from the founding era. American government merely needed to embrace, as he would later say, "the new terms of the old social contract."[8]

This belief that some core principles remained outside of time to be appropriated in new ways had been a persistent aspect of liberal politics and constitutionalism. Abraham Lincoln, for example, had asserted that the ideals of equality and liberty could be detached from the historical circumstances of the American Revolution in order to inspire later generations in vastly different contexts to completely different ends. Woodrow Wilson believed that the founders' ideas of freedom had continuing resonance in his time even if the specifics of their vision were no longer relevant. A century later Barack Obama would invoke "the timeless spirit once conferred to us in a spare Philadelphia hall" that politicians needed to take up and apply anew. For Roosevelt, the old principles were anchors to ground his program.[9]

Once he won election, he continued the theme. In his inaugural address, Roosevelt pledged to work with Congress in his first one hundred days to pass a comprehensive program in agriculture, industry, and finance. The idea was to use the full force of government to fight the Great Depression. But he claimed that such a program would be in keeping with the founding principles because the Constitution was "so simple and practical" that it enabled him "to meet extraordinary needs by changes in emphasis and arrangement without loss of essential form."[10]

But he also introduced a new perspective in his inaugural address. Arguing that the businessmen's creed of the past decade had taken the nation off track, Roosevelt charged that business leaders were betrayers of principle. Once the Depression hit, they "fled from their high seats in the temple of our civilization." Their abandonment opened up a space for action. "We may now restore that temple," he told the crowd, "to the ancient truths." At the center of the old truths, he said, was a set of social values that went beyond the profit motive and drew inspiration from the Scriptures. His rhetoric of restoration also worked, on a deeper level, with the civic republican tradition, which had long affirmed public-mindedness as a core value and foresaw the continual falling away and then return to principle as a central dynamic in the life of a republic. This cyclical sense of time stood in some contrast to his previous statements.[11]

By his inaugural address, in other words, Roosevelt had presented three different and not entirely compatible conceptions of historical time. The first was a secular notion of time that emphasized linear development, the progressive and accumulative evolution of social systems that occurs over eras. The second was a flirtation with timelessness, an assertion that principles stood outside of time and could be appropriated in new ways in different circumstances without violating those principles. The third was the cyclical notion of time that emphasized that ideas were promulgated, betrayed, and then restored.

Each story had a different strategy of legitimation. The secular notion of time emphasized a disjunction with the past in order to free government officials from past constraint. The assertion of timeless principles freed officials from past policy constraint but claimed some tether to tradition. The cyclical notion of time legitimated action by painting his predecessors as betrayers of core principles that he sought to restore.

In the early part of his administration, he stuck with his first story, that the tremendous changes of the past required governmental renovation and reconstruction. That story underwrote the burst of legislative activity that would continue through much of his first year and beyond. But in July 1934 a group of businessmen who were opposed to the New Deal began to challenge him on this point. Their main concern was the protection of their property from the socialistic thrust of Roosevelt's programs. Yet they decided that their emphasis needed to be on what they saw as his betrayal of principle, not the protection of their interests. Principle could motivate the public, they hoped, in a way that the protection of their property would not. So when the businessmen formed the American Liberty League a few months later, they used the new organization to claim that Roosevelt was a constitutional usurper.[12]

Their basic story was an inversion of Roosevelt's own historical justifications. Taking issue with the idea that past change had demanded governmental reconstruction, the League argued that Roosevelt had departed from the tried and true principles of previous eras. They put out pamphlets in the millions claiming that Roosevelt's New Deal was "gnawing at the vitals of the Constitution," "wrecking the Constitution," undermining "Constitutional Liberty," and "carving out vital portions of the Constitution by direct attack and subtle usurpation." The League also encouraged legal challenges to the New Deal, which began to bear fruit in late 1934 and 1935. In case after case the Supreme Court began striking down key components of Roosevelt's program, thereby reinforcing the League's narrative.[13]

Roosevelt did not at first have a clear response to the attacks. Because he had focused on the tremendous changes of the past as the key justification for his New Deal policies, he could not really disavow his program of reconstruction. But in responding to his critics he did emphasize that principle could be applied in new ways depending upon differences in time. For example, in a remarkable press conference in May 1935, after the Court struck down the National Recovery Administration, Roosevelt complained that his opponents had lost any sense of historical reality. They had closed their eyes to the tremendous changes of the last 150 years. When the Constitution was written, Roosevelt told the reporters, "the country was in the horse-and-buggy age." Commerce was slow, local, and largely preindustrial. "And if you go back to the debates on the Federal Constitution," he continued, "you will find in 1787 that one of the impelling motives for putting in that [interstate commerce] clause was this: There wasn't much interstate commerce at all." The framers hoped to generate commerce that could be regulated at some point in the future. They succeeded. But those changes in the last 150 years did not mean that the Constitution could now be used to thwart reform or regulation. The opposite was the case. It meant that the Constitution was intended to be interpreted in new ways, extracting principle to be applied anew. Yet rather than recognizing the changes between 1787 and 1935—and the subsequent necessity of new interpretations—the Court acted as though the Constitution was fixed in time. Such a posture would not do, Roosevelt said, because it debilitated the government and made it unable to solve national economic problems.[14]

The Court, unsurprisingly, was unmoved. As it continued its opposition in case after case, Roosevelt's advisers began to suggest that he might need to rethink his rhetorical posture. The most forceful suggestion came from Thurman W. Arnold, a Yale law professor who was in frequent contact with the administration and who would soon head up the antitrust division within the Justice Department. Roosevelt's emphasis on secular time and linear progress ran up against what Arnold called "the irrational elements" of legal and economic institutions within American society. Law and economics were particularly backward-looking disciplines that, to some extent, ignored the onward flow of time. It was endemic to their disciplines to look for answers from the past to apply to the present, even if the past was not really applicable. So rather than railing against the Court's obtuseness, as Roosevelt was inclined to do, Thurman believed that Roosevelt needed to acknowledge the irrational elements of these institutions and to adjust his rhetoric accordingly.[15]

When others began to echo Arnold, Roosevelt began to change his story, but not always in a consistent fashion. As he reworked New Deal programs to try to get around the Court, he bounced between narrative strategies without really abandoning his call for governmental renovation. A month after his press conference, Roosevelt proposed a new series of taxes on the rich that showcased the narrative confusion. In explaining the necessity of such taxes, he first told a story that focused on the increasing interdependence of society that was the result of industrial consolidation. In recognition of this social interdependence, he explained, American policy makers had adopted a progressive taxation scheme that sought to distribute the tax burden in an equitable manner. "The movement toward progressive taxation," Roosevelt said, "has accompanied the growing diversification and interrelation of effort which marks our industrial society." If one were to extend the trend line forward, he argued, it was evident that his newest tax proposals were simply outgrowths of the secular changes over time that had given rise to these new tax forms.[16]

But in the same message Roosevelt also turned to timeless principle, at least implicitly. Because he was proposing for the first time a tax on inheritances, he argued that the great fortunes passed down between generations had begun to create a moneyed aristocracy in the United States. "Such inherited economic power," he said, was "inconsistent with the ideals of the generation which established our Government." Precisely because the founders' ideals were still relevant to national life, at least when extracted from their context, his taxes were in keeping with core American principles.[17]

As he pressed for legislative action through 1935, he continued to move between these two rhetorical justifications for his policies. A few months after he proposed new taxes for the rich, for example, Roosevelt signed the Social Security Act and issued a signing statement that pointed to the extensive changes in secular time as the impetus for the legislation. Because "the civilization of the past hundred years" had involved such "startling industrial changes," he said, American life had tended toward greater degrees of insecurity. The Social Security program was a straightforward and necessary response to those changes, bringing government in line with new social realities.[18]

That same month, in a radio address to the Young Democratic Clubs of America, he continued the story and sought to counter the League head-on. Answering criticism from his opponents that he was taking the nation off course, Roosevelt claimed to honor "the heritage, spiritual and material," that had come down from the past. But he thought it obvious that "this modern economic world . . . is governed by rules and regulations vastly more complex than those laid down in the days of Adam Smith and John Stuart Mill." The world of the past was simpler. The business corporation, as it existed in the 1930s, was unknown 150 years earlier. Industrial relations, banking practices, social conditions were all different. "There was a day," he concluded, "when political sages, or those who controlled them, took the attitude that anything new, or what they called 'new-fangled,' would lead to dire results." But he rejected that attitude. He looked instead to what he called "the spirit of America"—a timeless spirit of inquiry, adjustment, and improvement—that would guide the nation going forward.[19]

Looking merely at his legislative achievements, Roosevelt's efforts were unquestionably a success. The sum total of his accomplishments in this period—which ranged from new taxes to Social Security legislation to support for labor unions and more—was so impressive that the historian William Leuchtenburg has called this period the "Second New Deal." Yet in the midst of his success Roosevelt remained worried about the American Liberty League. As he was putting the finishing touches on his latest round of legislation, the League ramped up its campaign against Roosevelt by using his frequent invocations of historical change against him. Since Roosevelt's poll numbers had been falling through 1935, he had reason for concern. As he looked ahead to the coming election, he and his advisers recognized that they needed some way to answer the League and that his usual narratives were not working. When he emphasized historical change, he remained susceptible to the charge that he was abandoning principle. When he invoked timeless American principles that could adapt depending on circumstance, he invited refutation that he was invoking abstractions while in fact abandoning the past.[20]

He decided to make a full-scale shift in rhetoric. To accomplish that move, he needed to change dramatically his dominant historical posture. He sought a way to downplay his secular sense of transformation in favor of a more cyclical vision in which core principles were elaborated, threatened, and then restored.

After some experimentation, he arrived at his new narrative. His advisers decided to use the 1936 State of the Union address to begin the rhetorical shift. In order to maximize the radio audience, Roosevelt requested the nearly unprecedented occasion of an evening address to Congress. His careful preparations signaled the importance that the administration placed on the message. Almost everyone believed, the *New York Times* reported, that his speech would "set the pattern for the administration re-election campaign."[21]

On the night of the event, Roosevelt fulfilled those expectations. Bracing himself before the radio microphones, he told the packed chamber that his goal was the maintenance of democratic institutions in the face of autocratic threats, both abroad and within American borders. Controversy over the New Deal, Roosevelt said, proved that "popular opinion is at war with a power-seeking minority." "That is no new thing," he told the crowd. In fact, it had occurred on a cyclical basis since the American Revolution and the Constitutional Convention. "From time to time since then," he said, "the battle has been continued, under Thomas Jefferson, Andrew Jackson, Theodore Roosevelt, and Woodrow Wilson." Successive generations had faced the threat and had overcome it. Seen in the light of that history, his efforts in the New Deal were in no way revolutionary. Nor were his struggles new. They were but the latest battle "to restore power to those to whom it rightfully belonged."[22]

This cyclical view of the past became the dominant theme of his 1936 campaign. Although he occasionally still referenced changes in secular time and emphasized the need for adaption of governmental forms to new realities, his dominant message was that he fought in a long line of those who had defended fundamental principles against those seeking autocratic power. His new story did not try to legitimate governmental action so much as it sought to preserve his existing legislative accomplishments. But it also moved him beyond his earlier campaign posture, in which he had portrayed himself as an anti-Hoover. By placing himself in line with Jefferson, Jackson, Wilson, and others, he exploited, in the words of the historian Alfred Haworth Jones, "parallels with the past for his own political advantage." Roosevelt's basic assertion was, as he put it a few days later, "History repeats."[23]

Yet even here he was inconsistent. In his State of the Union address, he emphasized the continual ebb and flow of history, a cyclical process that was renewed on a constant basis. But at other times he argued that the founding moment had been a singular time to which he was trying to return. At the Thomas Jefferson Dinner a few months after his State of the Union address, he described the founding era as a straightforward moment of national consolidation followed by a long period of betrayal. The founders' vision, he explained, conceived of the country "as an economic unity." Their purpose in creating the government was to regulate this unity. But over the next one hundred or so years "the country . . . was cut up into segments." The nationalistic vision that looked to government to bring good into people's lives had given way to distrust of government. That distrust had created paralysis during the Great Depression at the moment when government was most needed. "It is only in these comparatively recent days," he argued, "that we have been turning back to the broader vision of the Founding Fathers." This was still a cyclical conception of the past, but one in which he alone was responsible for completing the cycle.[24]

These inconsistencies, bothersome though they may be to the historian, did not matter politically. The stories themselves all pointed in the same direction. He abandoned talk of governmental reconstruction to meet the realities of a new time and worked instead within a consistent narrative structure that had the character of a fable. Roosevelt told a story with heroes (Jefferson,

Jackson, Wilson, and especially Roosevelt himself) and villains (above all the American Liberty League and the conservatives on the U.S. Supreme Court). He emphasized that the villains abandoned core principles and that the heroes upheld them. In that way, he gave his disagreements with the League historical significance, maybe even world-historical significance, by abandoning his conception of change over linear time and instead reducing history to a series of engagements between the forces of good and the forces of evil.

The new strategy was especially apparent at the Democratic National Convention that year. Just as he used his previous convention speech to dramatize his sense that the party needed to break from the past, he used the new speech to claim that the fight over the New Deal was one that confirmed his historical fidelity. Although he kept important elements of his previous story, he submerged those elements with his new claim. As he put it, "the rush of modern civilization" had created "new difficulties, new problems which must be solved if we are to preserve to the United States the political and economic freedom for which Washington and Jefferson planned and fought." Those problems had created new means by which the perennial enemies of freedom could maintain their privilege. In resisting the New Deal his enemies were really defending the unequal structure of society and the freedom of a small few. The "economic royalists" of the League and the Court were essentially modern Tories who sought to defend elite rule against the power of the people. Roosevelt told the crowd that he was confident that the American people could see that it was he who fought on the side of the founders, and that it was the League and their puppets that constituted "the resolute enemy within our gates."[25]

His speech was largely incommensurable with the one he had given at the Democratic National Convention four years earlier. In that speech, he spoke as a progressive. In the new speech, he spoke as a conservative. In the previous speech, he emphasized accumulative change. In the new speech, he spoke of perennial battles over principle. Both argued from historical time, but conceived of that time in different ways.

These contradictions did not trouble his partisans. As the cheers rained down on him after the speech, it became clear that Roosevelt had motivated his followers in a way that the League and the Republicans could not. Although there was still some uncertainty on election night, due mainly to an early vote in Maine that had gone to his opponent, once the votes were counted the effectiveness of Roosevelt's campaign became clear. He demolished his

Republican opponent, Alf Landon. He won every state but two. He won the popular vote with 60.8 percent to Landon's 30.5 percent. It was the most sweeping victory since James Monroe's unopposed election in 1820.[26]

FDR then used the election to expand his narrative, shifting once again his sense of time. In his second inaugural address, he returned to the idea that the founding principles were timeless in spite of the changes over the past centuries. "This year marks the one hundred and fiftieth anniversary of the Constitutional Convention which made us a nation," he said at the beginning of the speech. But instead of emphasizing the difference in historical circumstance that had grown over that time, as he surely would have done four years earlier, he drew parallels between the founding era and his own:

> At that convention our forefathers found the way out of the chaos which followed the Revolutionary War; they created a strong government with powers of united action sufficient then and now to solve problems utterly beyond individual or local solution. A century and a half ago they established the Federal Government in order to promote the general welfare and secure the blessings of liberty to the American people. Today we invoke those same powers of government to achieve the same objectives.[27]

His new rhetoric looked, at first, to be working. Within a few months of his inauguration, Roosevelt threatened to reorganize the Court in order to get his measures through, and his opponents on the Court capitulated to his belief that the government had expansive powers with which to regulate the economy. But Roosevelt's new rhetoric was ultimately unsuccessful. His major legislative accomplishments were largely over. His new rhetoric was unable to accommodate his ambitions to reconstruct the government, partly because he had to continually undersell his goals in order to proclaim fidelity to the original terms of the Constitution.

In early 1937, for example, he proposed to reorganize the executive branch. That desire had long been part of progressive thought. Woodrow Wilson in particular had argued that the founders' separation of powers had limited the ability of the executive to take decisive action that was necessary given the fast-moving nature of the industrial economy. Roosevelt was now in a position to achieve what two generations of progressives had desired. But rather than pointing to the changes in time that had made such executive action necessary, he emphasized that his proposal for reorganization was essentially conservative. "You and I are taking up in our generation the battle to preserve that freedom of self-government which our forefathers fought to establish and hand down to us," he said. "They struggled against tyranny, against non-representative controls, against government by birth, wealth or class, against sectionalism. Our struggle now is against confusion, against ineffectiveness, against waste, against inefficiency." To claim that his ambitions could be reduced to the streamlining of administrative processes and that his organizational efforts were in line with the founders' struggle against tyranny was, as the political scientist Stephen Skowronek has said, "woefully inadequate to his reconstructive ambitions."[28]

Roosevelt's loss of rhetorical coherence coincided with his loss of legislative momentum. Although he won a sweeping electoral victory, Congress soon turned hostile and was unwilling to treat his office with the deference of a prime minister in a parliamentary system. His legislative victories slowed to a trickle and then stopped altogether. During the second session of 1937, Congress did not pass a single bill that Roosevelt requested. Although Roosevelt would soon try to purge recalcitrant leaders from the Democratic Party and then would turn to the troubles in Europe, he was never able to reacquire the synchronicity between his historical rhetoric and his legislative accomplishments that he achieved in his first term.[29]

And yet that does not mean that Roosevelt's efforts did not matter. Although the New Deal largely came to an end as a policy program after 1937, the historian Alan Brinkley has pointed out that it nevertheless "continued to develop as an idea." Roosevelt's various notions about historical time—that secular processes justified governmental reconstruction, that timeless principle could be applied in new ways, that he took part in a cyclical process in which principles were proclaimed, betrayed, and then restored—sought to justify whatever action he wished to take at the moment while at the same time supporting a novel reading of American liberalism and the American political tradition. As that reading grew in importance after 1937, his second notion of time—that timeless principle could be applied in new ways depending on historical circumstance—proved to be the most significant.

Roosevelt had always relied on that notion to disavow any revolutionary intentions. He was tethered, he claimed, to the American political tradition. But as the New Deal faded in policy terms and grew as a political idea, Roosevelt drew upon this notion of timeless principle to rework basic categories of American political thought, especially received ideas about freedom and rights. As early as his 1936 nomination acceptance speech, Roosevelt had asserted that "necessitous men are not free men," which had been a truism going back to before the founding of American government. According to the civic republic tradition, which was a familiar if not central political persuasion among the Revolutionary generation, freedom required the capacity of self-government. A person who was incapable of self-government was incapable of participating in the political process in a way that preserved freedom. And because necessitous men—that is, men without a certain amount of property who worked for wages and therefore relied on others—were not self-reliant and were incapable of self-government, they were accordingly prevented from voting during the early republic.[30]

But Roosevelt drew a different conclusion from the truism while still upholding freedom as he understood it. Rather than excluding necessitous men from government, in the New Deal Roosevelt decided that government needed to make them free by providing a minimum measure of security. Freedom meant one thing in the founding era, but it meant another given the economic concentrations of modern life and the systemic risks of capitalism that no individual could control. So, as Cass Sunstein has argued, Roosevelt "attempted to provide security in the face of a wide range of social risks—and to see that security as a basic right, a condition of freedom."[31]

This reworked conception of freedom did not betray the American constitutional order, Roosevelt claimed, because meaning changes over time. Property requirements for voting had been dropped within a generation or two of the founding era, and the meaning of freedom had expanded from that point forward. Nowhere was this argument more obvious than his 1941 State of the Union address, where Roosevelt first articulated what became known as his Four Freedoms. With the world increasingly under the sway of fascism, Roosevelt asserted that the fight of the Allied powers was one of enormous consequence for both the United States and the world. Their victory, which was then hardly assured, would bring forth "a world founded upon four essential freedoms": freedom of speech, freedom of religion, freedom from want, and freedom from fear. He recognized that, in aligning the United States with this vision, he was not seeking to preserve political ideals as they existed in the past. But that was not, according to Roosevelt, in any way problematic. "Since the beginning of our American history," he said, "we have been engaged in change—in a perpetual peaceful revolution—a revolution which goes on steadily, quietly adjusting itself to changing conditions—without the concentration camp or the quick-lime in the ditch."[32]

Of those four freedoms, the freedom from want was the animating principle of the New Deal. But rather than leave it there, Roosevelt returned to the issue in his 1944 State of the Union address, just over two years after the United States had, in his words, "become an active partner in the world's greatest war against human slavery." Looking ahead to the conclusion of the war, he believed that certain things were now understood. "We have come to a clear realization," he said, "of the fact that true individual freedom cannot exist without economic security and independence." Because "these economic truths" were "self-evident," he continued, "we have accepted, so to speak, a second Bill of Rights under which a new basis of security and prosperity can be established for all." Those rights included access to a remunerative job, a decent home, a good education, and protection from the economic fears of old age, sickness, and accident. He called upon Congress to implement the economic bill of rights, "for it is definitely the responsibility of the Congress so to do."[33]

Although Congress did not respond immediately, the Democratic Party spent the next half-century and more building upon Roosevelt's reconstruction of the American political tradition. John F. Kennedy's New Frontier, Lyndon Johnson's Great Society and War on Poverty, even Barack Obama's health care proposals grew out of Roosevelt's transformative assertion that core principles of the American tradition remained out of time to be appropriated in new ways.[34]

And yet there was always a potential weakness in Roosevelt's formulations, one that in retrospect appears to be a strategic error. In proposing the second Bill of Rights, Roosevelt asserted a change in what Sunstein has called the nation's "constitutive commitments," the values that sustain the American political order and American society more generally. He did so while claiming to honor the timeless principle of freedom that has long been central to the American political tradition. That was why he suggested that Americans had already accepted the second Bill of Rights and called upon Congress to implement the values that were "self-evident" to the American people. But Roosevelt did not require a corresponding change in the form of government through constitutional amendments. Unlike the generation earlier, when progressives' commitment to addressing new historical realities resulted in four major constitutional amendments, Roosevelt's far more sweeping reconstruction relied on no amendments at all.[35]

To some extent this was a pragmatic decision. He told a reporter in 1937 that he was worried that a "thoroughly skilled and organized opposition directed at the point of least resistance" could easily prevent the ratification of an amendment. That risk made him disinclined to engage the fight. But his shift in rhetoric also played a part. His early assertion that changes in secular time had resulted in the need for governmental reconstruction would have seamlessly meshed with a corresponding set of constitutional amendments. But his argument that ideals like freedom could grow and change, floating outside of time and altering their meaning according to circumstance, precluded or at least worked against a formal constitutional amendment. To advocate such an amendment would be to admit a rupture between past and present large enough to justify a change in constitutional form. Instead, Roosevelt appealed to a living tradition and relied upon what the progressive Walter Weyl derisively called "amendment by interpretation."[36]

Roosevelt's strategy worked so long as it was, in fact, self-evident that government should provide a measure of security as a precondition of freedom. But the American Liberty League never believed that assertion. Neither, it turned out, did the League's successors. The modern conservative movement was built upon the notion that an empowered government tended not to the promotion of freedom but to its detriment. As Ronald Reagan said in a 1964 speech in support of Barry Goldwater for the presidency, "A government can't control the economy without controlling people."[37]

Because Roosevelt did not formally amend the Constitution, the disagreement between liberals and conservatives inevitably became not just a disagreement over political principles but also a disagreement over the legitimacy of Roosevelt's actions within the wider history of the American political tradition. In that disagreement, conservatives gained the upper hand in the 1970s. They mimicked Roosevelt's rhetoric while reversing the political and ideological import of the stories that he told. Reagan in particular borrowed from Roosevelt's cyclical notion of time while putting it toward more consistently conservative ends. "I think it's time we ask ourselves," Reagan said in his 1964 speech, "if we still know the freedoms that were intended for us by the Founding Fathers." His argument rhetorically undermined the twentieth-century welfare state by returning to the more primeval past of the nation's founding. This was another fable, but it was one that comported with his wider political project in a way that it really never did for Roosevelt.[38]

To look at Roosevelt in this way is to see some of his political innovativeness but also to appreciate his limits. He sought to renovate from within the American political tradition while reconstructing, sometimes wholesale, American political institutions. His justification for that reconstruction shifted over time and deployed varying historical stories to various ends. Roosevelt was at his best—which is to say his most politically successful—when making a straightforward case for political transformation that responded to changes in secular time. His cyclical notion of time and his flirtations with timelessness worked less well. They muddied the case for political reconstruction. And because he failed to institutionalize his innovations with a set of constitutional amendments, his political reconstruction was always susceptible to the challenges that we see today.

## *Notes*

1. For an account of Roosevelt's historical abilities that focuses on his use of the Founding Fathers, see David Sehat, *The Jefferson Rule: How the Founding Fathers Became Infallible and Our Politics Inflexible* (New York: Simon and Schuster, 2015), 119–55.

2. Herbert Hoover, *American Individualism* (New York: Doubleday, Page, 1922), 8.

3. Walter E. Weyl, *The New Democracy: An Essay on Certain Political and Economic Tendencies in the United States* (New York: Macmillan, 1912), 108 (first and second quotations); Walter Lippmann, *A Preface to Politics* (New York: M. Kennerley, 1913), 31 (third and fourth quotations). For more on progressivism, see Sehat, *Jefferson Rule,* 109–19.

4. Franklin Delano Roosevelt, "Address at Oglethorpe University," May 22, 1932, in Franklin Delano Roosevelt, *The Public Papers and Addresses of Franklin D. Roosevelt,* ed. Samuel I. Rosenman (New York: Random House, 1938–1950), 1:645 (second and third quotations), 646 (first quotation).

5. I have taken this idea of secular time from Stephen Skowronek, *The Politics Presidents Make: Leadership from John Adams to Bill Clinton* (Cambridge, MA: Belknap Press of Harvard University Press, 1997), 30.

6. Franklin Delano Roosevelt, "The Governor Accepts the Nomination for the Presidency," July 2, 1932, in Roosevelt, *Public Papers,* 1:647 (first and second quotations), 648 (third quotation), 649 (fourth quotation).

7. Ibid., 1:648 (second quotation), 659 (first quotation).

8. Franklin Delano Roosevelt, *Looking Forward* (New York: John Day, 1933), 14.

9. See Abraham Lincoln, "Speech at Springfield, Illinois," June 26, 1857, in Abraham Lincoln, *The Collected Works of Abraham Lincoln,* ed. Roy P. Basler (New Brunswick,

NJ: Rutgers University Press, 1953–1955): 2:398–410; Woodrow Wilson, *Constitutional Government in the United States* (New York: Columbia University Press, 1908); "President Obama's Inaugural Address," *New York Times,* Jan. 21, 2013, http://www.nytimes.com/interactive/2013/01/22/us/politics/22obama-inaugural-speech-annotated.html.

10. Franklin Delano Roosevelt, "Inaugural Address," Mar. 4, 1933, in Roosevelt, *Public Papers,* 2:15.

11. Ibid., 2:12. On the notion of republican restoration, see J. G. A. Pocock, *The Machiavellian Moment: Florentine Political Thought and the Atlantic Republican Tradition* (Princeton, NJ: Princeton University Press, 1975).

12. Kim Phillips-Fein, *Invisible Hands: The Making of the Conservative Movement from the New Deal to Reagan* (New York: Norton, 2009), 10–11.

13. George Wolfskill, *The Revolt of the Conservatives: A History of the American Liberty League, 1934–1940* (Boston: Houghton Mifflin, 1962), 112 (quotations); William E. Leuchtenburg, *Franklin D. Roosevelt and the New Deal, 1932–1940* (New York: Harper & Row, 1963), 143–45.

14. Franklin Delano Roosevelt, "Two Hundred and Ninth Press Conference," May 31, 1935, in Roosevelt, *Public Papers,* 4:209.

15. Thurman W. Arnold, *The Symbols of Government* (New Haven, CT: Yale University Press, 1935), 1–30 (quotation on 18).

16. Franklin Delano Roosevelt, "A Message to Congress on Tax Revision," June 19, 1935, in Roosevelt, *Public Papers,* 4:271.

17. Ibid., 4:272.

18. Franklin Delano Roosevelt, "Presidential Statement upon Signing the Social Security Act," Aug. 14, 1935, in ibid., 4:324.

19. Franklin Delano Roosevelt, "Radio Address to the Young Democratic Clubs of America," Aug. 24, 1935, in ibid., 4:337 (first quotation), 339 (second quotation), 342 (third and fourth quotations), 343 (fifth quotation).

20. Leuchtenburg, *Franklin D. Roosevelt,* 162.

21. Turner Catledge, "Roosevelt Speech Politics, Says G.O.P.," *New York Times,* Jan. 2, 1936, 1.

22. Franklin Delano Roosevelt, "Annual Message to Congress," Jan. 3, 1936, in Roosevelt, *Public Papers,* 5:12 (first three quotations), 12–13 (fourth quotation), 13 (fifth quotation).

23. Alfred Haworth Jones, *Roosevelt's Image Brokers: Poets, Playwrights, and the Use of the Lincoln Symbol* (Port Washington, NY: Kennikat Press, 1974), 3; Franklin Delano Roosevelt, "Address at the Jackson Dinner," Jan. 8, 1936, in Roosevelt, *Public Papers,* 5:41.

24. Franklin Delano Roosevelt, "Address at the Thomas Jefferson Dinner, New York City," Apr. 25, 1936, in Roosevelt, *Public Papers,* 5:178. For variations on the story, see Franklin Delano Roosevelt, "A Greeting on the Centenary of the Death of James Madison," May 8, 1936, in ibid., 5:185–86; Franklin Delano Roosevelt, "Address at Little Rock, Arkansas," June 10, 1936, in ibid., 5:195–202.

25. Franklin Delano Roosevelt, "Acceptance of the Renomination for the Presidency," June 27, 1936, in Roosevelt, *Public Papers,* 5:231 (first two quotations), 232 (third quotation), 234 (fourth quotation).

26. Leuchtenburg, *Franklin D. Roosevelt,* 195–96.

27. Franklin Delano Roosevelt, "Second Inaugural Address," Jan. 20, 1937, in Roosevelt, *Public Papers,* 6:1–2 (first quotation), 2 (second quotation).

28. Franklin Delano Roosevelt, "A Recommendation for Legislation to Reorganize the Executive Branch of the Government," Jan. 12, 1937, in Roosevelt, *Public Papers,* 5:669; Skowronek, *Politics Presidents Make,* 322. See also Wilson, *Constitutional Government,* 200–203, 221–22.

29. Leuchtenburg, *Franklin D. Roosevelt,* 231–51.

30. Franklin Delano Roosevelt, "Acceptance of the Renomination for the Presidency," June 27, 1936, in Roosevelt, *Public Papers,* 5:233.

31. Cass R. Sunstein, *The Second Bill of Rights: FDR's Unfinished Revolution and Why We Need It More Than Ever* (New York: Basic Books, 2004), 95.

32. Franklin Delano Roosevelt, "Annual Message to Congress," Jan. 6, 1941, in Roosevelt, *Public Papers,* 9:672.

33. Franklin Delano Roosevelt, "Message to Congress on the State of the Union," Jan. 11, 1944, in Roosevelt, *Public Papers,* 13:32 (first quotation), 41 (second through sixth quotations), 42 (seventh quotation).

34. For a now-classic interpretation of the New Deal as a political order, see Steve Fraser and Gary Gerstle, eds., *The Rise and Fall of the New Deal Order, 1930–1980* (Princeton, NJ: Princeton University Press, 1989). On Obama's use of the second Bill of Rights, see James T. Kloppenberg's essay in this volume.

35. Sunstein, *Second Bill of Rights,* 61.

36. Franklin Delano Roosevelt, "The Three Hundred and Forty-Fourth Press Conference," Feb. 12, 1937, in Roosevelt, *Public Papers,* 6:76; Weyl, *New Democracy,* 109.

37. Ronald Reagan, "A Time for Choosing," *Reagan Foundation,* https://www.youtube.com/watch?v=qXBswFfh6AY.

38. Ibid. For a longer account of Reagan's use of the Founding Fathers, see Sehat, *Jefferson Rule,* 157–208. On Reagan's turn toward fable, see Rick Perlstein's chapter in this volume.

# 9 Profiles in Triangulation

## *John F. Kennedy's Neoliberal History of American Politics*

Jeffrey L. Pasley

Though still one of the most familiar names in popular history and selling briskly in multiple formats at the John F. Kennedy Library, it has been a long while since scholars or journalists took Kennedy's Pulitzer Prize–winning book *Profiles in Courage* very seriously. In the decades since baby boomers stopped getting the book as a graduation gift, it has become far better known for the controversy over its authorship, launched by columnist Drew Pearson and chin-stroked over by Kennedy watchers ever since. Yet the traditional concern with parsing John F. Kennedy's percentage of authorship, in an openly staff-produced book, misses the larger significance of *Profiles in Courage.* Understood in a broader context than who really deserved to win the Pulitzer Prize for Biography in 1957, *Profiles in Courage* represents one of the most striking and detailed uses of history in the history of presidential politics. Along with its accompanying publicity campaign, the book mapped out and helped shape the future development of American politics, especially in the Democratic Party: by reading John F. Kennedy's own centrist, nationalistic, and individualistic values and triangulating strategies into the American past, it sought to legitimate and ennoble them for the present and future.[1]

Kennedy's prominent place in the popular historical imagination of post-1960s America had often obscured the political mythology he helped shape for himself as he rose to power in the 1950s. Attending to the details of *Profiles in Courage* helps us recapture that. Though in the short run, in the wake of his assassination, Kennedy's memory seemed to authorize the liberal statism of Lyndon Johnson and his youngest brother, his longer-term legacy was different. Quite a few of the young politicians who grew up reading *Profiles in Courage* and became national figures in the Democratic Party would turn out to be the neoliberal government reinventors and triangulators of the 1980s, 1990s, and after. Although none were as good as the original at the "Kennedy-esque" soaring oratory, Gary Hart, Al Gore, Bill Clinton, and even Barack Obama had all the boyish good looks, middle-straddling policies, and cult of political "courage" to show for it.

The fascination with the Kennedys as pop cultural icons has often tended to obscure and overshadow John F. Kennedy as an actual political figure, and *Profiles in Courage* is no exception. Scholars tend to disregard popular history when they are not trying to write it, so the political project of the book has been missed. Released in early 1956 just as that year's presidential race was shaping up, it was part of a long Kennedy family campaign to give Jack's reputation the weight he would need to be a successful national contender. His youthful playboy image and relative lack of political accomplishments needed to be countered with evidence of his seriousness. The theme of "courage" called back to the lovingly fostered stories of Kennedy's wartime heroism; copies of John Hersey's 1944 *New Yorker* article on the P.T. 109 incident had been distributed by all of his campaigns from the beginning. It silently ignored a pre-presidential political career that was far more ambitious than heroic, and invoked the Hemingway-style quiet machismo—"grace under pressure"—that Kennedy and the popular publishing industry greatly admired and promoted. The use of history was even more appealing to Kennedy himself. Despite his swinging lifestyle and tousled-haired image, Jack was considered the intellectual of the family and had first come into the public eye with a book of historical interpretation: *Why England Slept,* on the appeasement policy of the 1930s. Politically, however, there was much more to *Profiles in Courage* than rubbing shoulders with Hemingway and Churchill.[2]

## *Triangulating Race and Region*

The courage that Kennedy and his aide and amanuensis Ted Sorensen celebrated in *Profiles* was specifically *political* courage, not really Hemingway's "grace under pressure" at all. All of the examples in the book were senators "whose abiding loyalty to their nation triumphed over all personal and political considerations." Most of Kennedy's senatorial vignettes revolved around a political sacrifice made, typically by crossing party and regional lines in some way, at the cost of a lost campaign or criticism from erstwhile allies, in the name of maintaining the stability and power of U.S. institutions, especially the presidency. Usually (but not always) the choice defined as *less* courageous was loyalty to party, home, or cause, with the subject's stand carefully defined as brave and sacrificial even when long-range ambition was also at work. First up in the book is John Quincy Adams, praised for being the only New England Federalist to support the Louisiana Purchase and Jefferson's embargo Act of 1807, which devastated New England's maritime economy. "You are supported by no party," Kennedy quotes Adams's father writing to him. "You have too honest a heart, too independent a mind, and too brilliant talents, to be . . . trusted by any man who is under the domination of party maxims or party feelings." John Quincy Adams was apparently the only one of the *Profiles* for which JFK did much of the research and writing himself, rather than academic researchers or Ted Sorensen, and his section perhaps best encapsulates the kind of putatively high-minded but ambitious triangulation that Kennedy both admired and tried to practice. Siding with Thomas Jefferson may have cost John Quincy Adams his Senate seat, but it also put him in line, as a newly minted Democratic Republican, for a string of diplomatic posts, including secretary of state, that eventually led to the presidency.[3] Similarly, though Kennedy would have to play down some of his isolationist father's conservative connections later, Ambassador Joseph P. Kennedy's loyal friends—*New York Times* columnist Arthur Krock, a fellow conservative Democrat, and arch-Republican publisher Henry Luce, owner of *Time* and *LIFE*—were instrumental in the heavy, adulatory publicity Jack Kennedy the man, politician, and author received throughout his life.[4]

*Profiles in Courage* was published in early 1956 just as that year's presidential race (and more relevant for Kennedy, the process of publicly mentioning contenders for the second spot on the Democratic ticket) was beginning. Glowingly reviewed in publications large and small, national and regional, it was excerpted in the *New York Times* and popular magazines such as *Reader's Digest* and *Collier's*. In May, only a few weeks before the Democratic Convention, one of the Golden Age of Television's most respected live anthology shows, *Kraft Television Theatre,* lavishly dramatized a chapter of the book, with seventy-six actors, twenty-eight sets, and Senator Kennedy himself on hand to open and close the hour.[5]

The book's usable history worked hard on particular Kennedy political problems, finding worthy historical precedents for Jack's own patterns. Party discipline and respect for seniority had never suited him. As a young senator, Kennedy had angered Majority Leader Lyndon Johnson by constantly straying on party-line votes and setting his sights for higher office almost immediately. More seriously, he had been the only Democrat not to vote for the censure of Republican demagogue Joe McCarthy, a Kennedy family friend and fellow Irish American whose rabid anti-Communism actually suited Jack the presidential candidate's tough foreign policy stance. Kennedy's chapter on John Quincy Adams emphasized the nationalism and expansionism of his younger years rather than his late-life stint as "Old Man Eloquent" doggedly fighting slavery in the House of Representatives. The younger John Adams became the original model of the brainy son of New England privilege brashly forging his own path in the nation's capital. "Arriving in Washington," Kennedy wrote, "[John Quincy] Adams promptly indicated his disregard for both party affiliations and customary freshman reticence." The chapter did double duty by taking on the Kennedy-cognate task of mainstreaming a politician from New England, possibly the North's most distinctive and alienating region for outsiders.[6]

Kennedy also sought to mainstream the South, despite his genuine but somewhat nominal support for African American civil rights. In common with most 1950s northern Democrats who were not "A.D.A. [Americans for Democratic Action] liberals," John F. Kennedy still looked for votes from the southern segregationist wing of the party. ("ADA liberal" was generally a term of abuse in the Kennedy family, at least before they brought ADA cofounder Arthur Schlesinger Jr. onto their staff to placate and occasionally misdirect liberals.) Indeed, like his rival Adlai Stevenson, Kennedy generally kept to the right on race issues of even moderately liberal southern figures in the party like Harry Truman, Lyndon Johnson, and Tennessee's Estes Kefauver. Stevenson, for his part, was often wrongly seen and remembered as a liberal because of his urbane, "egghead" image and fan base of educated reformers in New York and other cities, a confusion between style and substance that was not uncommon in that milieu. Though the cool approach to civil rights was at least partly strategic, neither of the Democratic aristocrats took much personal interest in the matter. Kennedy, writes biographer Robert Dallek, "could not empathize, and only faintly sympathize, with pains felt by African Americans. . . . The only blacks he knew were chauffeurs, valets, and domestics, with whom he had minimal contact." Along with legislative procedure and constitutional interpretation, history was a convenient way for Kennedy to clasp the South to his bosom without completely alienating white liberals and blacks, whose votes would be crucial in the North. In

*Profiles,* Kennedy wooed the segregationist South not by defending racism, slavery, or Jim Crow, but by finding common cause with southerners and their allies (including many racists and slaveholders) at moments when they could be depicted as principled, noble, and nationalistic; sometimes two out of three was good enough. This wasn't too difficult, as the leading academic historians of the day tended to take the same approach.[7]

The most popular and paradigmatic of Kennedy's profiles, used in a separately published magazine article, adapted for a television special even before his presidency, and then adapted again for the follow-up television series, concerned Senator Edmund G. Ross, a Kansas Republican whose departure from a party-line vote saved President Andrew Johnson of Tennessee from impeachment. Kennedy and Sorensen played Ross's defiance of his party as a pure sacrifice for the good of the Republic. This was a revealing reinterpretation. The real life Ross was a former Democrat, who, while he had been a fiery "Free State" editor and Union officer, was like many other former Democrats in developing qualms about the Radical Republicans' willingness to use federal government authority to remake southern society and punish the ex-Confederates. In other words, Ross had much in common politically with Andrew Johnson himself, making his vote an act of ideology as much as courage. He also stood to lose all his influence over Kansas patronage appointments if Johnson was removed. While the failed Johnson impeachment *eventually* helped finish off Ross as a Kansas Republican, he had a long career ahead in Democratic politics, including a stint as territorial governor of New Mexico. While not unbrave, Ross's defection from Radical Republicanism actually followed the arc of the Democratic Party and the country in the late nineteenth century toward less activist government and a reconciliation of northern and southern whites that was indifferent—or much worse—to the fate of former slaves and their children.[8]

These attitudes were far from completely absent from the 1950s world in which *Profiles in Courage* was written. *Kraft Television Theatre* chose the Ross chapter as the one to stage. Ace screenwriter Wendell Mayes (an Oscar nominee for *Anatomy of a Murder*) turned out a Dunning school epic about the horrors of Reconstruction that went much farther than the book in depicting a "shattered," hungry South beleaguered by "the curse of a vengeful North," with carpetbaggers luring the freed slaves to vote Republican with candy, promises, and "jungle rhythms." Even that Senator Kennedy did not find strong enough, penciling his own words into the narrator's dialogue about the "fanatical" plans of Thaddeus Stevens (played by villain specialist Victor Jory) to give suffrage to "the liberated slaves, whether they were ready for it or not, and to crush the South, its political leaders and its economy, whether it was constitutional or not." Ted Sorensen was still concerned that the show might hurt Kennedy with southern viewers and voters. He forced Mayes to rewrite Act II of the show "to avoid concentration on the race issue."[9]

The type of courage that does stand out in Kennedy's southern stories was a certain flinty, attractively obstinate amorality that allowed the senator in question to focus on higher national interests over the carpings of various hacks and fanatics. While pontificating moralists were not absent from *Profiles,* making a strong stand on social and moral issues did not count for much. The two antislavery heroes in Kennedy's book were Thomas Hart Benton and Sam Houston, whose manly southern indifference to the moral questions is emphasized to create mini-melodramas about two lions in winter (actors Brian Keith and J. D. Cannon chewed the scenery gloriously in the 1964–65 television series) angrily shaking off the reins of party discipline and thrashing around at the secessionist upstarts in their midst. The book and television script find Benton, a slaveholder fighting to save his Senate seat from proslavery forces back in Missouri and defend the Compromise of 1850, declaring himself "the natural enemy of all rotten politicians" and a man who would rather sit down with dead cholera victims than the "gang of scamps" who criticized him. As Kennedy doubtless saw himself, Benton and Houston are depicted as personally free of racial prejudice, but primarily motivated by nationalistic rather than humanistic concerns: the unforgivable sin of proslavery extremists was not racism but the danger they posed to the expanding territorial integrity of the United States.[10]

The stories of northerners like Edmund G. Ross who went soft in the fight against slavery and racism were used to turn the abandonment of regional and party loyalties, in the interests of national influence, into stories of dramatic sacrifice. It was the well-triangulated approach of a historian-politician who supported African American civil rights but still sought the good opinion of southern whites. In his chapter on Daniel Webster, Kennedy lauded Black Dan for having the courage to *not* follow his conscience, supporting the Compromise of 1850 instead, at the behest of his old friend Henry Clay. Unlike the last stands of Benton, Houston, and Webster, which really did ruin them each politically, Kennedy's triangulations always seemed to work out for the better of his reputation. In 1954, he came out for the

St. Lawrence Seaway, a free trade project many believed would divert business from the port of Boston and put many Kennedy constituents out of work; speechwriter Ted Sorensen pulled out a Daniel Webster quote for the occasion. Instead of ignominy, Jack was rewarded with a *Meet the Press* appearance and increased national standing.[11]

## *Politicians above Party*

The Kennedy ideal of political courage valorized leaders who flouted democratic pressures from party ideologues or their own constituents in the name of more "responsible" measures favored by national elites in Washington, D.C., or else followed the whims of their own consciences. Kennedy threw another bouquet to the South in his profile of Sen. Lucius Quintus Cincinnatus Lamar of Mississippi, a proslavery racialist college professor and former Confederate general. Lamar won Kennedy's plaudits for agreeing to the deal that officially ended Reconstruction, and giving a nice eulogy for an opponent, abolitionist senator Charles Sumner (despite still accepting none of Sumner's ideals), thus healing the nation with no mention of the fate of southern blacks. Lamar's other claim to "courage" was a fiscally responsible vote against a free silver bill that was popular among his impoverished constituents. Lamar's "sacrifices" included never losing his place in Mississippi's white oligarchy and becoming the first ex-Confederate on the Supreme Court.[12]

A more defensible Kennedy favorite was Progressive Republican George W. Norris of Nebraska, suggested by Ted Sorensen, whose father had worked with Norris and had some relevant letters and clippings in his possession. Norris had many exploits, but what Sorensen and Kennedy chose to highlight was his habit of undermining whatever political party he happened to be working with at a given time: leading the overthrow of the old Republican boss of the House of Representatives, Joe Cannon, then filibustering Democrat Woodrow Wilson's Armed Ships Bill, and finally earning true Kennedy family honors by crossing back over again to support Al Smith, a "wet" Catholic Democrat, in 1928, even though Norris himself was a long-time "dry." As quoted by Kennedy, in the book and other venues, Norris wanted to "abolish party responsibility and in its stead establish personal responsibility."

Severely underplayed or left out entirely was the economic liberal statism that actually tied all of Norris's zig and zags together—he was especially devoted to the old Progressive crusade for public ownership of utilities, and later (after *Profiles in Courage* drops the story) left the Republican Party for good in the 1930s to become an ardent New Dealer and legislative founder of the Tennessee Valley Authority (TVA). Norris managed to avoid any tragic sacrifices until, after serving forty consecutive years in Congress, he ran for reelection one last time as an independent in 1942. Norris's last stand demonstrated one of the dangers of his brand of "personal responsibility" politics to the causes he supported; his candidacy split the liberal vote, and facilitated the victory of shouting conservative Kenneth S. Wherry, a self-described "fundamentalist" Republican who thought all government programs were socialist (including the Marshall Plan) and earned latter-day infamy as a leader of the Cold War campaign to purge homosexuals from the federal bureaucracy.[13]

On the one hand, the underlying message of the celebration of bi-, non-, and antipartisanship in *Profiles in Courage* was simply that elite rule was best, as long as the great men had integrity and intelligence, as they always did in *Profiles in Courage.* This was a natural enough attitude for a politician to the manor born like John F. Kennedy, and one that suited the increasingly imperial powers of the United States in the Cold War era. In one of *Profiles'* more honest passages, the introductory chapter that by all accounts he was most directly involved in writing, Kennedy struck a decidedly martial note, admitting that the purpose of political "courage" as he understood it was enabling a leader to use power (even force) harshly and broadly "for future glory" whether the people understood and supported it or not: "In the days ahead, only the very courageous will be able to take the hard and unpopular decisions necessary for our survival in the struggle with a powerful enemy."[14]

On the other hand, and on a more self-conscious level, Kennedy was simply trying to produce an inspirational book that would help readers see the good in the American political tradition and hold politicians in higher estimation. This was a recurring theme of the barrage of articles that Ted Sorensen wrote under Kennedy's byline, for a hilariously bewildering array of publications. If popular respect for politics and politicians was not increased, "Senator John F. Kennedy of Massachusetts" wrote in the *Alumnews,* a local Catholic newsletter in Cleveland, "we cannot fail to have mediocre people making the vital decisions that affect us all. *Our best young men and women will not choose a career in which they can look forward only to abuse and scorn.*" The reader might have inferred it was a good thing that at least one Harvard-educated Pulitzer Prize–winner was still available.[15]

From a twenty-first-century vantage point, it is refreshing to see a politician campaigning with such relative high-mindedness, but Kennedy's elision of power, celebrity, and political philosophy from the possible list of motivations for going into politics is striking. As the popularity of *Profiles in Courage* attests, Kennedy was tapping into something deep in the heart of American political culture, a self-image of political individualism and a concomitant, almost automatic suspicion of parties, partisanship, and political organization that defies the assumptions of midcentury political scientists and contradicts the polarization found in mass voting behavior. As an early Americanist by trade, it is hard not to notice the way that many of the approvingly quoted sentiments in *Profiles in Courage* echo the "republican virtue" ideal of patriotic leadership espoused at least on some occasions by the founding elite of the United States. Kennedy and Sorensen were undoubtedly not invoking this tradition consciously—historians were only just then unearthing it—but it does show the depth of the independent ideal Kennedy and Sorensen were appealing to. An advocate for European-style mass-membership parties with coherent social visions and policy agendas, the political scientist Walter Dean Burnham lamented in 1965 "the failure of political organizations more advanced than the 19th-century middle-class cadre party to develop in this country," underlying which was a "deeper failure of any except middle-class social and political values to achieve full legitimacy." Instead, Americans were gripped with an "ideological individualism which continues so deeply to pervade our political culture." Burnham was still active at the time of Donald Trump's election in 2016, and his analysis was still in full force.[16]

The problem, with the founders and with JFK, was that this ideal could be self-serving as well as noble, suitable for elevating the man above the people who elected him, and the executive authority he commands over other parts of the government and the political process. This dovetailed with the longtime concern Kennedy had, going back to *Why England Slept,* with whether democracies could be strong and stable enough to compete with totalitarian states. The Cold War era answer in circles like the Kennedys was quite possibly not, and this was one impulse behind the ever-expanding powers and pretensions of the presidency.

If floating above parties was the political ideal within the world of *Profiles in Courage,* the real world of the 1950s had to be satisfied with gentrifying the parties that existed. Kennedy's message clearly had a strong appeal to young, educated professionals, who were a growing force in the Democratic Party in the 1950s, and who had increasingly less patience for the grubby, transactional politics and unquestioning partisanship of the urban ward-heeler and other denizens of the regular Democratic Party organizations. The gentrification movement took off in New York and other cities, where "amateur Democrats" organized themselves into reform clubs to take on their local party bosses and organizations. The club activists felt that candidates and officeholders should act on their principles, not for money, patronage, or just to keep their party in power. Conceiving themselves as liberals but lacking much substance to their ideas, they flocked to the genteel banners of the relatively conservative Adlai Stevenson in response to stylistics: according to the political scientist James Q. Wilson's sociological study of the clubs, the members found Stevenson poised, urbane, and witty, "a true intellectual, and more than that, a true American aristocrat." As Thomas Jefferson or John Adams might have put it, Stevenson came off as a "natural aristocrat," a product of inborn talent, good breeding, and a fine education, the son of a vice president. Adlai the "egghead" was catnip to young professionals who were just then emerging from the higher ends of America's rapidly expanding system of educational meritocracy, culminating in prestigious universities and professional schools. Kennedy was actually regarded as a bit of an arriviste by many of the club people, who looked down on his youth, Catholicism, and what seemed to them his crass use of his family's wealth in politics. Yet Kennedy himself was drawn to Stevenson, and partly by attaching himself to the Democratic front-runner, and partly with the message of *Profiles in Courage,* Kennedy would eventually win the urban amateurs and people like them over. An important Stevenson-Kennedy connection was Harvard history professor Arthur Schlesinger Jr., a Stevenson speechwriter and cofounder of ADA, whose switch to Kennedy in 1960 gave JFK cover with self-styled Stevenson liberals.[17]

With *Profiles in Courage* in the bookstores, 1956 was John Kennedy's year to move in on the Stevenson constituency and help out with its gentrification of the Democratic Party. Contrary to Nixonian myths about organized crime and the city machines fixing elections for Kennedy, his relationship with such elements of the party was actually quite distant and hostile. While hardly a reformer himself, Kennedy had little taste for the rough Irish pols who dominated Democratic politics in Massachusetts and many other northern places, and in most cases the bad feelings were mutual. He avoided dealing with them as much as possible, but if he did it was often to confront and make them foils. In 1956, he personally involved himself in the overthrow of Massachusetts state Democratic chairman William "Onions" Burke. Burke had engineered a favorite-son victory for Representative John McCormack over Adlai Stevenson in the 1956 state presidential primary, and made the mistake of casting Stevenson and his supporters as left-wing Communist sympathizers who "ought to be down in Princeton listening to Alger Hiss." Kennedy personally drove out to western Massachusetts, where "Onions" had his namesake onion farm, and told Burke he was out as state chairman. Then Kennedy and his aides furiously lined up candidates to run against Burke and his allies on the state committee, and pushed them through to start "a new era for the Democratic Party in Massachusetts." Jack's chief Boston political cronies, Dave Powers and Kenny O'Donnell, thought the battle with Onions was a political coming-of-age for Kennedy, and credited the reflection and study of great leaders that went into *Profiles in Courage* with granting Jack newfound wisdom and toughness.[18]

It would be unwise to uncritically accept the word of John F. Kennedy's two most devoted sycophants, but it seems clear that *Profiles in Courage* did help set his course for the next few years. Appealing to young people and professionals against the old parties and party leaders, even if they were nearly the same age as he was and just *looked* older, Kennedy pursued a candidate-centered style of campaigning that his victories would popularize. After riding his wave of prestige publicity into the 1956 vice-presidential race against the wishes of Adlai Stevenson, Ambassador Kennedy, and other party elders, Jack was selected to give the speech nominating Stevenson at the Democratic Convention, as a way of softening the rejection. He adopted the suprapartisan rhetoric of *Profiles in Courage* for the occasion, amped up with his own heroic notions of the presidency. He cautioned the delegates not to "forget the grave responsibilities" they possessed. "We are selecting the head of the most powerful Nation on earth, the man who literally will hold in his hands the power of survival or destruction, of freedom or slavery, of success or failure for us all." Hence they needed a man "who must be something more than a good candidate, something more than a good speaker, more than a good politician, a good liberal or a good conservative."[19] Later, during a Stevenson-sanctioned floor fight over the vice presidential nomination, Governor Abraham Ribicoff of Connecticut put Kennedy's name in nomination with explicit reference to his appeal to "the large number of independent voters" who lurked in the electorate. The older "ardent Democrats" on the convention floor needed to be "realistic" and let the "fresh and clean breezes" of JFK blow over them. Kennedy lost the veepstakes to the original front-runner for the second spot, Estes Kefauver, but with the Democratic ticket destined to be crushed by Eisenhower and Nixon in the fall, he was the unquestioned star of the party thereafter, if not yet its accepted leader.[20]

To a degree that has been understandably overshadowed by the many, many more sensational events that followed the Kennedy family through history, one of John F. Kennedy's most durable legacies has been the inexorable rise of candidate- (as opposed to party-) centered presidential politics that came in the wake of his success as a politician and pop-culture icon. By emerging in the public eye based on media coverage, and then becoming the first president perceived to gain the nomination by damaging more established contenders in the primaries (only a handful of states held them in 1960, but Kennedy's defeats of Hubert Humphrey in Wisconsin and West Virginia were considered decisive), Kennedy established candidate-centered campaigning as the norm in American presidential politics, sapping significant prestige and influence from the national party organizations. After Eugene McCarthy and President Kennedy's own brother both followed his example in 1968, only to have the nomination end up with the party establishment's candidate, Hubert Humphrey, reforms were brought in that damaged the party organizations institutionally, making primary campaigns driven by the media and especially by the candidates themselves loom larger and larger in the process. After the Kennedys, the national party organizations would increasingly act as little but conduits for campaign funds and advertising, in competition with many others. Nominations would be determined entirely in the primaries, with the candidates' personal organizations controlling every aspect of the campaigns, including (by the late twentieth century) even the national party conventions.[21]

## *"Edward Youngfellow" and the New Economics: Kennedy's Neoliberalism*

Part and parcel of the trend toward a candidate-centered politics pitched to the professional classes, especially in the Democratic Party, was the declining prestige and coherence of the party's ideological program. In the 1950s, that meant the New Deal liberalism that had reshaped U.S. government and American society in the previous two decades, especially as it was further developed by the Truman administration. Combining Keynesian economics, infrastructure development, protection of labor rights, and federal government interventions to support housing, education, old-age pensions, and other basic forms of social welfare, the New Deal order would actually see its greatest expansion under Kennedy's immediate successors, Lyndon Johnson and Richard Nixon. The New Deal proper was largely entailed away from southern blacks by Franklin D. Roosevelt's southern allies, but through the pressure of the civil rights movement and its attendant Supreme Court decisions, African Americans would come to be included in the New Deal coalition, too, as beneficiaries as well as voters.

Yet before he and his brother became the fallen saviors of 1960s liberalism, John F. Kennedy was a committed centrist, at best. He famously outflanked Nixon to the right in 1960 on national security, accusing the Eisenhower administration of allowing a "missile gap" to develop, and his conservatism actually went much deeper than that. His roots were in the Irish Catholic right of the northern Democratic Party, traditionally hostile or indifferent to public schools and other government programs that were often (correctly) perceived as Protestant assimilationist plots and unfriendly to the aspirations of competing ethnic groups, especially African Americans and Jews. He was also a child of wealth who, by his own admission, never personally experienced the Great Depression or took any serious personal interest in domestic affairs. Like his father, he was a fiscal traditionalist who pined for balanced federal budgets and chafed at the popularity of New Deal social programs among his constituents. Part of John F. Kennedy's anti-Communism was antistatism. In a speech at Notre Dame in 1950, he condemned the "resignation of major problems into the all absorbing hands of the great Leviathan—the state" as "the scarlet thread that runs throughout the world." The "New Frontier" he offered the country in 1960 was distinctly one that pointed toward individual striving and away from New Deal liberalism, despite the shared adjective.[22]

The ideological groundwork for this move, including the manly but soaring rhetoric that ennobled it, was laid by *Profiles in Courage* and its offshoots. Kennedy, Sorensen, and their collaborators fashioned a history of American politics that almost completely omitted the New Deal or any other kind of social reform cause, or indeed any struggles for equality or democracy, from the annals of American political courage. On the contrary, as we have seen, the reverse was usually true. Only southern slaveholders got to stand up, sideways, against slavery. By the same token, racism was only addressed in a one-page tribute to a southern Democrat. In the "Other Men of Courage" chapter at the end of the book, Kennedy saluted forgotten presidential candidate Oscar Underwood of Alabama for favoring (or rather, not opposing) a failed anti–Ku Klux Klan platform plank at the 1924 Democratic convention, the "Klanbake" where the Klan marched outside the hall and actively politicked within it.[23]

The only other major chapter not mentioned so far celebrated another of Ambassador Joseph P. Kennedy's curious friends, "Mr. Republican" Robert A. Taft. Taft had given a speech in Ohio questioning the constitutionality of the Nuremberg Nazi war crimes trials a few days before the executions in 1946. This was at a time when it was not uncommon for the old isolationist Republicans, including the aforementioned lavender-baiter Kenneth Wherry, to voice surprising sympathy for the defeated Germans. "The hanging of the eleven men convicted will be a blot on the American record we shall long regret," Taft told the assembled at Kenyon College. He suggested exiling the Nazi leaders as Napoleon Bonaparte had been. According to Kennedy, these were sentiments shared by "a goodly number" of Americans at the time, but only Taft was brave enough to say so in public. More than likely, one of the goodly number was old Joe Kennedy, whose views on many topics were quite close to those of Mr. Republican. The private political understanding between the two had helped Jack beat Henry Cabot Lodge Jr. (even amid a Republican landslide) in the 1952 Senate race. Lodge was a supporter of the Truman administration's internationalist foreign policy, and Joe had activated the angry Taft forces in Massachusetts against Lodge through Basil Brewer, the editor of the New Bedford *Standard-Times.* The word had gone forth that young Jack was stronger against the Reds than Lodge.[24]

The *Profiles in Courage* Taft tribute shows how much more palatable such triangulations could seem when projected between the lines of inspirational historical stories. The political intentions become more obvious when the papers relating to the drafting of the book are examined. Originally the preface to the book was to contain an epistolary dialogue between Kennedy, or "Senator Edward Youngfellow," and "Senator J. P. Oldtimer," who urges him to vote against some unnamed "national" bill, possibly a defense appropriation or a potentially economically dislocating infrastructure project like the St. Lawrence Seaway, because his constituents were against it. For "Oldtimer," politics was about democracy, not the individual senator's ideas of right and wrong: "How can you come along and say you know better than they that it's in their interest? That's a mighty dangerous doctrine, son—smacks of aristocracy and demagoguery. . . . When you've been in the Senate as long as I have, you'll understand that we don't play the game that way, no matter how noble and courageous it looks to the newspapers." Of course, Kennedy's whole strategy was to look noble and courageous and attractive to the national media and its audience and to the idealistic young middle-class professionals, joiners of Stevenson clubs, and eager readers of *Profiles in Courage* who admired a high-minded approach to politics and government. Their interests hardly seemed to match up with the union workers, the indigent elderly, and others who were perceived to be most dependent on New Deal–era government programs in any case. Piously, Kennedy replied to "Oldtimer" by quoting Edmund Burke and arguing that, along with "party responsibility," he had "a personal responsibility" to "my nation and my conscience," not owed "to our constituents" alone but to "our God as well." If the mores of party and Senate did not change and allow "independent conduct or insurgent members," they would "wither and waste away until no one would be left but those few whose ideas had never changed." All of this may have been too on-the-nose, because while the Burke quotation and a few of the specific points appeared in Kennedy's published first chapter, the Youngfellow-Oldtimer dialogue and its explicit attack on the played-out politics of Democratic Party elders were replaced with Hemingway and "grace under pressure."[25]

Without contesting the nobility and attractiveness of such sentiments, they need to be seen in the context of the Kennedy goal of building a political profile against potential Democratic primary opponents such as Stevenson, Lyndon Johnson, Stuart Symington of Missouri, and especially the man who was then the liberal torchbearer for civil rights and the expanding New Deal order, Hubert Humphrey.

Throughout the mid-to-late 1950s, Kennedy and Sorensen were producing a steady stream of articles and columns for the popular press that first previewed and then reechoed and expanded on the themes of *Profiles.* Particularly telling was a cover article on the future of the Democratic Party for *LIFE* magazine (almost a Kennedy family album by this point) published in early 1957 in the wake of Adlai Stevenson's defeat. "Author Kennedy," as he was coyly identified in the cover caption, called in essence for the gentrification and nationalization of the Democratic Party, de-emphasizing the

"Grand Alliance" of workers and farmers and retooling itself in ways that would appeal better to suburbanites and youth and the newly urbanized South. Building on his new fame as a historian, Kennedy spun out a capsule history of American political parties. His historical analysis was that the Democrats needed to retire "the tired or tarnished holdovers from another era"—the Senator Oldtimers and Onions Burkes and tut-tutting liberals he had sparred with or been suspected by in the past—or they would go the way of the Federalists and Whigs. The Federalists had rested on their accomplishments in government and refused to face the future, Kennedy argued, while the Whigs had flopped "by going to the other extreme to seek favor by appealing to the current demands of every group in the nation." Kennedy implicitly offered himself as the type of new Democrat who could counter the modern Republicanism of Eisenhower and Nixon, said to be making dangerous inroads into the Democrats' bases in the South and the cities, including the African American vote. It was all illustrated with a cartoon spanning two pages with various types of Democrats running to the right side of the spread to collect ice cream bars from a truck labeled "Ike and Dick's Frozen 'Good Times.'"[26]

According to Kennedy, the Democrats needed to avoid both radicalism (as they traditionally had, often more effectively than their opponents, before the mid-1930s) and conservatism—the party should not be "'the captive of the A.D.A.' or the 'victim of Confederate vengeance.'" Nor should it fall back on simply propitiating its parochial interest groups, "the farm vote, the Negro vote, the veterans' vote, and all the rest." Interestingly, the "Negro vote" for the Democrats was a relatively new development at that point, and only in the immediately previous Democratic administration (Truman's) had African Americans' problems gotten much serious attention. Yet already they were being triangulated against.[27]

Given this swipe at what would later be called identity politics, it should be noted that one parochial interest group Kennedy was eager to cultivate was the female voter. As JFK's 1958 senatorial reelection campaign and expected presidential run loomed, the cycle of *Profiles* spin-offs turned to women. In a heavily publicized January 1958 article for the women's magazine *McCall's,* "Three Women of Courage," Kennedy honored "womanhood" (said the newspapers) by adding Jeannette Rankin, Anne Hutchinson, and Prudence Crandall to his Hall of Fame. The article did double-duty by both diversifying the ennobling quality of courage and including a remarkably tousled-haired mug shot of Jack. (Not that *McCall's* was ever going to take its feminism too far: adjacent to Kennedy's article in that issue were a screed against sex manuals and a featurette on how folksy entertainer Burl Ives met his wife.)

Rankin was a natural Profile in Courage: she was the first woman in Congress, but did not make Kennedy's cut for that. Instead, she was another heroic isolationist like Bob Taft, having voted against U.S. entry into *both* world wars. Besides this continuing theme of sympathy for a certain type of Republican, there were subtle political messages in the other choices as well. By including Prudence Crandall, a Connecticut teacher persecuted for opening her school to African American girls, Kennedy addressed racism for the first time, without the need of a black character. (The *McCall's* people still sent out a special release to the black press.) With Kennedy facing questions about the electability of a Catholic from several quarters of the party, including the liberals, the story of Anne Hutchinson's stand against religious intolerance had some obvious utility, although Hutchinson herself would perhaps have been shocked to learn she had helped a papist win power.[28]

In the 1960 presidential election, Kennedy weaved the themes and rhetoric of *Profiles in Courage* in with other elements that were better remembered later—a new generation of leader with better hair poised to "get the country moving again." In doing so, he took the Democratic Party out from under the New Dealers and liberals—and then the country from Richard Nixon—by exploiting recent innovations that would become mainstays of presidential campaigning because of him: primaries and the network-controlled television debates that have been inflicted on us in every election cycle since the Nixon-era reforms. Strikingly, Kennedy directly reinvoked and in some ways closed out his *Profiles in Courage* campaign just before he took office in a speech to the Massachusetts General Court in January 1961. In front of the Bay State's assembled pols, history seemed to virtually demand a policy of triangulation against the midcentury Democratic Party: "For of those to whom much is given, much is required. And when at some future date the high court of history sits in judgment on each one of us—recording whether in our brief span of service we fulfilled our responsibilities to the state—our success or failure, in whatever office we may hold, will be measured by the answers to four questions." I will only mention the first: "were we truly men of courage—with the courage to stand up to one's enemies—and the courage to stand up, when necessary, to one's associates—the courage to resist public pressure, as well as private greed?" That democracy and corruption could be treated as equally in need of courageous resistance said volumes about the kind of elitist leadership Kennedy advocated.[29]

The top-down orientation showed in his preferred approach to economic policy as well. John and Robert Kennedy's "New Economics" was much discussed in the early 1960s, but has been remembered only sporadically and selectively since then. While Keynesian in its theoretical foundations, the Kennedy approach was frankly labeled "Supply-Side Economics" by one of its architects, Council of Economic Advisers chair Walter W. Heller, who distinguished it from the Ronald Reagan version only in terms of Heller's less Panglossian revenue estimates. In response to the occasional economic doldrums of the late 1950s and early 1960s, and their sense that the president might be required to address them, the Kennedys became attracted to the idea that cutting taxes might be the most effective and congenial way to stimulate the economy. Top tax rates would be lowered, ideally but not necessarily as part of a package of reforms that would also close various business loopholes, as a way to put more money back into the private economy. Early twenty-first-century conservatives are wrong to claim John F. Kennedy as the father of their movement, based solely on his interest in tax cuts, but perhaps not completely wrong. By deleting the New Deal from political history in *Profiles in Courage,* Kennedy had imaginatively restored the laissez-faire status quo of the old Democratic Party his father Ambassador Joseph P. Kennedy grew up in, as close to Hoover as F.D.R. on economics. Kennedy's new economic approach did not turn back the clock that far, but it did display great interest in boosting the economy through its most powerful economic players and winning the favor of the business community.[30]

Understood in his full 1950s context, then, John F. Kennedy presaged the future of the Democratic Party on policy as well as methods. Kennedy, and often *Profiles in Courage* itself, was quite literally the inspiration for the well-coiffed baby boomer–aged "Atari Democrats" who emerged in the late 1970s and 1980s with rise of Gary Hart, and came to power in the 1990s in the guise of Bill and Hillary Clinton, Al Gore, and many of their Democratic Leadership Council associates. For a time, their preferred term for themselves was "Neoliberal," popularized by one of their favorite magazines, the *Washington Monthly,* edited by an old Kennedy hand named Charles Peters. Drawing on younger, white, educated elements of the party, Neoliberals did not espouse Reaganomics per se, but they loved JFK-style "tax reform," criticized Washington's sclerotic bureaucracies, and represented what then seemed to be a new market-oriented departure in Democratic politics. Their new Democratic Party was to become much closer to corporate interests, especially in banking and technology, and less friendly to government entitlement programs and by then traditional Democratic constituencies like the unions and African Americans. The type of government programs they did like were Kennedy-inspired "national service" programs such as Bill Clinton's AmeriCorps, and its education initiative Teach for America (TFA), designed to send college students into poor school districts where they could help reform the public school system. TFA graduates in turn became the backbone of the charter school movement that has ended up privatizing large chunks of many big-city public school systems.[31]

Ironically, or maybe not so ironically, it was Al Gore's father, the ardent southern New Dealer Senator Albert Gore Sr., who registered one of the clearest and strongest reactions to Kennedy's economic approach. Gore was the kind of Democrat who rhapsodized about the TVA and wept when the Interstate Highway System was opened to his hometown of Possum Hollow. As an influential member of the Senate Finance Committee, Gore was nonplussed to be accosted by President Kennedy at Eleanor Roosevelt's 1962 funeral, of all places, about supporting a tax cut to get the economy moving again. (In June, Kennedy had proposed 40 per cent cut in the corporate tax rate and substantial relief for the top income tax brackets.) Later Senator Gore was awarded an impromptu lobbying ride on Air Force One over the same issue. Presciently, he argued that tax cuts would force spending cuts, and once that train was rolling, it would be impossible to stop. Democrats would be better off defending "the value and validity" of federal spending "or the balance of public sentiment will be lost to the conservatives" through the tacit admission that there was something fundamentally wrong or unnecessary about public expenditure. JFK complained that Gore was being a "son of a bitch" about his economic program, and Gore in turn expressed his dismay with a "Democratic administration" pushing "a trickle-down tactic as old as Herbert Hoover."[32]

## *Television Afterlife*

Kennedy's neoliberalism has been obscured by the course of events during and after his presidency that forced his policies and especially his reputation steadily leftward. Southern violence against the civil rights movement forced the Kennedys to be more aggressive domestically, and the failures of President Kennedy's early experiments with Cold War confrontation, which transformed Soviet missiles from a campaign talking point into a terrifying reality in Cuba, inspired a growing interest in disarmament and world peace that might or might not have brought U.S. involvement in Vietnam to an earlier close. *Profiles in Courage* was caught up in this process, too, its commercial exploitation potential renewed by the Kennedy presidency and even more so by the president's untimely death. It was brought to the screen again by television producer Robert Saudek, creator of the prestigious *Omnibus* series, hosted by Alistair Cooke and featuring such improving fare as Shakespeare plays, dramas about Abraham Lincoln, and classical music conducted by Leonard Bernstein. *Omnibus* was often held up as a shining example of quality programming in an age when tube executives were writhing under the brickbats of Federal Communications Commission head Newton Minow (Adlai Stevenson's law partner), who famously condemned TV as a "vast wasteland." In the months leading up to the assassination, Saudek was working on an ambitious adaptation of *Profiles in Courage* as a weekly drama for NBC. Work was suspended in November 1963 but then awkwardly resumed a few months later so the show could premiere in time for the 1964 fall television season, with public interest in John F. Kennedy higher than ever.[33]

The series extended and expanded Kennedy's vision with a wider array of heroes and an increased sense of social concern, especially about bigotry and violence, worries that Saudek's program shared with the other early 1960s drama series (for example, *Twilight Zone, Wagon Train*) it often resembled in style and casting. The additions were drawn from stray mentions in the book and ancillary articles or from Ted Sorensen's notes, so they could be billed as "selected by President Kennedy." The fallen president's brother-in-law Peter Lawford got a turn as Missouri's Alexander Doniphan, saving the lives of Joseph Smith and other Mormon leaders during the 1838 "Mormon War," and the 1915 Leo Frank lynching case was also dramatized, bringing anti-Semitism into the issue mix. David McCallum of *The Man from U.N.C.L.E.* played the youngest and most dashing John Adams ever put on screen, defending the accused British soldiers after the Boston Massacre. The politics of *Profiles in Courage* were somewhat updated to fit the civil rights year of

1964. Nonsenators such as Anne Hutchinson and Prudence Crandall (from the *McCall's* article) got spots in the series, and one episode even centered on a nonwhite character, Frederick Douglass. L. Q. C. Lamar was mercifully left behind, and the Edmund G. Ross story was no longer set against a *Birth of a Nation*–style version of Reconstruction.

Yet, if anything, the changes made *Profiles*' nationalist, centrist, free-market approach to politics, government, and economics stand out even more starkly. The Douglass and Crandall episodes both managed to make radical abolitionist William Lloyd Garrison into a sinister fanatic and secondary villain, played by a character actor who had a recurring role as a ghost U-boat captain on *Voyage in the Bottom of the Sea* that quite suited actor Alfred Ryder's ghoulish demeanor. Andrew Johnson got a particular admiring hour, in addition to the Ross impeachment saga, with Walter Matthau, decked out in a curly Andrew Johnson wig, hamming hard. Grover Cleveland, played by the future Archie Bunker, Carroll O'Connor, got an entire episode for courageously standing against veterans' pensions for war widows and orphans. "Government lives by the people," Cleveland mansplains to his young wife—Barbara Feldon, Agent 99 from *Get Smart!*—but pensions for dependents would mean "people lived off the government . . . and that would be wrong."

The TV version of *Profiles* lasted only one season. Perhaps too many other episodes featured elderly actors lecturing the supporting cast as the colorless likes of Oscar Underwood, Robert Taft, and bonus codger Hamilton Fish, facing down injustices that either could not be shown or properly explained. Yet true to its source material, the show managed to tell twenty-six stories from American political and social history in which New Deal liberalism played no role, and radicalism no constructive one. It was all too appropriate material for the middle-American classroom staple many of the films became, distributed to the educational market through the Social Studies School Service. It paved a straight path, now largely forgotten, from the conservative Democratic Party of Thomas Hart Benton, Andrew Johnson, and Grover Cleveland, through John F. Kennedy, to the cautiously triangulating, instinctively centrist one of Jimmy Carter, Bill Clinton, and Barack Obama.

## *Notes*

1. John F. Kennedy, *Profiles in Courage,* 50th Anniversary Edition (New York: Harper Perennial, 2006), xxi–xxii (hereafter cited as *PiC*). Perhaps the use of ghostwriters and research assistants was just one more way in which the Kennedys were ahead of their time, but to the modern eye accustomed to the idea that books published under the names of wealthy, important people in nonliterary walks of life are almost inevitably staff productions, there is not much to see here as a scandal. The heavy contributions of Jacqueline Kennedy's Georgetown University history professor, Jules Davids, and Jack's chief aide and speechwriter, Theodore Sorensen, along with a host of others, were acknowledged up front in the original 1955 preface. There definitely was some political interference involved in the book winning the Pulitzer Prize over the heads of the selection committee, but it seems quite unlikely to be the only time that politics was ever played in a journalistic prize competition, or the only type of politics that could be played.

2. Though covered to some extent in almost all of the hundreds of texts covering John F. Kennedy's rise to power, the literature on *Profiles in Courage* itself is surprisingly sparse, perhaps conveying something about how self-selectively blind scholars are about the cultural and political force of popular history. Two that flog the Hemingway angle are John Hellman, *The Kennedy Obsession: The American Myth of JFK* (New York: Columbia University Press, 1997), 63–85; and John Michael, "Profiles in Courage, JFK's Book for Boys," *American Literary History* 24 (2012): 424–43. For unusually full and balanced historical accounts of *Why England Slept, Profiles in Courage,* and other Kennedy literary productions, see Herbert S. Parmet, *Jack: The Struggles of John F. Kennedy* (New York: Dial Press, 1980).

3. *PiC,* 18, 29–48; Parmet, *Jack,* 330–33.

4. Michael O'Brien, *John F. Kennedy: A Biography* (New York: Thomas Dunne Books/St. Martin's Press, 2005), 328. The *New York Times* in those days called itself an "Independent Democratic" paper that "placed chief emphasis on the word 'Independent.'" It endorsed Franklin D. Roosevelt in 1936 primarily as a bulwark against radicalism, but turned to Republicans Wendell Willkie, Thomas Dewey, and Dwight Eisenhower after that, before finally coming back to the Democrats with our hero in 1960. *New York Times,* Oct. 1, 1936, linked at "New York Times Endorsements Through the Ages," https://www.nytimes.com/interactive/2016/09/23/opinion/presidential-endorsement-timeline.html.

5. O'Brien, *John F. Kennedy,* 285–89; Harry Harris, "'Profiles in Courage' Brings Praise to Kraft," *Philadelphia Inquirer,* May 17, 1956, 18.

6. Robert Dallek, *An Unfinished Life: John F. Kennedy, 1917–1963* (New York: Back Bay Books, 2004), 189–92; quotation from *PiC,* 37.

7. Dallek, *Unfinished Life,* 170, 180, 215–17.

8. *PiC,* 115–32; Ralph J. Roske, "The Seven Martyrs?," *American Historical Review* 64, no. 2 (1959): 323–30; Eugene H. Berwanger, "Ross and the Impeachment: A New

Look at a Critical Vote," *Kansas History* 1, no. 4 (Dec. 1978): 235–42; Mark A. Plummer, "Profile in Courage? Edmund G. Ross and the Impeachment Trial," *Midwest Quarterly* 27 (Sept. 1985): 30–48. For a biography of Ross, see Richard A. Ruddy, *Edmund G. Ross: Soldier, Senator, Abolitionist* (Albuquerque: University of New Mexico Press, 2014).

9. *Profiles in Courage* television adaptation [1956], act 1, pp. 4, 9B, act 2, revised, p. 2, John F. Kennedy Personal Papers, John F. Kennedy Presidential Library, Boston; Memorandum on Suggested Changes in TV Script [1956], Theodore C. Sorensen Papers, Subject Files 1953–1960, Kennedy Library; *Philadelphia Inquirer,* May 17, 1956, 18.

10. *PiC,* 75–108, quotations on 86 and 87. Ironically, William Nisbet Chambers's excellent biography of Thomas Hart Benton, *Old Bullion Benton, Senator from the New West: Thomas Hart Benton, 1782–1858* (Boston: Little Brown, 1956), quite possibly a source for Kennedy's researchers, was one of the final scholarly jury selections that the Pulitzer Prize board of newspaper editors leapfrogged over to give the biography prize to *Profiles in Courage.* Parmet, *Jack,* 394–97.

11. *PiC,* 18, 57–108; Dallek, *Unfinished Life,* 182–83; Ted Sorensen, *Kennedy: The Classic Biography,* new ed. (New York: Harper Perennial, 2009), 58–59.

12. *PiC,* 139–62.

13. Ibid., 170–92, quotation on 187; Ted Sorensen, *Counselor: A Life at the Edge of History* (New York: Harper Perennial, 2009), 146–47. On Norris's liberalism, see Richard Lowitt, "'Present at the Creation': George W. Norris, Franklin D. Roosevelt and the TVA Enabling Act," *East Tennessee Historical Society's Publications* 48 (Jan. 1976): 116–26; Richard Lowitt, "George W. Norris and the New Deal in Nebraska," *Agricultural History* 51, no. 2 (Spring 1977): 396–405. On his defeat and the rise of Kenneth Wherry, see Harl A. Dalstrom, "The Defeat of George W. Norris in 1942," *Nebraska History* 59, no. 2 (June 1978): 231–58; David K. Johnson, *The Lavender Scare: The Cold War Persecution of Gays and Lesbians in the Federal Government* (Chicago: University of Chicago Press, 2004), 80–99; Wherry's obituary, *New York Times,* Nov. 30, 1951, 1, 24.

14. *PiC,* 17.

15. "Politics and Citizenship," *Alumnews* (Nov.–Dec. 1958): 2–3, in Theodore C. Sorensen Papers, Subcollection 1, Series 1: Subject Files, 1953–1960, Box 3: Articles, Kennedy Library. A similar item in Box 5 is "Politics as a Career," from the University of Florida *Peninsula,* July 1957.

16. On the antipartyism of the founders and its continuing power in American political life, see, among others, Ralph Ketcham, *Presidents above Party: The First American Presidency, 1789–1829* (Chapel Hill: University of North Carolina Press for the Institute of Early American History and Culture, 1984); Richard Hofstadter, *The Idea of a Party System: The Rise of Legitimate Opposition in the United States, 1780–1840* (Berkeley: University of California Press, 1969); Ronald P. Formisano, "Political Character, Antipartyism and the Second Party System," *American Quarterly* 21 (1969): 683–709; Walter Dean Burnham, *The Current Crisis in American Politics* (New York: Oxford University Press, 1982); Nina Eliasoph, *Avoiding Politics: How Americans Produce Apathy in Everyday Life* (Cambridge: Cambridge University Press, 1998). Quotation from Walter Dean Burnham, "The Changing Shape of the American Political Universe," *American*

*Political Science Review* 59 (1965): 28. Burnham's take on the 2016 election was published on the London School of Economics website: "In 2017, Trump and the Ultra-Right Wrecking Crew Will Continue to Roll Back History," *USAPP* (blog), Dec. 29, 2016, http://blogs.lse.ac.uk/usappblog/2016/12/29/in-2017-trump-and-the-ultra-right-wrecking-crew-will-continue-to-roll-back-history.

17. James Q. Wilson, *The Amateur Democrat: Club Politics in Three Cities,* new ed. (Chicago: University of Chicago Press, 1966), esp. 52–58.

18. Kenneth P. O'Donnell, David F. Powers, with Joe McCarthy, *"Johnny, We Hardly Knew Ye": Memories of John Fitzgerald Kennedy* (Boston: Little, Brown, 1972), 103–17.

19. Ruth Aull and Daniel M. Ogden Jr., eds., *Official Report of the Proceedings of the Democratic National Convention, Chicago, Illinois, August 13 through August 17, 1956* (Richmond, VA: Beacon Press, 1956), 342.

20. Ibid., 435–36.

21. Nelson W. Polsby, *Consequences of Party Reform* (New York: Oxford University Press, 1983); Martin P. Wattenberg, *The Rise of Candidate-Centered Politics: Presidential Elections of the 1980s* (Cambridge, MA: Harvard University Press, 1991); Martin P. Wattenberg, *The Decline of American Political Parties, 1952–1984,* 2nd ed. (Cambridge, MA: Harvard University Press, 1986); Thomas E. Patterson, *Out of Order,* vol. 2 (New York: Vintage, 1994). There are always political scientists and journalists ready to argue for the continued relevance of parties in presidential politics, and there are plenty of good arguments for that position. Yet it seems indisputable that candidates using their personal organizations to contest primary campaigns has become the default mode of presidential candidate selection. On the Democratic side, there has not been a successful non-incumbent presidential candidate who started the nomination campaign as the front runner with party regulars since Franklin D. Roosevelt. The Republican Party has done a bit better holding its organizational choices in place, with the two George Bushes, but Trump 2016 will likely stand for some time as the most catastrophically unexpected example of candidate-centered presidential primary politics in history.

22. Dallek, *Unfinished Life,* 142–43.

23. *PiC,* 207–8; David Nasaw, *The Patriarch: The Remarkable Life and Turbulent Times of Joseph P. Kennedy* (New York: Penguin Books, 2013), 666.

24. *PiC,* 193–205, quotations on 199–201.

25. Manuscripts: *Profiles in Courage,* Related papers: Item 4-materials for introduction and conclusion, John F. Kennedy Personal Papers, Kennedy Presidential Library, https://www.jfklibrary.org/Asset-Viewer/Archives/JFKPP-031-004.aspx. The dialogue (and its replacement) was called to my attention by Hellman, *Kennedy Obsession,* 63–64.

26. Senator John F. Kennedy, "A Democrat Says Party Must Lead—Or Get Left," *LIFE,* Mar. 11, 1957, 155–78.

27. Ibid., 171–72.

28. *McCall's,* Jan. 1958, 36–36, 54–55; Christine Sadler to Ted Sorensen, Jan. 7, 1958, and other material in Articles file, Sorensen Papers, Kennedy Library.

29. Address of President-Elect John F. Kennedy Delivered to a Joint Convention of the General Court of the Commonwealth of Massachusetts, The State House, Boston, Jan. 9, 1961, MR65–221, John F. Kennedy Presidential Library, https://www.jfklibrary.org/Asset-Viewer/OYhUZE2Q00-0gdV70k900A.aspx.

30. Walter W. Heller, "Kennedy's Supply-Side Economics," *Challenge* 24, no. 2 (1981): 14–18. Robert Dallek's account of Kennedy's tax policy emphasizes its Keynesian side, and the administration's effort to break through older prejudices against deficit spending. Yet Dallek also invites the reader to "recapture the boldness" of the Kennedy tax cut requests, which he compares to "Republican advocacy under Reagan and both George Bushes." Dallek, *Unfinished Life,* 507, 583–589.

31. For conservatives claiming Kennedy, see Ira Stoll, *JFK, Conservative* (Boston: Houghton Mifflin Harcourt, 2013); Scott Farris, *Kennedy and Reagan: Why Their Legacies Endure* (Guilford, CT: Lyons Press, 2013); Lawrence Kudlow and Brian Domitrovic, *JFK and the Reagan Revolution: A Secret History of American Prosperity* (New York: Portfolio, 2016). We badly need a full scholarly history of the Neoliberals or "Atari Democrats" of the 1980s, but until that time, see Randall Rothenberg, *The Neoliberals: Creating the New American Politics* (New York: Simon and Schuster, 1984). On Charles Peters and the *Washington Monthly,* see his memoir *Tilting at Windmills: An Autobiography* (Reading, MA: Addison-Wesley, 1988). For a balanced account that covers the Neoliberals' impact on public education, see Dana Goldstein, *The Teacher Wars: A History of America's Most Embattled Profession* (New York: Anchor, 2015). "Neoliberalism" is used here in a much more specific way than is typically found in academic discourse, to denote a certain faction of the U.S. Democratic Party rather than the global reimposition of capitalist values over the past fifty years, as summarized in such works as David Harvey, *A Brief History of Neoliberalism* (New York: Oxford University Press, 2007). Yet the "Atari Democrats" could certainly be seen as part of that larger trend, and some of them key players.

32. Albert Gore, *Let the Glory Out: My South and Its Politics* (New York: Viking Press, 1972), 154–60, 170–72; Kyle Longley, *Senator Albert Gore, Sr.: Tennessee Maverick* (Baton Rouge: Louisiana State University Press, 2004), 170–71. On the 1962 proposals, see Dallek, *Unfinished Life,* 506–508.

33. On Robert Saudek and the *PiC* television series, see Daniel Marcus, "Profiles in Courage: Televisual History on the New Frontier," *Film & History* 30 (2000): 38–49, and the extensive materials on the series in the Sorensen Papers, Kennedy Library. All the details about the plots and cast of the various episodes below are based on video recordings of the series in the author's personal collection, obtained from the Social Studies School Service of Culver City, CA.

# 10 Ronald Reagan's Allegories of History

Rick Perlstein

The most useful demonstration about how Ronald Reagan used history is not precisely historical at all. In the spring of 1975, North Vietnamese forces easily overran the South Vietnamese army, conquering the nation America had spent billions of dollars and 58,000 lives defending. The *Economist* ran a cover story entitled "The Fading of America." *Time* asked, "Is This What America Has Left?" The *New Yorker* wrote, "Our noble commitments, our firm stands, our global responsibilities—how frequently, in recent years, have they served as a cover for self-interest and greed?" The *New Republic* observed that it was the 200th anniversary of the Battle of Lexington and Concord. "If the Bicentennial helps us focus on the contrast between our idealism and our crimes, so much the better."[1]

Vietnamese refugees were treated with shocking cruelty. A radio poll in a town by the name of Niceville, in the Florida panhandle, found 80 percent opposing their resettlement at nearby Elgin Air Force Base. The Associated Press reported, "Children in one school joked about shooting a few." In San Diego, California, a congressman told a reporter of his constituents, "They think of the Vietnamese as nothing but diseased job seekers." In San Francisco, an army building providing shelter for war orphans had to be guarded around the clock for fear of vigilante attacks.[2]

But in one of the daily radio commentaries the former governor and future president delivered over hundreds of radio stations, Ronald Reagan told a different story. He recounted a letter he claimed to have seen, to an unidentified publication, from an unnamed American missionary.

> The reverend described a 20-foot craft adrift in the Gulf of Thailand with no fuel, no food, no water, barely afloat and sinking with its

> cargo of 82 refugees. Towering over it was the aircraft carrier the USS Midway. The reverend described the Midway as tired. It had already deposited some 2,000 refugees on other ships. . . . Once onboard they had one question: would they be handed over to an unfriendly government, perhaps to be eventually murdered? The executive officer of the ship . . . said, "Our job is to keep you as comfortable as possible, heal the sick, and feed you to your hearts' content." That was the official policy of our nation and therefore of the Midway.

Reagan next described a series of veritable miracles.

> A tiny baby with double pneumonia was cured. People without clothes were given American clothing . . . children were being given piggyback rides on the shoulders of American seamen, and Navy T-shirts bearing the Midway decal began appearing on the little ones. . . . Ads went into the ship's paper asking for toys. Charity begat more charity.

Reagan concluded:

> In the dark days right after World War II, when our industrial power and military power were all that stood between a war-ravaged world and a return to the dark ages, Pope Pius XII said, "America has a genius for great and unselfish deeds. Into the hands of America God has placed the destiny of an afflicted mankind." I think those young men on the Midway have reassured God that he hasn't given us more of an assignment than we can handle.[3]

In its eight years in Southeast Asia, the USS *Midway* had actually operated as a death-dealing juggernaut—a launching pad for air strikes responsible for killing thousands of civilians. Listening to Ronald Reagan, you could imagine its only job had been rescuing widows and orphans. Others told you Vietnam was a crime, a waste. It took Ronald Reagan to explain how simple and noble the whole thing was: charity begetting more charity.

The introduction of "optimism" was among Reagan's signal contributions to the evolution of American conservatism. In the popular imagination, conservatives had been seen as ineluctably dour: "mossbacks" was one common description of them in the middle of the twentieth century. They were American politics' penny-pinching bookkeepers, its spoilsports, its Scrooges. Liberals, on the other hand, were the forces of youthful dynamism: think of John F. Kennedy, promising on the campaign trail to "get America moving again." Liberals were also seen by definition as generous. Ever since the New Deal and the rise of Keynesianism as a governing philosophy, conservatives, frustrated by their electoral defeats at the hand of liberal politicians promising goodies from the U.S. Treasury, had been uttering an agonized plaint: "No one shoots Santa Claus." One of the ways that Reagan rendered conservatism attractive for the first time to a majority of Americans, in time for his 1980 landslide presidential victory—following the agonizing "malaise" of the post-Vietnam, post-Watergate, energy crisis 1970s—was by fashioning a way for Republican politicians to embody Santa Claus and for Democrats to become the Scrooges. He rejected, as he put it in a 1978 column, "the pessimistic belief of those who today control the Democratic Party that we must lower our expectations."

One way he achieved this transformation of conservatism was on the level of policy. He adopted the doctrines of supply-side economics, which held (dubiously, as it turned out) that across-the-board tax cuts would inject a new dynamism into the American economy. Even before that, however, he did it on the level of rhetoric. And key to this rhetoric was a vision of history. This vision was comprised of two broad components.

The first component was positive. It maintained, in contrast to the fashionable narratives of American decline, that America *could not* decline. America was God's chosen nation. America's people were "the most generous people on earth."[4] America was ineluctably grounded in an ideology of individual liberty and radical skepticism toward government that, in Reagan's telling, was the universal formula for producing the greatest good for the greatest number.

The second component, however, was negative. It sought to provide an explanation for all those moments in which America and Americans did *not* behave decently, and when it embraced government solutions over individualist ones. His explanation was that this happened when naive (but usually well-intentioned) Americans surrendered to the blandishments of forces that were *foreign.* This Ronald Reagan was a world historian—invoking the rest of the world's history as an instructive contrast to the American way.

The first component shows up in his rhetoric as early as 1952, when he said in a commencement speech, "I, in my own mind, have always thought of America as a place in the divine scheme of things that was set aside as a promised land"—a "shining city on a hill," to cite a formulation he first uttered in that dark year of 1974 and returned to again and again.[5]

For Ronald Reagan, whether it was 1774 or 1974, whether his lesson was derived from events the day before yesterday or back beyond the dawn of time, the story was exactly the same. To demonstrate those lessons, however, Reagan took liberties with the truth—or, perhaps it is more accurate to say, refashioned scattered scraps of information within his imagination to coincide with what he saw as higher truths. For Reagan, Cleo was a god of allegory, not inquiry.

To demonstrate how Americans were always honorable and loyal to one another, for example, he liked to tell a story from 1853 of a Hungarian revolutionary, Martin Koszta, who had declared his intention on U.S. soil to become an American citizen and later was kidnapped by an Austrian warship in the Mediterranean. "Koszta's manservant had been taught what our flag looked like," Reagan explained. "He saw an American flag. It flew from a tiny war sloop. [The manservant] went aboard and told his story to the commanding officer." According to Reagan, the American ship's captain, Duncan Nathaniel Ingraham, boarded the Austrian ship and demanded to see the prisoner. He asked Koszta, "Do you seek the protection of the American flag?" When Captain Ingraham learned that Koszta affirmed that he did, Ingraham made ready to attack the Austrian vessel unless the aspiring American was released.[6]

Reagan told this story in a 1975 broadcast, and again in a speech aboard the USS *Constellation* in 1981, when he dated it to 1840. That time he added melodramatic dialogue. He also added the embellishing detail that three *more* Austrian warships had sailed in to reinforce the first by the time Captain Ingraham made his threat.[7] Both times, the narrative as related was confusing and self-contradictory. But both times he delivered the same soul-stirring conclusion: when Captain Ingraham offered his resignation for embarrassing his country, the U.S. Senate rejected it, with a resolution that included the following words: "This war that was never fought may turn out to be the most important battle in this nation's history."

Reagan's version of events bore scant relation to documented history. The phrase "This war that was never fought may turn out to be the most important battle in this nation's history" never appears in any congressional record.[8] The House and Senate joint resolution in Captain Ingraham's honor says nothing like this. Ingraham never appears to have offered his resignation; and, as President Franklin Pierce explained in his State of the Union address in 1853 in a version that only vaguely resembles Reagan's tale of derring-do on the high seas, he was following official U.S. policy.

Now Ronald Reagan was famous for not getting facts right. But he was consistent in his allegorical purpose—in this case, that Americans never left Americans behind. Allegories, of course, always serve a moral purpose. Implicitly, the reason Reagan told this story in the spring of 1975 was to decry what he saw as the fact Americans *were* leaving other Americans behind. Reagan firmly believed the conspiracy theory that Americans missing in action were still languishing in Communist prison camps in Vietnam. Shortly before he retold the Captain Ingraham story on the USS *Constellation,* he told Clint Eastwood, who was sponsoring a mission led by retired colonel Bo Gritz to raid one of those alleged camps, "If you bring out one U.S. POW, I will start World War III to get the rest out."[9] Calling America back to this part of its better angels was Captain Ingraham's allegorical purpose—and likely why the story was called back to Reagan's own mind in 1981, when Gritz was planning his raid.

But that raises a paradox. Reagan told stories affirming Americans' inherent honor in precisely those moments he believed they were *not* behaving honorably. If Americans never left other Americans behind, even at risk of war, how to explain that Americans *were* leaving other Americans behind? Similarly, if Americans believed in the individual and were skeptical of centralized government, why was it that Americans so often *did* fall to the snares of liberalism and its statist cousin, socialism? Fighting that, after all, was why Reagan pursued a political vocation in the first place.

Thus we arrive at the second component of Reagan's allegorical vision: to explain why Americans sometimes did not act like Americans. They did so, his stories explained, when they let the way the rest of the world thought intrude on their thinking, when they were visited upon by influences that were not precisely American at all. In the case of locating and rescuing Vietnam POW/MIAS, it was "the government bureaucracy," which he tended to frame as a dangerous and foreign imposition upon the American commonweal.

It was certainly foreign, in his telling, to America's Founding Fathers, whom he spoke of in celestial terms, and whose authority he referred to in what I think might be one of the most telling quotes in his lexicon, which he attributed to Thomas Jefferson: "The American people won't make a mistake if they are given all the facts." The assertion itself, however, was not factual: Thomas Jefferson never said it. It shows how, in Reagan's reasoning, *stories* made facts, rather than the other way around—obviating the need for historical fact-checking or even historical inquiry as such.

Perhaps the most striking example of Reagan deploying a version of world history to allegorize the foreignness of government solutions to social problems was his version of the fall of Ancient Rome. In 1978, he introduced his radio listeners to libertarian journalist H. J. Haskell's 1939 book, *The New Deal in Old Rome: How Government in the Ancient World Tried to Deal with Modern Problems.* "Haskell wondered," Reagan explained, "how a civilization that could build such wonders would simply disappear into the dustbin of history." The answer: "the growth of government intervention . . . extensive public works like our New Deal WPA," even a Roman version of the Agricultural Adjustment Administration, "which plowed under half the grapes to stop overproduction of wine." Like the U.S. Treasury printing money to pay debts and creating inflation, the Roman treasury "debased their currency by adding copper to silver coins."

Reagan explained, "They even tried wage and price controls with capital punishment for violations but even then they didn't work as they don't work now. By that time government in Rome had brought commerce and industry to a halt with confiscatory taxation and a network of regulations." In a 1976 statement on behalf of Gerald Ford's reelection campaign he referred to Jimmy Carter's supposed ambition for "'national economic planning." Again citing the fall of Rome, he called this "a modern version of this same ancient folly. . . . [W]henever that temptation has been given in to, human freedom has been lost and human misery followed."

Two words here are key: "ancient" and "modern." These terms suggest a stark structural contrast between an atavistic, out-of-time moment when humanity had not yet achieved the enlightenment to understand that statism portended disaster and a modern period in which humanity had come to comprehend the wisdom of libertarianism. We are now modern, and so know better; and we are *American.* We thus have the power to avoid the temptation to be seduced by statism. "Temptation" was another word to suggest that the un-American way is the atavistic, almost pre-rational way. For if you are modern and rational, and also mature and self-possessed, you will realize that libertarianism is the only logical way for a society to proceed. It is a brilliant rhetorical performance.

Reagan found a similar lesson in England's Poor Laws. Drafting off a news report that one out of six people in San Francisco received public assistance, he explained, "We can look to history if we don't recognize what we are doing and where we are going": welfare always hurts "the very people we are trying to help." It is worth quoting Reagan's historical account at length:

> England embarked on its first welfare program in 1547. By the end of the 17th century nearly one-fifth of the English nation was receiving aid at least part of the time. . . . In England the dole was often three times as much as the laborer could afford for himself and his family. By the end of the 18th century at a place called Speenhamland [officials] decided that wages below a certain level should be supplemented according to the price of bread and the number of children in the family. (Sound familiar?) In the next twenty years the cost of the program doubled and redoubled until it was one-sixth of the total national expenditure . . . riots and fires swept the countryside.

Then and now, the story was exactly the same.

> In 1832 a Royal Commission was appointed to study the problem. At the end of two years the commission reported "the worker need not bestir himself to work." So they recommended that relief should not be made more attractive than the pay for the most menial of jobs. They said "We do not believe that a country in which every man whatever his conduct or character is insured a comfortable living can retain its prosperity or even its civilization." In commenting on the social workers they said, "Their feelings are all on one side. Their pity for the pauper excludes any for the taxpayer."

Again, exactly the same:

> Some time back a Rutgers University professor discovered what the English Royal Commission learned 150 years ago. He said, "The billions of dollars that are being spent on the urban poor by

> all levels of government go mainly to support a growing welfare bureaucracy of teachers, aides, youth workers, clerks, supervisors, key punchers, and people's lawyers. The bureaucracy is sustained by the plight of the poor. When the old programs demonstrably fail, they are re-baptized and refunded."[10]

This was by then the boilerplate neoconservative argument, and indeed Reagan's citation is urbanist George S. Steinlieb, who pioneered neoconservatism's now familiar revival of early Victorian explanations of urban disorder and poverty as the product of the soul-dissipating character of government provision. Reagan's broader account of the Poor Laws, meanwhile, is derived from the mid-twentieth-century libertarian writer Henry Hazlitt, whose work was a fundamental source of Reagan's economic thinking.

When I first heard this broadcast, archived at the Hoover Institution, I asked for an evaluation of it from two historical experts on the English Poor Laws, without identifying its author. George Boyer of Cornell said of Reagan's (and Hazlitt's) claim that the dole was three times higher than wage levels, "I know of no evidence that this was the case."[11] He said cases of welfare benefits being higher than wages would have been "rare." And he noted the economic historian R. W. H. Tawney's conclusion that the 1832 Royal Commission's account of the Poor Laws was "wildly ahistorical." Interestingly, that same phrase—"wildly ahistorical"—appeared in the response of the other historian I consulted, Lynn MacKay, the author of *Respectability and the London Poor, 1780–1870:* "There was no dole; were no social workers, and the poor law system was funded by a rate, not a tax," she wrote me. She called it "a trite and mediocre effort by a banal and lazy thinker."[12]

It's not news that one shouldn't rely on Ronald Reagan for accurate accounts of history. In one infamous example, President Reagan regaled a convention of Congressional Medal of Honor winners with the tale of B-17 pilot who told a wounded tail-gunner unable to bail out of their dying plane, "Never mind, son, we'll ride it down together." Since Reagan claimed the pilot was posthumously awarded the Medal of Honor, that one proved easy for journalist Lars-Erik Nelson to check: there had never been such an award. After he said so in his *New York Daily News* column, a reader pointed out that the same story appeared in the 1944 film *A Wing and a Prayer.*[13]

The telling of heroic tales was central to Reagan's rhetorical vocation. It is not incidental that both these inventions concern World War II, an event that naturally formed a touchstone of his imagination. As he once put it, "During that time my generation defeated totalitarianism. As a result, your world is poised for better tomorrows."[14]

Reagan was especially obsessed with evoking the World War II generation during the 1960s, when his stand against student protesters was central to his rise to national political prominence. Broadcasts at the Vanderbilt Television News Archives reveal that of the sixty-seven times Reagan was featured on the three network newscasts between 1967 and 1970, over half concerned his stands on campus militancy. As much as his introduction of optimism into conservative discourse, his rise to national political prominence was conditioned by his aggressive rhetoric against student militancy—a discourse in which, again, Americans' moral errors were attributed to their seduction by a foreign ideology. Frequently labeled a "fascist" for his crackdowns on protest, Reagan used World War II to reply that he himself had seen fascism, and knew of what he spoke when he called his *adversaries* a "cowardly fascist band."[15]

He also used this history to push back against the hegemonic construction of the baby boom generation as uniquely moral, which reached its apotheosis when *Time* magazine, in the year he became governor, named Americans twenty-five years and younger its "Man of the Year." In such praise, Reagan saw a rebuke of his own generation, and he fought back: "As for our generation, I have no intention of apologizing. No people in all history paid a higher price for freedom. And, no people have done so much to advance the dignity of man."[16]

For decades afterward, he would relate a zinger he said he had delivered in response to a student leader who lectured him: "Governor, you didn't grow up in an age of instant electronics, of jet travel, of space travel, and journeys to the Moon."[17] He gave as his response: "You're absolutely right. Our generation, we didn't have those things when we were your age. We invented them." Decades before Tom Brokaw thought to call it the "Greatest Generation," Reagan got there first. It was his allegory for America at its finest moment: America at its most American—which, in his telling, coincided with America's unapologetic embrace of an establishment value, which is again reframed as ineluctably modern and, in this case, scientifically and technologically advanced, and even cosmopolitan. "We are called materialistic," he said during his reelection campaign in 1970. "Maybe so. . . . But our materialism has made our children the biggest, tallest, most handsome and intelligent generation of Americans yet. They will live longer with fewer illnesses, learn more, see more of the world, and have more success in realizing their personal dreams and ambitions than any other period in our history—because of our 'materialism.'"[18]

He derived another oft-repeated argument from Europe's bloody mid-century history. In an interview with *Time* in 1976, he was asked what would be the key policy issues if he became the presidential nominee. He cited Jimmy Carter's "approach to unemployment: he's for the Humphrey-Hawkins bill." The bill mandated the federal government provide jobs unless the unemployment rate was 3 percent or less. "If ever there was a design for fascism, that's it. Fascism was really the basis for the New Deal. It was Mussolini's success in Italy, with his government-directed economy, that led the early New Dealers to say, 'But Mussolini keeps the trains running on time.' The Humphrey-Hawkins bill calls for the same kind of planned economy, and that would mark the end of the free marketplace in this county."[19]

Now, the argument for policy similarities between the early New Deal and fascism is not foreign to serious historical literature: both shared a fondness for the economic arrangement known as "corporatism," a technical term referring to shared economic decision making by cartels made up of representatives of business, labor, and government. Alonzo Hamby, in his 2004 comparative history *For the Survival of Democracy: Franklin Roosevelt and the World Crisis of the 1930s,* wrote that "[t]he Nazi recovery program organized the economy in ways that bore a clear surface resemblance to the early New Deal."[20] The argument was pioneered by the distinguished Columbia University historian John A. Garraty,[21] and developed at book length by the German historian Wolfgang Schivelbush.[22] But they didn't quite mean what Reagan meant, when he said in a *60 Minutes* interview in 1975, "You know, someone very profoundly once said many years ago that if fascism comes to the U.S.A. it will come in the name of liberalism." He continued, "And what is fascism? Fascism is private ownership, private enterprise, but total government control and regulation. Well, isn't this the liberal philosophy?"[23]

Liberalism, for Reagan, could not be but an entirely *alien* philosophy—and thus destined, in another repurposed phrase he used again and again, for the "dustbin of history." This, above all, was what he understood the annals of humanity to show. Conveying this was a pursuit he took with great seriousness.

Reagan's untruths were always in the service of a higher truth. To Reagan's acolytes, this was nothing to apologize for. In his influential 1990 hagiography *Ronald Reagan: How an Ordinary Man Became an Extraordinary Leader,* Dinesh D'Souza cites a story from Jimmy Carter's memoir. Preparing to hand over the Oval Office to his successor, Carter briefed "him on some of the major issues that new president would have to face. . . . Reagan listened politely but did not write anything down or ask any questions. The information was 'quite complex,' Carter writes, 'and I did not see how he could possibly retain all of it merely by listening.' Yet when Carter asked him if he wanted to take notes, Reagan said no."[24] Unlike Carter, Reagan did not understand his leadership in terms of getting the facts or details right. D'Souza tells another story. At a meeting of big-city mayors early in his term, Reagan didn't recognize his own secretary of housing and urban development, referring to him as "Mr. Mayor."

In these examples D'Souza spies virtue. "Like Lincoln, Reagan had an unerring capacity to separate things that mattered from things that were peripheral. . . . He understood the importance of the big picture and would not be distracted by petty details. He was wrong not to recognize Sam Pierce, but the reason for his oversight was that he had no interest in the Department of Housing and Urban Development, which he saw as a rat hole of public policy. He knew that if he went in, he might never come out. By and large, he was right."[25]

Concludes D'Souza, "Reagan's greatness derives in large part from the fact that he was a visionary—a conceptualizer who was able to see the world different from the way it was. . . . He saw the world through the clear lens of right and wrong. This kind of knowledge came not from books but from within himself. . . . He understood the moral power of the American ideal and saw how it could be realized most effectively in his time."[26] I've called this Reagan's "liturgy of absolution," and frame it as central to his political appeal.[27] It reached to an imagined past to tell an imagined future; but what kind of future did it tell?

The social critic Thomas Geoghegan points out that John Winthrop's actual 1630 "City on a Hill" address, whose title was "A Model of Christian Charity," was precisely not about America's superiority but its vulnerability. "The speech makes clear that humility is our only hope. . . . According to Winthrop, God put us up high, not to have the whole world bow down to us—but to give everyone a front row seat to view our example. Should we no longer be meek and humble, God would rain down fire on our heads before their upturned eyes."[28]

Ironically, it was precisely this profound moral reckoning that, at bottom, Reagan's deployment of history was designed to head off. It was a moral imagination that insisted upon forgetting as a virtue, and calling that forgetting "history."

## *Notes*

1. "The Fading of America," *The Economist,* Apr. 4, 1975, 12; "Special Section: Is This What America Has Left?" *Time,* Apr. 7, 1975; "Notes and Comment," *New Yorker,* Mar. 31, 1975; "Editorial," *New Republic,* May 3, 1975.

2. "HEW: Refugees' Health Good: Protesters Fear Disease, Job Loss," *Daytona Morning Journal,* May 1, 1975, 1A; Agency for International Development, *Operation Babylift: Report,* Apr.–June 1975.

3. Kiron K. Skinner, Martin Anderson, and Annelise Anderson, eds., *Reagan In His Own Hand: The Writings of Ronald Reagan That Reveal His Revolutionary Vision for America* (New York: Free Press, 2001), 48–50.

4. Ibid., 390, quoting "Welfare," a radio commentary recorded Dec. 22, 1976.

5. Anne Edwards Papers, Special Collections, University of California–Los Angeles, Folder 18, reprinted in Anne Edwards, *The Reagans: Portrait of a Marriage* (New York: St. Martin's Press, 2003), 369; speech to first Conservative Political Action Conference, Jan. 25, 1974, reagan2020.us/speeches/City_Upon_A_Hill.asp.

6. "London #2," recorded Apr. 1975, album 75–07, Track 02, Hoover Institution, Stanford University, Ronald Reagan Sound Recording Collection.

7. Ronald Reagan, "Remarks on Board the U.S.S. *Constellation* Off the Coast of California," Aug. 20, 1981, online by Gerhard Peters and John T. Woolley, The American Presidency Project, http://www.presidency.ucsb.edu/ws/?pid=44172.

8. Technically, there was no official "Congressional Record," just several publications that provided transcripts of congressional debates.

9. H. Bruce Franklin, *Vietnam and Other American Fantasies* (Amherst: University of Massachusetts Press, 2001), 191.

10. "Welfare Program #1," recorded Apr. 1975, album 75–07, Track 09, Hoover Institution, Stanford University, Ronald Reagan Sound Recording Collection.

11. Email correspondence with George Boyer, author of *An Economic History of the English Poor Law, 1750–1850* (New York: Cambridge University Press, 1990).

12. Email correspondence with Lynn MacKay, author of *Respectability and the London Poor: The Value of Virtue* (New York: Rutledge, 2013).

13. Lou Canon, *President Reagan: The Role of a Lifetime* (New York: Public Affairs Books, 2008), 39.

14. Speech to the Oxford Union, Dec. 4, 1992, in James C. Humes, ed., *The Wit and Wisdom of Ronald Reagan* (Washington, DC: Regnery Publishing, 2007).

15. "Reagan Jeered and Cursed by 300 Students," *Chicago Tribune,* Mar. 12, 1970.

16. "Reagan Calls for Rejection of State's Prophets of Doom," *Los Angeles Times,* Sept. 7, 1970, A10.

17. Ronald Reagan, "Remarks and a Question-and-Answer Session with Senior Citizens in Los Angeles, California," July 6, 1982, online by Gerhard Peters and John T. Woolley, The American Presidency Project, http://www.presidency.ucsb.edu/ws/?pid=42708.

18. Steven V. Roberts, "Ronald Reagan Is Giving 'Em Heck," *New York Times Magazine,* Oct. 25, 1970.

19. "The Nation: I've Had a Bum Rap," *Time,* May 16, 1976.

20. Alonzo Hamby, *For the Survival of Democracy: Franklin Roosevelt and the World Crisis of the 1930s* (New York: Free Press, 2004), 205.

21. John A. Garraty, "The New Deal, National Socialism, and the Great Depression," *American Historical Review* 78, no. 4 (Oct. 1973): 907–44.

22. Wolfgang Schivelbush, *Three New Deals: Reflections on Roosevelt's America, Mussolini's Italy, and Hitler's Germany, 1933–1939* (New York: Picador, 2007).

23. *60 Minutes,* Dec. 14, 1975, viewed at Ronald Reagan Ranch Center, Santa Barbara, CA.

24. Dinesh D'Souza, *Ronald Reagan: How an Ordinary Man Became an Extraordinary Leader* (New York: Free Press, 1999), 16.

25. Ibid., 29.

26. Ibid., 28.

27. Emmett Rensin, "A Liturgy of Absolution," *Los Angeles Review of Books,* Aug. 14, 2014.

28. Thomas Geoghegan, "Our First and Scariest Inaugural Address, Courtesy of the Puritans," *Atlantic,* https://www.theatlantic.com/politics/archive/2013/01/our-first-and-scariest-inaugural-address-courtesy-of-the-puritans/267299/.

# 11 Barack Obama's Use of American History

James T. Kloppenberg

The books Barack Obama wrote before his election to the presidency, *Dreams from My Father* (1995) and *The Audacity of Hope* (2006), are directed toward an audience of American citizens rather than American historians. But Obama's sensibility was shaped by developments in American academic culture since the 1960s, and this essay draws on that underappreciated connection to examine the ways in which he has deployed historical evidence in his writings and speeches. Obama was trained in two of America's leading colleges, Occidental and Columbia. He earned his law degree at one of its leading law schools, Harvard, then taught law for a decade at another top-flight institution, the University of Chicago Law School. In his books Obama never explicitly addresses his education or his teaching, but it is not necessary. His writing clearly reflects his experiences as a student and as a professor in turbulent times and manifests his serious engagement with the life of the mind in general and U.S. history in particular.[1]

Obama the writer, even before he became involved in electoral politics, preferred flesh-and-blood characterizations to extended historical analysis. Even so, his understanding of American history comes into focus in his written work and in many of the speeches he gave as president of the United States. Also in evidence are many of the ideas debated in the academy in the late twentieth century, including the discourse ethics of deliberative democracy and the antifoundationalism of thinkers who challenged the notion of timeless, universal truths and stressed instead the particularity and historicity of all human experience. Obama's worldview emerged not only from his family, his friends, and his colleagues in the sharp-elbowed worlds of community organizing and political struggle, decisive as those surely were. His worldview was also shaped by the debates that rocked the campuses where he studied and taught, debates about history and ideas as well as politics.

Of Obama's two principal books, many people prefer *Dreams from My Father,* a meditation on Obama's personal identity and the problems of race and cultural diversity in America. To understand Obama's ideas about American culture and politics, however, his personal story must be placed in the framework provided by *The Audacity of Hope,* a book in which one can identify the echoes of earlier and more recent voices in American history. Obama's most incisive biographer, David Remnick, wrote in *The Bridge* that one of Obama's Senate staffers told him that Obama's "whole soul went into" *The Audacity of Hope,* a serious book that deserves scholars' close attention.[2] Particularly important are his discussions of the Constitution, antebellum American democracy, Lincoln and the Civil War, and the reform movements of the progressive, New Deal, and civil rights eras. From his analysis of those issues emerges a particular conception of democracy.

Perhaps not surprisingly for someone who studied and taught constitutional law, Obama writes incisively about the U.S. Constitution. Near the end of *Dreams from My Father,* he describes the law as the record of "a long-running conversation, a nation arguing with its conscience."[3] His former teacher at Harvard Law School, the distinguished legal scholar Laurence Tribe, and Tribe's coauthor, Michael Dorf, attributed to Obama and Robert Fischer the conception of the Constitution as a conversation, the argument they advance in their book *On Reading the Constitution* (1993).[4] For that reason the first part of that phrase should come as no surprise, but the second hints at the differences between Obama's writing and the wooden prose that deadens much legal discourse. In *The Audacity of Hope,* Obama's argument is less lyrical but even more provocative. Against those conservatives who invoke the idea of the founders' so-called original intent, a set of determinate meanings that are said to limit what legislatures and judges can legitimately do, Obama points out that the Constitution resulted from a series of compromises made necessary by the depth of disagreement at the Constitutional Convention and during the process of ratification. Moreover, Obama correctly observes that the decision to leave the document open to amendment testified to the framers' realization that the nation's Constitution would have to change, albeit slowly, with American culture in order to survive.

The failure to provide a mechanism for such alterations, the framers understood, had doomed earlier republics to failure—as we can see now that it doomed later republics, such as the first several republics proclaimed in France—when they proved incapable of adapting to changed circumstances. Obama quotes a crucial passage from the nineteenth-century U.S. historian Jared Sparks concerning the value and the necessity of open-mindedness in the Constitutional Convention. "No man felt himself obliged to retain his opinions any longer than he was satisfied of their propriety and truth," Sparks wrote. Everyone at the convention had to remain "open to the force of argument" in order to hammer out the Constitution.[5] That passage expresses Obama's understanding of democracy as deliberation.

Sparks's comment about remaining "open to the force of argument" served as the epigraph for Obama's longtime University of Chicago colleague and friend Cass Sunstein's *The Partial Constitution* (1993), where it was mistakenly attributed, as it often is, to James Madison. Sunstein's book offers a more ambitious, and much more fully fleshed out, version of the argument that Tribe and Dorf attributed to Obama: the Constitution is best understood as the start of a continuing, open-ended conversation rather than a document with a single, fixed meaning.[6]

In his description of the Constitution and the way it was constructed, Obama shows his familiarity with one of the most important developments in American scholarship since the 1970s, when Bernard Bailyn, Gordon Wood, and other historians sparked the republican revival and legal scholars such as Frank Michelman and Sunstein brought it to law schools. Not only constitutional lawyers but also political theorists are now rediscovering what Madison, Jefferson, and Thomas Paine understood: representative democracy is not a bastardized or second-best version but instead a distinctive variant of democracy that values persuasion over the rigid, unyielding defense of preferences or interests. Representative democracy is designed to substitute the dynamic process of making reasoned arguments for the simple tallying of votes dictated by constituents' preferences. In Obama's words, the size of the new nation meant that "an Athenian model of democracy was out of the question" and the "direct democracy" of New England town meetings was "unmanageable."[7] It was not, however, only practicality that dictated representation.

The process of deliberation, particularly when it brought together people with diverse backgrounds, convictions, and aspirations, made possible a metamorphosis unavailable through any other form of decision making. People who saw the world through very different lenses could help each other see more clearly. Just as Sparks identified the value of delegates' willingness to change their minds and yield to the force of the better argument, so Obama explicitly echoes the arguments of Madison—and, strikingly, of Alexander Hamilton in *Federalist* 70—concerning the importance of encouraging the "jarring of parties" because such differences of opinion could "promote deliberation and circumspection." Although Obama does not explicitly invoke the scholarship of the republican synthesis, which he first encountered at Occidental and then again in law school, nor the work of his Harvard Law School professors or those who published in *the Harvard Law Review* during the years he helped edit it, he does point out that scholars now agree that the Constitution was "cobbled together" from heated debates and emerged not just from debates over abstract principles "but as the result of power and passion."[8] The ideas of Madison were never identical to those of Hamilton, nor those of Robert Morris the same as those of James Wilson. No unitary meaning or intent can be found. Instead the Constitution shows traces of competing arguments drawn from sources including the Bible, English common law, Scottish philosophy, civic republican traditions, and the Enlightenment idea of natural rights.[9]

Obama the law professor concedes that such a conception of the founding appeals to him because it encourages us to emphasize the contingency of the original document and to appreciate the contingencies that lie beneath our own invocations of high principle. His constitutionalism fits neatly into the historicist framework that was displacing older verities in the academic communities of Los Angeles, New York, Cambridge, and Chicago during the 1980s and 1990s. Such historicism, he writes, might free us to "assert our own values unencumbered by fidelity to the stodgy traditions of a distant past."[10] In other words, it might tempt us to describe constitutional interpretation as a question of shifting conventions or changing paradigms. When it comes to the Constitution, we might conclude, to use the story from the cultural anthropologist Clifford Geertz that Obama invokes near the beginning of *Dreams from My Father,* that there are no unchanging ideas and all our stories rest on other stories: "it's turtles all the way down."[11] But Obama admits that such freedom makes him uneasy. He describes it as "the freedom of the relativist, the rule breaker," or "the apostate," and he concedes that "such apostasy leaves me unsatisfied."[12] Caught between the pressures of Geertz and the historian of science Thomas Kuhn, on the one hand, and the persistent yearning for stable principles of justice, on the other, where could Obama turn?

He could, and he did, turn to the tradition of philosophical pragmatism and to American history. What we need, he suggests, is a "shift in metaphors," a willingness to see "our democracy not as a house to be built, but as a conversation to be had." The framers of the Constitution did not give us a "fixed blueprint." Instead they provided a flexible framework that cannot resolve all our differences but offers only "a way by which we argue about our future." The institutional machinery of the Constitution was intended, Obama argues, not to solve our problems once and for all but "to force us into a conversation." The Constitution gave birth to a "'deliberative democracy' in which all citizens are required to engage in a process of testing their ideas against an external reality, persuading others of their point of view, and building shifting alliances of consent."[13] It would be hard to find in William James or John Dewey, or in Hilary Putnam, Richard Rorty, or Richard J. Bernstein, a clearer statement of the conceptual and historical connections between philosophical pragmatism and deliberative democracy in the American political tradition.[14]

Obama's arguments about American democracy rest on a solid scholarly foundation. Sunstein argued in an article published in the *Harvard Law Review* in 1989, "Interpreting Statutes in the Regulatory State," that Madison envisioned the clashing of arguments in American legislatures as a uniquely productive process whereby representatives found their own convictions, and those of their constituents, challenged and changed. Madison sought, as the historian Marvin Meyers argued decades ago in a brilliant essay cited by Sunstein, not merely stability but new understandings of the common good, understandings unavailable to any individual but emerging from the processes of contestation and deliberation.[15] In Obama's formulation of this crucial point, the founders wanted above all to avoid "all forms of absolute authority," and the most perilous moments for the new nation occurred when that fallibilism was threatened by attempts to freeze the dynamic process of democratic deliberation by stifling debate. Through this process of making arguments, encountering objections, rethinking our positions, forging compromises, and testing our ideas against a resistant reality in which our schemes succeed or fail, Obama concludes, we learn "to examine our motives and our interests constantly." We learn, in short, that "both our individual and collective judgments are at once legitimate and highly fallible."[16]

Balancing the historicism of cutting-edge constitutional scholarship against his lingering desire for something more substantial than quicksand (or a tower of turtles), Obama makes use of the American tradition of philosophical pragmatism: we should debate our differences, and test provisional interpretations of principle, not by measuring proposals against unchanging dogmas but through trial and error, by trying to solve problems creatively and then democratically deliberating, yet again, on the consequences of our experiments. "We hang on to our values, even if they seem at times tarnished and worn," even if we realize that "we have betrayed them more often than we remember." Our democratic values, deliberation and truth testing, constitute the American people as a nation developing over time. Our commitments to freedom and equality are "our inheritance, what makes us who we are as a people."[17] As individuals and as a nation, we are constituted by the values we cherish, the principles we seek to realize, and the democratic process whereby we attempt to reach those goals.

We must not pretend that the meaning of those shared principles has ever been anything but contested. As Madison understood, as the pragmatists James and Dewey insisted repeatedly, and as more recent philosophical pragmatists have confirmed, democratic principles should not be confused with unchanging dogmas. They must remain subject to criticism and revision. In Obama's words, "our values must be tested against fact and experience."[18] Freedom and equality had one set of meanings in the agrarian settlements of the seventeenth century, another set in the eighteenth and nineteenth centuries, and they are destined to have new meanings for every generation. That is the challenge of democracy, and that is the reason why the philosophy of pragmatism is uniquely suited to democratic decision making. When our understandings no longer conform to the facts of lived experience, as has been the case over and over in American history, it is time for critical inquiry and substantive change. Ritual invocations of earlier nostrums, as if such formulas could help solve problems earlier generations could not have imagined, deflect attention from the hard work of democracy.

The need for such hard work derives, at least in part, from the deeply flawed institutional structures put in place by the Constitution. Although subject to amendment, the Constitution nevertheless erected formidable barriers in the way of those who would alter the framework of American governance. Of all the flaws, the most serious was the founders' failure to address the outrageous practice of slavery. In Obama's words, the generation of Adams, Jefferson, and Madison bequeathed to their successors "a form of government unique in its genius—yet blind to the whip and the chain."

A second antidemocratic feature of the "grand compromise" between the North and the slaveholding South was the provision for electing two senators from each state.[19] That arrangement has given those chosen to represent small, sparsely populated states—then Rhode Island and Delaware, now Vermont and Wyoming—equal power with the most populous. In 1790, Virginia had ten times the population of Rhode Island; California now has more than seventy times the population of Wyoming. Madison himself—a Virginian—opposed this feature of the Constitution because of its antidemocratic quality, as does Obama, but without the bargain struck between the large and small states, there would have been no Constitution. Not surprisingly, from the beginning the Senate has tended to resist change more vigorously than has the more representative House of Representatives.

The way in which the structure of the Constitution has facilitated some forms of change and blocked others remains as clear as ever in the twenty-first century. As president, Obama demonstrated repeatedly the depth—and the perils—of his commitment to open-endedness and deliberative democracy, particularly in his handling of the stimulus package and the protracted debate over health care. His flexibility and his willingness to compromise on both measures infuriated some of his supporters on the left, and the refusal of his intransigent Republican opponents caused many observers to mock the president's repeated appeals to negotiation, bipartisanship, and creative compromise. As savvy pundits left and right pointed out repeatedly, and as we saw demonstrated throughout the Obama presidency, it takes two to compromise. Efforts to negotiate prove futile when the other side shows no interest. But Obama's steadfast insistence that he was open to suggestions, that he was willing to meet with his adversaries and consider their ideas, and his repeated invitations to Republicans to propose alternatives served a purpose that few commentators seemed to notice as the debate wore on. He was displaying, over and over, a patience that outraged his allies and bewildered his opponents left and right, an iron fortitude that his critics mistook for weakness.[20]

As the fate of the Affordable Care Act, still so uncertain in 2018, makes clear, Obama was right to observe, in *The Audacity of Hope,* that in a democracy "no law is ever final, no battle truly finished."[21] Obama's books demonstrate that he was dissatisfied with universalism yet remained uneasy with relativism. Searching for guidance about the traditions he could tap to advance his ideals of freedom and equality, he turned to American history. What did he find there?

During the years between the Puritans' arrival in North America and the decade of the 1780s, Obama observes in *The Audacity of Hope* that Americans embraced an ideal of "ordered liberty" patterned on the Puritans' model. They pioneered a particular kind of democracy premised on what he calls "a certain humility" and "a rejection of absolute truth." Although the Puritans surely cherished the absolute truth of their Christianity, the institutions they put in place in New England towns enabled them to govern themselves, which had the unintended effect of destabilizing hierarchical authority in the public sphere and empowering the people. Instead of truth descending from on high, it would bubble up from the unruly deliberations of citizens gathering together in meetinghouses to decide for themselves on issues of public concern.

The experience of having to accept the results of elections, as unpalatable as those results might be, can help individuals appreciate the power and, at least occasionally, the value of other points of view. Only through that discursive process, as Madison observed, as Alexis de Tocqueville confirmed in the 1830s, and as Obama argues in *The Audacity of Hope,* did Americans come to know—or rather to create—what they called a common good. They understood that the ideal of a common good appeared and then receded along the horizon. It did not exist before they argued about it, and it changed shape as they tried to implement it. In Obama's words, the framers set up "a community in which a common culture, a common faith, and a well-developed set of civic virtues" enabled citizens to contain the inevitable "contention and strife" on which democracy depends. By experiencing such struggles, he concludes, Americans learned that the individual's "self-interest" is "inextricably linked to the interests of others."[22]

Obama the community organizer turned professor of constitutional law has a solid grasp of the dynamics of American democracy. He knows the process whereby individual interests can become transformed into something larger. He learned the theory in college and law school from the civic republican revival; he saw—and for several years helped shape—the practice in the Far South Side of Chicago. Democracy means squabbling about differences, reaching tentative agreements, then immediately resuming debate. Obama understands that disagreement is more American than apple pie. The hallmarks of early national American political culture, as sketched in *The Audacity of Hope,* mirror those that appeared in articles published in the *Harvard Law Review* in the early 1990s and updated in the Saguaro seminars that Robert Putnam convened, and in which Obama played a decisive role, a few years later: civic republicanism, deliberative democracy, communitarianism, and the forced practice of experimentation and testing.[23]

Obama shares with Tocqueville a conviction that some of Obama's supporters on the left have had as much trouble accepting as his critics on the right: the willingness to endure acceptable compromises instead of demanding decisive victory over one's opponents has been a recurring feature of American democratic culture. Tocqueville never tired of contrasting that characteristic to the fatal unwillingness of his fellow French citizens to reach accommodations with each other. Tocqueville explained the success of American democracy by inverting the lessons of France's failure. Whereas the French Revolution foundered on the civil wars that erupted between monarchists and republicans, between champions of the old regime and the new, and between Enlightenment fundamentalists intolerant of religion and Catholics who remained equally intolerant of atheism, Tocqueville marveled at the willingness displayed by Americans of different backgrounds to find common ground—or at least to tolerate their differences. From a variety of experiences ranging from barn raisings to service on juries, Americans were learning to learn from each other. From the perspective of Tocqueville, born into an aristocratic family but intrigued by the magic of democratic equality, that transformation both demanded and further developed an ethical sensibility that recognized the legitimacy of difference and the productive potential of disagreement.

In a similar vein, Obama observes that he became committed to American politics, and to running for elective office, because he believes that something lies beyond the undeniable cynicism and partisanship that prompts so much unpalatable political maneuvering. His inoculation against that cynicism has been tested again and again. Obama's persistent wariness of partisan stridency has been among the defining features of his political career, and he knows that civility has become more difficult to sustain amid what he calls the "industry of insult" that now drowns out more moderate voices. Obama accounts for his continuing allegiance to compromise by invoking a "tradition that stretched from the days of the country's founding to the glory of the civil rights movement, a tradition based on the simple idea that we have a stake in one another, and that what binds us together is greater than what drives us apart."[24]

Appropriately enough for someone who has lived and worked on the South Side of Chicago, in neighborhoods not that far from Jane Addams's

Hull House, Obama's reference to "that which binds us together" echoes the almost identical words that Addams wrote to explain the settlement house movement in her memoir, *Twenty Years at Hull House* (1910). Using a phrase she attributed to the founder of the English settlement house movement, Addams professed her belief "that the things which make men alike are finer and better than the things that keep them apart, and that these basic likenesses, if they are properly accentuated, easily transcend the less essential differences of race, language, creed, and tradition." Addams, like Tocqueville, derived her cultural cosmopolitanism from her democratic ideal. "Hull-House was soberly opened on the theory that the dependence of classes on each other is reciprocal." Because "the social relation is essentially a reciprocal relation, it gives a form of expression that has peculiar value," the value added by expanding the appreciation of individuals for those unlike themselves. Obama's fondness for this formulation became even clearer during his presidency. He used it in his Cairo address to the Islamic world; in his Nobel acceptance speech in Oslo; at the fiftieth anniversary march over the Edmund Pettis Bridge outside Selma, Alabama; and after the murders in the Mother Emanuel AME Church in Charleston, South Carolina; and it has been a staple of the message he took to meetings around the United States. For him, it captures the heart of democracy.[25]

Hull House inspired a generation of well-to-do native-born women to live and work with recent immigrants from a wide range of different cultures. Since the 1960s, critics have maligned and satirized the efforts of such progressive reformers, both men and women, because beneath their language of uplift and harmony many skeptics see schemes of cultural imperialism and social control. Some progressives did participate in efforts to enforce racial segregation, restrict immigration, and prohibit the sale of alcohol, but the progressives were a diverse coalition that also included democratic socialists and the founders of the National Association for the Advancement of Colored People (NAACP). Some commentators sagely contrast the supposedly elitist progressives and the supposedly democratic populists, a distinction almost always made to the detriment of the former that neglects the continuity in central aspects of the groups' agendas. Finding veiled, sinister impulses beneath the efforts of those involved in settlements or in the social gospel, concerted efforts to ameliorate conditions of urban poverty, seems to me difficult to do. Settlement house workers such as Addams, whatever else they achieved, did at least begin the process of transforming middle-class attitudes toward cultural diversity and urban poverty, helping to make the former more acceptable and the latter a scandal. In an essay published before Obama left the world of community organizing for Harvard Law School, "Why Organize? Problems and Promise in the Inner City," he argued that social activists such as Saul Alinsky's community organizers should draw as heavily on Jane Addams's empathy as they do on John L. Lewis's intransigence.[26]

If Obama refers only indirectly to the ideas and example of Jane Addams in *The Audacity of Hope,* he does much more explicitly invoke the progressives' ideas of graduated taxation and government regulation of the economy. These two ideas, embraced by Democrats from the election of Woodrow Wilson in 1912 through the presidency of Lyndon Johnson, have been repudiated by Republicans since the election of Ronald Reagan in 1980. In recent decades a bipartisan consensus has formed about the desirability of lowering taxes and around the theory—which the catastrophic recession that began in 2008 failed to shake—that state regulation of the economy is less efficient than reliance on free markets. There is also widespread agreement among economists, whether they applaud or deprecate the fact, concerning one of the consequences of deregulating the economy and reducing taxes on the wealthy: the distance between the richest and the poorest Americans has grown dramatically in recent decades, a phenomenon Obama emphasized in his speeches and his books.[27]

That gap separating the wealthiest Americans not only from those at the bottom but from those in the middle of the range of income distribution shrank from the New Deal until the oil crisis of 1974. It shrank not by accident or through simple economic growth but, as Obama points out, because of four deliberate strategies: progressive taxation, economic regulation, support for unionization, and massive investment in higher education. In the aftermath of Reagan's election in 1980, all of those strategies have been deemed inconsistent with American principles. At least partly as a consequence, inequality has soared to levels unseen at least since the late nineteenth century and perhaps unprecedented in American history.[28]

Like the progressives and New Dealers before him—and like the founders of the American Republic before them—Obama sees such increasing economic inequality as inimical to democracy. His sustained critique of inequality in *The Audacity of Hope* might seem to place him at the edge of twenty-first-century American political debate, but he knows that it descends from a long tradition. Although the great champions of independence John Adams and Thomas Jefferson eventually disagreed with each other about many things, they never wavered from their shared conviction that the American experiment with self-government would succeed only if the nation's citizens remained roughly equal in their economic standing. For that reason, both opposed the standard European practices of primogeniture and entail. Both saw that such techniques, which provided for passing down estates and fortunes intact to first-born sons, had enabled European aristocrats to consolidate their wealth and their power at the expense of everyone else. Adams and Jefferson, like Franklin and Madison, agreed that democracy could survive in the United States only if the nation prevented the emergence and persistence of extremes of wealth and poverty such as those of the Old World.

Both Adams and Jefferson distrusted Hamilton's scheme in the 1790s for consolidating the power of bankers, because they valued producers of wealth—whether farmers or artisans—over those who, in Adams's phrase, only "moved money around." Given that the financial sector's share of the U.S. economy has increased dramatically in recent years, perhaps the time has come to resurrect this observation from the pen of contemporary conservatives' favorite founder. Whatever the reasons behind investment banks' dramatic increase in revenues, ever-increasing inequality, as Adams and Jefferson agreed and as Obama has pointed out repeatedly, is disastrous for democracy. Adams, Jefferson, and other members of their generation took the first steps toward securing equality when they ensured that the United States would never permit a hereditary aristocracy to develop.[29] Progressives and New Dealers contributed the ideas of a minimum wage, graduated taxation, estate taxes, economic regulation, collective bargaining, and expanded access to higher education in order to update that original American commitment to economic equality—at least relative to the nations of Europe.

Obama explicitly endorsed the judgment of progressive reformers such as Louis Brandeis, the "people's attorney," who wrote that "no office in a democracy is more important" than the office of citizen.[30] Progressives argued that democracy requires all individuals to see beyond their narrow personal interest and attend to the common good. Obama's approach to economic and political reform essentially extends that of the progressives, who sought to rein in corporate power by various means. Brandeis wanted to attack "bigness" directly, through antimonopoly measures. Others preferred the "Wisconsin idea" of nonpartisan public servants engaging in research to identify problems and mobilize public resources to address them. From that orientation emerged the independent regulatory agency. The idea of a body operating in the interest of consumers originated in the Interstate Commerce Commission in 1887. It was reborn in Wisconsin in the 1910s, then exported to other states and the federal government.[31]

Progressive reformers adopted a wide range of strategies, but in the economic realm they built on that idea of regulation in the public interest until the retrenchment of government in the 1920s. Herbert Hoover's "associative state," which effectively empowered business and enriched business owners at the expense of government authority, contributed to the skewed income distribution that helped deepen the catastrophic Great Depression by reducing the buying power of most Americans. Franklin D. Roosevelt, after initially resisting the progressives' approach, resurrected it in the New Deal. In Obama's words, the Social Security Act of 1935 was "the centerpiece of the new welfare state, a safety net that would lift almost half of all senior citizens out of poverty, provide unemployment insurance for those who had lost their jobs, and provide modest welfare payments to the disabled and the elderly poor."[32] Although it was full of holes, the Social Security Act represented a beginning, and as it expanded it has provided much wider coverage, particularly for senior citizens. Obama has suggested that the process of gradual expansion and consolidation might provide a model for health care reform in the coming decades.

Roosevelt proposed a more dramatic expansion of the New Deal when he laid out his plan for a more generous scheme of social provision in his second Bill of Rights, a program he announced in his State of the Union address in 1944. In *The Audacity of Hope,* when Obama listed the concerns that animated citizens he met while preparing to run for the U.S. Senate in 2002, he outlined essentially the same program on which Roosevelt campaigned for reelection almost six decades earlier: a living wage, health insurance, good schools, safety from criminals at home and enemies abroad, a clean environment, "time with their kids," and "a chance to retire with some dignity and respect."[33] Like Roosevelt, Obama judged those hopes modest and, for a nation as rich as America, achievable. Roosevelt died before he had the chance to fight for those programs at the end of World War II. Many historians doubt he would have made the effort, or that he would have succeeded had he tried, primarily because of the intractability of racism. Southern congressmen, through strategies detailed by Ira Katznelson in his study of New Deal legislation, *Fear Itself: The New Deal and the Origins of Our Time* (2013), managed to blunt all attempts to establish programs of social provision that might puncture white supremacy. But FDR did achieve such goals in the GI Bill, and that investment helped transform the experience of a generation of white American males in the years after 1945. Obama's friend Sunstein made an ambitious and convincing case for the significance of FDR's plans in his book *The Second Bill of Rights* (2004), and his account there is fully consistent with Obama's observations in *The Audacity of Hope* concerning the ambitions, and the still-unfulfilled promise, of the New Deal.[34]

Obama has no illusions about the mid-twentieth-century Democratic Party. He understands it harbored and humored vicious racists who weighed every initiative against their overriding commitment to preserving white rule in the South. He knows that the Democratic Party coalition was held together by inspiring ideals—"a vision of fair wages and benefits"—and hard-nosed calculations—"patronage and public works"—and above all by "an ever-rising standard of living." Although Obama applauds the achievements of the New Deal, he acknowledges its limitations—and not only its failure to tackle institutionalized racism. In the early 1930s, Roosevelt was denounced as too timid by John Dewey, Reinhold Niebuhr, and their allies on the radical left, who criticized him for failing to make America socialist when he had the chance. He has been denounced by conservatives ever since for doing just that. Rejecting both of those exaggerated characterizations, Obama credits the New Deal for achieving what was politically possible. His interpretation faithfully echoes and updates Carl Degler's still persuasive account, in *Out of Our Past,* which was the interpretation of the New Deal to which the political scientist and Tocqueville scholar Roger Boesche first exposed Obama when he was an undergraduate at Occidental. According to Degler and other historians who share this judgment, including William Leuchtenburg and, more recently, David M. Kennedy, Roosevelt brought to the United States lasting measures such as the Social Security Act, unemployment insurance, assistance for people with disabilities, and regulation of the failed banking system, all of which prevented the nation's economy from slipping further into chaos. As Obama observes, the New Deal addressed the scandal of child labor, established the forty-hour work week and the minimum wage, and provided unprecedented support for unionization.[35]

Such steps were intended, in the words of Roosevelt that Obama endorses, to ensure "freedom from want" and "freedom from fear."[36] Although accomplishing all of that took not just a couple of years but most of Roosevelt's four terms in office, and necessitated very skillful negotiating with adversaries within as well as outside his own party, the accomplishments of the New Deal nevertheless fell far short of Roosevelt's ultimate goals, a second Bill of Rights, on which he campaigned successfully for reelection in 1944. These programs did establish a precedent, however—the legitimacy of social provision—that enabled later generations to extend those principles and expand the range of Americans covered by those programs. Obama reports in *The Audacity of Hope* that he carried with him similar aspirations as he entered the U.S. Senate.[37] Although he made clear that his goals did not change after his election in 2008, he had few opportunities to make progress toward them after the election of 2010.

During his presidency, Obama repeatedly emphasized the responsibility of the federal government to return to its earlier practice of regulating the American financial sector. It has become clear to many observers that the bipartisan mania for deregulation during the 1990s helped usher in the worst economic crisis since the 1930s. Obama pledged to address the problems caused by that deregulation, and he brought Sunstein, Tribe, and Elizabeth Warren to Washington to help spearhead the effort. If the founders were right to believe—as did progressives, New Dealers, and champions of the Great Society, and as Obama himself wrote in *The Audacity of Hope* that he believes as well—that democracy requires at least rough economic equality, then the United States for several decades has been slipping steadily away from one of its central animating principles. Whatever Obama's own legacy proves to be, he patterned his diagnosis of the problems of financial malfeasance and his initial proposals for its solution in *The Audacity of Hope* after those of the progressives and New Dealers who constructed the regulatory apparatus that has been largely dismantled since 1980.[38]

Unlike most of his colleagues in the Democratic Party, however, Obama has also acknowledged that regulation can fail, or go too far. In one of the most striking passages in *The Audacity of Hope,* he credits the Reagan revolution with removing some constraints that had ceased to serve a purpose but persisted only because of inertia and dogma. Distinctive among Democrats in recent decades, Obama has criticized members of his own party who have allowed themselves to be boxed in by their automatic opposition to all Republican Party initiatives. As a result, Democrats often resist using market principles even when they are the appropriate tool for solving some social problems. Obama concedes that even the firmest of progressive principles yield only rough guidelines, not recipes or rule books.[39] Like many of his teachers at Occidental, Columbia, and Harvard Law School, and like his friend Sunstein in particular, Obama recommends escaping ideological straitjackets of multiple hues and experimenting with different policies to see what works.

Obama's conviction that justice as fairness should be considered in economic terms—rather than merely as equal treatment before the law—is hardly novel. Nor is it un-American. Instead, such concerns have surfaced repeatedly in American history from the eighteenth century until the present. Insistence that successful democratic government requires not only political equality but at least rough economic equality has been a persistent feature of American political thought and practice ever since the Puritans' strictures against excessive wealth. Contemporaries who hearken back to a simpler time of firmer principles might want to ponder the Puritans' strict sumptuary laws, the rules they used to guard against excessive consumption or displays of wealth as signs of sinful indulgence. From the days when John Winthrop urged his fellow Puritans to "abridge ourselves of our superfluities" so that every member of the community could have enough to survive, the impulse to ensure that wealth is shared fairly is a fundamental American value that has only recently—and in increasingly brazen terms—been decried. It is also, as Winthrop pointed out, the central message of the Christian Scriptures. To pretend otherwise, which has been one of the most shrill and insistent claims of many self-proclaimed American traditionalists in recent decades, is to ignore not only the Beatitudes but also a central feature of American history that dates back to the early seventeenth century. Hatred of the privileges accompanying great wealth has driven Europeans to emigrate to America since the early seventeenth century, and anxiety about the consequences of enormous fortunes for popular government has animated American political movements ever since the 1770s, when the first American patriots challenged the prerogatives of wealthy British merchants and aristocrats whom they sent scurrying back to Britain or north to Canada. No citizen of the United States need apologize for criticizing inequality; it is instead the defense of inequality as beneficial that betrays the traditional American ideal of equality.[40]

Obama also speaks the language of the social gospel, one of the most vigorous of the strands in the progressive reform coalition. In *The Audacity of Hope,* he criticizes his fellow Democrats for turning away from America's rich religious traditions in terms similar to those he used in his 2006 Washington address to Jim Wallis's conference "Building a Covenant for a New America." In many of his recent speeches, including those at the Edmund Pettis Bridge in Selma and at Mother Emmanuel AME Church in Charleston, Obama has invoked the tradition of African American religiosity as one of the sturdiest pillars on which the struggle for civil rights stood.[41] In *The Audacity of Hope,* Obama recounts his own decision to join the Chicago congregation of the Reverend Jeremiah Wright, the fiery preacher whose stinging criticism of American racism was to cause Obama such trouble in the spring of 2008. During the three years he spent working as a community organizer in Chicago, Obama became acquainted with ministers, priests, and church-based social activists. Although many of them earned his grudging admiration, he remained "a reluctant skeptic," unsure of his motives, "wary of expedient conversion, having too many quarrels with God to accept a salvation too easily won." While he was thinking about law school, Obama decided to investigate Wright's church, the Trinity United Church of Christ. He was impressed by Wright's straightforward embrace of the traditions of black Christianity and his deliberate attempt to blend Christian and African elements in his church services. Listening to Wright, Obama writes that he felt for the first time the desire to surrender himself to a divine power that could help him, as it seemed that others in the church and in the broader movement for racial justice had been helped, to recover from the knowledge that they had reached "a spiritual dead end," that they had been "cut off from themselves," that on their own they could not escape the desperation enveloping their communities. The black church embodied centuries of struggle, Obama realized, and Trinity seemed to him "a vessel carrying the story of a people into future generations and into a larger world." As one Trinity church service concluded, through tears that surprised him, Obama "felt God's spirit beckoning me." On the basis of that experience, Obama joined Wright's congregation, and although he wears his faith much less ostentatiously than some of his predecessors, he continues to describe himself as a "Christian and skeptic."[42] That tradition, which grows from a hardy strain of nondogmatic Christian political and social activism originating in the Gospels, seems alien to many Americans, but it ranks among the oldest in the history of Christianity. It bears a striking resemblance to the form of religiosity that Lincoln expressed in the final years of his life, as Obama himself has noted.[43] American history (like every nation's history) is distinctive for many reasons, but the presence of multiple religious traditions, none of which can plausibly claim official status, is surely among the most striking features of the United States, as Obama understands.[44] Inasmuch as the recent cross-denominational split dividing liberals from conservatives erodes that long-standing tradition of religious pluralism, it threatens to weaken Americans' toleration of diversity. It also reinforces the polarization that Obama, like Robert Putnam and other students of civil society, considers so debilitating, and it impedes the operation of the ethic of reciprocity on which democracy depends.[45]

Obama has faced head-on the challenge of discussing the implications of his beliefs for politics. He reiterates in *The Audacity of Hope* his conviction that "shared values" ought to be "at the heart of our politics." In that spirit he aggressively disputes a familiar distinction, which dates from the era of the Cold War, between what the philosopher Isaiah Berlin called negative and positive liberty. Obama echoes instead the arguments that Dewey and other progressives made repeatedly from the 1890s through the 1940s, arguments that seem less familiar in twenty-first-century American and European academic debates than they were in the United States during the first half of the twentieth century. Obama contends that "freedom from," or negative liberty, makes no sense in the absence of "freedom to," or positive liberty, which he describes as "the ideal of opportunity and the subsidiary values that help realize opportunity."[46] Formal freedom is meaningless unless individuals possess the resources, both economic and cultural, that enable them to make use of their freedom.

This formulation hearkens back to the understanding of freedom shared by Adams, Jefferson, and Madison, emphasized by Tocqueville, and updated by Brandeis, Addams, and Dewey in the era of progressive reform. From this point of view, freedom has never been a matter of simply being left alone to do whatever one wants to do. It has always been a question of disciplining impulses according to ethical principles and considering the demands of the common good. Ronald Reagan opened a new era in American history when he invited Americans to ask whether they were better off, as individuals, than they were four years earlier, and to vote accordingly. Although William McKinley's "full-dinner-pail" campaign in 1896 offered a similar promise of personal prosperity, and some Republican candidates in the 1920s had followed his lead, the unvarnished appeal to economic self-interest has been rare in American politics. No eighteenth-century candidate for office would have considered such an appeal to individual self-interest; it was inconsistent with the civic virtue required for republican government, and it eroded the self-sacrifice citizens were expected to show. All the founders' appeals were couched in terms of the public good, which was understood to transcend the desires or the well-being of any single individual.

In Obama's effort to shift American public discourse away from obsessive concern with freedom *from* government, famously defined by Reagan as "the problem" of American life rather than a means to its solution, Obama knows he is trying to resuscitate a much older way of thinking about politics.[47] His invocations of the public good have roots that stretch much more deeply into American history than do the strident appeals to individual self-interest that have become almost reflexive across the political spectrum in the last three decades. The American Revolution emerged from a constellation of ideas with religious and ethical as well as political and economic dimensions. Although Americans who flatten that rich body of ideas by emphasizing only the right to make and spend money sometimes call themselves conservatives, they show limited understanding of the complexity of their nation's founding ideals.

Also echoing that persistent American tradition of civic republicanism are the following words from *The Audacity of Hope:* "Our individualism has always been bound by a set of communal values, the glue upon which every healthy society depends." Obama insists that Americans value "community," "patriotism," "a sense of duty and sacrifice on behalf of our nation. We value a faith in something bigger than ourselves, whether that something expresses itself in formal religion or ethical precepts." Finally, he writes, "we value the constellation of behaviors that express our mutual regard for one another: honesty, fairness, humility, kindness, courtesy, and compassion."[48] A similar litany punctuated Obama's acceptance speech the night of the election and his inaugural address, and he continued to repeat that message as he attempted to reorient the Democratic Party toward the values of empathy and reciprocity, two of the central animating norms of American democratic culture. The reformist traditions Obama inherited, ranging from the antebellum crusade against slavery through the progressive, New Deal, and civil rights movements, all grounded their arguments on calls to community and the Christian ideal of brotherhood and sisterhood.[49]

Obama's willingness to compromise does not reveal a lack of principle but instead the conviction of a democrat committed to finding common ground rather than deepening disagreements. Whereas many radicals as well as many conservatives believe that they possess the truth and that their opponents are evil as well as misguided, Obama accepts different political perspectives as a normal and healthy sign of a vibrant culture. When he said, in his health care address of September 13, 2009, that "I still believe we can replace acrimony with civility," and when he praised Gandhi "because he ended up doing so much and changing the world just by the power of his ethics," he was signaling a different conception of politics than that with which most Americans have grown accustomed in recent years. In *The Audacity of Hope,* Obama offers as an illustration his own experience shepherding through the Illinois legislature a modified bill on capital punishment that eventually earned unanimous approval, then immediately concedes that such compromises often prove elusive.[50] His presidency certainly proved the point.

The issue of race remains uniquely volcanic in American history. In *The Audacity of Hope,* Obama observes, accurately, that slavery was the one question in American history on which there could be, finally, no compromise. Indeed, from the very beginning, when the first enslaved Africans arrived in Virginia almost four centuries ago, slavery and its legacy have provided the overwhelming, undeniable proof of the limitations of the American democratic project. Notwithstanding the "genius" of the amendable Constitution, its architects were, to repeat Obama's apt phrase, "blind to the whip and the chain."[51] The persistence of slavery mocked the ideals of freedom and equality and the ethic of reciprocity. It cast a shadow over Americans' boasts about the comparatively small gaps between their rich and their poor. Obama refers to the heroic struggles fought by slaves and abolitionists, who learned from experience that on the question of slavery, "power would concede nothing without a fight." The intransigence of Frederick Douglass and the moral integrity of those who demanded the immediate end of slavery—not the moderation urged by their antislavery allies—changed the climate of debate. Tellingly, Obama draws from the Civil War the lesson that "it has not always been the pragmatist, the voice of reason, or the force of compromise, that has created the conditions for liberty."[52]

Yet from his realization that the battle to end slavery was ultimately won by those who refused to compromise, Obama draws a lesson both unexpected and unconventional, especially for an African American on the left. He writes that he is chastened by the example of such antislavery absolutists whenever he encounters zealots today. He deprecates the extremism of some contemporary activists, as he did in his address to the graduating class of Howard University in the spring of 2016.[53] Yet in *The Audacity of Hope* he admits that such uncompromising radicals might someday be thought right and the rest of us wrong. He is very careful not to extend that observation to any particular contemporary controversy, but readers cannot help making that leap themselves. Nothing in Obama's books suggests that he has second thoughts about his stances on hot-button issues such as abortion, capital punishment, gun control, or gay rights. Yet his measured comments concerning the implications of our contemporary admiration for radical abolitionists shows yet again the sophistication of his historicism. "I'm reminded," he writes, "that deliberation and the constitutional order may sometimes be the luxury of the powerful, and that it has sometimes been the cranks, the zealots, the prophets, the agitators, and the unreasonable—in other words, the absolutists—that have fought for a new order." It was William Lloyd Garrison, Frederick Douglass, and John Brown, not their moderate opponents, who forced the issue of abolition. With that awareness, Obama continues, "I can't summarily dismiss those possessed of similar certainty today—the antiabortion activist who pickets my town hall meeting, or the animal rights activist who raids a laboratory"—or, we might add, the most unyielding champions of the Black Lives Matter movement—"no matter how deeply I disagree with their views." It is one thing to acknowledge that we have come a long way from slavery and from other cruelties of the past. All politicians can play that tune. It is quite another to extend that logic to one's own convictions, which Obama does by raising the open-ended question about how posterity will judge our own moderation—and our own forms of zealotry. In that brief, remarkable, and little noticed passage about his reaction to contemporary extremists in *The Audacity of Hope,* Obama again demonstrates his acute self-consciousness.[54]

Obama acknowledges, perhaps more fully than any prominent figure in twenty-first-century American public life, the undeniable undertow exerted by historicism and antifoundationalism on all of our most deeply held convictions. Yet he is not paralyzed by that understanding. Obama is able to interrogate his own convictions—to place them in a broader cultural and historical context by imaginatively scrutinizing them from a position centuries in the future—without abandoning them.

Self-scrutiny of the sort that Obama has shown remains rare in American public life. So is this striking admission in *The Audacity of Hope:* "I am robbed even of the certainty of uncertainty—for sometimes absolute truths may well be absolute." Primarily for the reasons embedded in that arresting sentence, Obama finds himself, in his words, "left then with Lincoln." Obama's discussion of Lincoln reveals the reasons why he so often invokes the words of the sixteenth president, the predecessor he most admires. His account of Lincoln in *The Audacity of Hope* engages the controversies that have swirled around Lincoln's political career and his legacy ever since he emerged as a prominent national figure in the 1850s.[55] After the Kansas-Nebraska Act of 1854, Lincoln insisted that the question of allowing slavery in the territories should not be submitted to popular vote. His Illinois adversary Stephen A. Douglas invoked the principle of popular sovereignty to justify allowing the people of the territories to choose for themselves whether to permit the extension of slavery. In speeches stretching from his 1854 Peoria, Illinois, address through his election to the presidency in 1860, Lincoln stood firm against Douglas's interpretation of American democracy. It is true, as Lincoln's critics correctly observe, that during those years Lincoln never allied himself with abolitionists who insisted on the immediate end of slavery everywhere. Yet his characterizations of slavery as "a great moral wrong" nevertheless cost him crucial support in 1858, when whites in southern Illinois swung the legislature to select Douglas for the U.S. Senate. After the election of 1860, even though Lincoln deliberately muted his earlier criticism of slavery in an effort to prevent secession, it was the South's perception of the promise implicit in Lincoln's earlier denunciations of slavery that sparked the Civil War.[56]

No one before or since, Obama writes, has understood as well as Lincoln "both the deliberative function of our democracy and the limits of such deliberation."[57] Lincoln wrestled with competing impulses. On the one hand, he was convinced that slavery was an unmitigated evil. On the other, he knew that it would end only if Americans reached a common understanding about the need to eradicate it. The result of that struggle was Lincoln's tortured decision to go to war to preserve the Union. But throughout the war he insisted that the guilt for its necessity had to be shared, by both the South that had embraced slavery and the North that had allowed slavery to survive. The power of Lincoln's sublime second inaugural address depends on that insistence. Less a declaration of victory than an act of contrition, it pledged the nation to redeem the bloody sacrifice of war by redeeming its promise of equality for all. Yet only a few years after Lincoln's death, northern and southern whites began stitching the nation back together with a shared commitment to white supremacy.

Obama's paragraphs on Lincoln, among the most powerful in *The Audacity of Hope,* reveal an incisive understanding of both the advantages and the tragic disadvantages of democracy. Unless the commitment to majority rule is balanced against an equally firm commitment to realizing the ideals of individual liberty and social equality, democracy can produce—indeed, it has produced—horrible forms of injustice. Without an ethic of reciprocity that requires individuals to look beyond their own self-interest and to sacrifice for the sake of the common good, any group of three can yield a majority of two committed to enslaving the minority of one. As Lincoln came to realize, weighing the evil of such injustice against the cost of ending it by waging war is among the most serious challenges a president can face. Obama has learned, from history and from his own experience, that deliberation can improve decision making. Multiplying perspectives can improve the odds of reaching a resolution that no individual might have seen. Yet the experience of Lincoln's generation also shows that not every decision can be put to a vote. Sometimes it is necessary to change the terms of the debate, as did Frederick Douglass, the abolitionists, and finally the Union army. It was swords, not words, that severed slaves' chains.[58] Although formidable challenges of racism and inequality at home and the looming threat of war abroad remain, moral clarity of the sort we now assign so easily to the issue of slavery is harder to find.

Obama's Christian humility, his antifoundationalism, and his nuanced appreciation of the complexities of American history all point toward the disconcerting but inescapable truth of human fallibility, a lesson learned by only the best—and only a few—of those elected to our nation's highest office. The necessary war that ended slavery also ended half a million lives, after which the nation abandoned former slaves to a century-long ordeal, an ordeal justified by passionately held assumptions concerning white male supremacy that continue to poison American life. Obama understands that our admiration for Lincoln's heroic convictions should not be separated from our awareness of the tragedies of Civil War battlefields, or of the lynch mobs that enforced the culture of inequality that came in the wake of Union victory. As the case of slavery shows, and as continuing struggles to uproot the tenacious hold of hierarchies of power and privilege confirm, compromise is not always possible in democracy. But Americans, including those who malign Obama's unsuccessful efforts to resolve rather than intensify conflicts at home and across the globe, should never forget the cost of its failure.

## *Notes*

1. This chapter draws on James T. Kloppenberg, *Reading Obama: Dreams, Hope, and the American Political Tradition,* 2nd ed. (Princeton, NJ: Princeton University Press, 2012).

2. David Remnick, *The Bridge: The Life and Rise of Barack Obama* (New York: Knopf, 2010), 444–45. After acknowledging the book's importance, Remnick does not examine its contents. Nor do the authors of the other two most comprehensive biographies of Obama; David Marannis, *Barack Obama: The Story* (New York: Simon and Schuster, 2012), and David J. Garrow, *Rising Star: The Making of Barack Obama* (New York: William Morrow, 2017), pay as much attention to what is in the book as they do to its extraordinary sales.

3. Barack Obama, *Dreams from My Father: A Story of Race and Inheritance,* 2nd ed. (New York: Crown Publishing Group, 2004), 437.

4. Laurence H. Tribe and Michael C. Dorf, *On Reading the Constitution* (Cambridge, MA: Harvard University Press, 1991), 31, 125 n.1.

5. Jared Sparks, journal entry, Apr. 19, 1830, in Max Farrand, ed., *The Records of the Federal Convention of 1787,* 3 vols. (New Haven, CT: Yale University Press, 1911), 3:479.

6. See Cass Sunstein, *The Partial Constitution* (Cambridge, MA: Harvard University Press, 1993). On the transformation of constitutional law in the years in which Obama was studying at Harvard Law School and teaching at the University of Chicago Law School, see Laura Kalman, *The Strange Career of Legal Liberalism* (New Haven, CT: Yale University Press, 1996); James T. Kloppenberg, "The Theory and Practice of Legal History," *Harvard Law Review* 106, no. 6 (Apr. 1993): 1332–51; James T. Kloppenberg, "Deliberative Democracy and Judicial Supremacy," *Law and History Review* 13 (1995): 393–411.

7. Barack Obama, *The Audacity of Hope: Thoughts on Reclaiming the American Dream,* 2nd ed. (New York: Vintage, 2008), 104.

8. Ibid., 109–13.

9. Obama's understanding of the Constitution and how it should be understood aligns closely with arguments advanced in James T. Kloppenberg, *The Virtues of Liberalism* (New York: Oxford University Press, 1998), chapters 1–5; and James T. Kloppenberg, *Toward Democracy: The Struggle for Self-Rule in European and American Thought* (New York: Oxford University Press, 2016), chapters 6–9.

10. Obama, *Audacity of Hope,* 109.

11. Clifford Geertz, *The Interpretation of Cultures* (New York: Basic Books, 1973). Cf. Obama, *Dreams from My Father,* 10.

12. Obama, *Audacity of Hope,* 109–10.

13. Ibid., 110–11.

14. Analysis of the parallels between many of Obama's arguments and those of the principal figures in the American tradition of philosophical pragmatism is central to Kloppenberg, *Reading Obama.* On the revival of pragmatism during the years of Obama's intellectual formation, see James T. Kloppenberg, "Pragmatism: An Old Name for Some New Ways of Thinking?" *Journal of American History* 83, no. 1 (June 1996), reprinted in Morris Dickstein, ed., *The Revival of Pragmatism* (Durham, NC: Duke University Press, 1998), 83–127; James T. Kloppenberg, "James's *Pragmatism* and American Culture, 1907–2007," in John Stuhr, ed., *100 Years of Pragmatism: William James's Revolutionary Philosophy* (Bloomington: Indiana University Press, 2010), 7–40.

15. Cass R. Sunstein, "Interpreting Statutes in the Regulatory State," *Harvard Law Review* 103 (1989); Marvin Meyers, A Reflection and Choice: Beyond the Sum of the Differences, in Marvin Meyers, ed., *The Mind of the Founder: Sources of the Political Thought of James Madison* (Hanover, NH: University Press of New England, 1981), xi–xlix.

16. Obama, *Audacity of Hope,* 111.

17. Ibid., 83–84.

18. Ibid., 84, cf. 72.

19. Ibid., 90.

20. On the congressional wrangling over the stimulus package and the Affordable Care Act and the constraints on Obama's options, see Michael Grunwald, *The New New Deal: The Hidden Story of Change in the Obama Era* (New York: Simon and Schuster, 2012).

21. Obama, *Audacity of Hope,* 91.

22. Ibid., 103–13.

23. On the shaping of Obama's sensibility from his formal education through his work as a community organizer in the Far South Side of Chicago to his participation in the Saguaro seminars and his entry into national prominence, see Kloppenberg, *Reading Obama,* chapter 1.

24. Obama, *Audacity of Hope,* 21, 4.

25. Jane Addams, *Twenty Years at Hull House* (1910; repr., New York: Signet, 1961), 89. For a splendid collection of Obama's speeches that contain all of these and many others, see E. J. Dionne and Joy-Anne Reid, eds., *We Are the Change We Seek: The Speeches of Barack Obama* (New York: Bloomsbury, 2017).

26. See Louise Knight, *Jane Addams: Spirit in Action* (New York: Norton, 2010); Ariane Liazos, "The Movement for Good City Government: Municipal Leagues, Political Science, and the Meaning of Progressive Democracy, 1880–1930" (Ph.D. diss., Harvard University, 2007); Lauren Brandt, "Social Intercession: The Religious Nature

of Public Activism among American Women Reformers, 1892–1930" (Ph.D. diss., Harvard University, 2009).

27. Obama, *Audacity of Hope,* 228–29.

28. Ibid., 181–83.

29. John Adams to Thomas Jefferson, Feb. 24, 1819, in Lester J. Cappon, ed. *The Adams-Jefferson Letters* (Chapel Hill: University of North Carolina Press, 1987), 534–35. The commitment of most members of the founding generation to economic equality is central to Kloppenberg, *Toward Democracy,* chapter 6.

30. Obama, *Audacity of Hope,* 161.

31. For a more detailed account of Obama's reliance on, and consistency with, the ideas and policies championed by twentieth-century progressives, see James T. Kloppenberg, "Barack Obama and Progressive Reform," in Stephen Skowronek, Stephen M. Engel, and Bruce Ackerman, eds., *The Progressives' Century: Political Reform, Constitutional Government, and the Modern American State* (New Haven, CT: Yale University Press, 2016), 431–52.

32. Obama, *Audacity of Hope,* 182.

33. Ibid., 10.

34. See Ira Katznelson, *Fear Itself: The New Deal and the Origins of Our Time* (New York: Liveright, 2013); Cass Sunstein, *The Second Bill of Rights: FDR's Unfinished Revolution and Why We Need It More Than Ever* (New York: Basic Books, 2004).

35. On Boesche and Obama, see Kloppenberg, *Reading Obama,* chapter 1; on the New Deal, cf. Carl N. Degler, *Out of Our Past: The Forces That Shaped Modern America* (1959; 3rd ed., New York: Harper, 1984), chapter 13; William Leuchtenburg, *Franklin D. Roosevelt and the New Deal, 1932–1940* (New York: Harper and Row, 1963); David M. Kennedy, *Freedom from Fear: The American People in Depression and War, 1929–1945* (New York: Oxford University Press, 1999).

36. Obama, *Audacity of Hope,* 375.

37. Ibid., 7–15.

38. Ibid., 84, 260–61, 373.

39. Ibid., 38–39, 185–88.

40. On the continuing salience of these issues, see Kloppenberg, *Toward Democracy;* Daniel T. Rodgers, *The Eyes of all People Are Upon Us: Inventing and Reinventing John Winthrop's Model of Christian Charity* (Princeton, NJ: Princeton University Press, 2018).

41. All of those speeches are reprinted in Dionne and Reid, *We Are the Change We Seek.*

42. Obama, *Dreams from My Father,* 153–54, 179, 274–95; Obama, *Audacity of Hope,* 240–46, 250–56.

43. Obama, *Audacity of Hope,* 116, 254.

44. Ibid., 258.

45. For detailed discussion of this theme in relation to Obama, see James T. Kloppenberg, "Barack Obama and the Paradoxes of Progressive Christianity," in Darren Dochuk and Marie Griffith, eds., *Beyond the Culture Wars: Recasting Religion and*

*Politics in the Twentieth Century* (forthcoming); more broadly, see Robert D. Putnam and David E. Campbell, *American Grace: How Religion Divides and Unites Us* (New York: Simon and Schuster, 2010).

46. Obama, *Audacity of Hope,* 63–72.

47. Ibid., 174.

48. Ibid., 67–68.

49. This emphasis reverberates from Obama's first inaugural address, "A New Era of Responsibility," Jan. 20, 2009, through his farewell address, "What Our Democracy Demands," Jan. 20, 2017, both of which are reprinted in Dionne and Reid, *We Are the Change We Seek.*

50. Obama, *Audacity of Hope,* 70–72.

51. Ibid., 90.

52. Ibid., 115–16.

53. Obama's speech at Howard University, "You See, Change Requires More Than Righteous Anger," May 7, 2016, is reprinted in Dionne and Reid, *We Are the Change We Seek.*

54. Obama, *Audacity of Hope,* 116.

55. Ibid., 116–17, 179–80.

56. The most incisive and thorough analysis of Lincoln's ideas is John Burt, *Lincoln's Tragic Pragmatism: Lincoln, Douglas, and Moral Conflict* (Cambridge, MA: Belknap Press of Harvard University Press, 2013). On the relation between Lincoln's ideas and the ethic of reciprocity required for the survival of democratic culture, see Kloppenberg, *Toward Democracy,* chapter 14.

57. Obama, *Audacity of Hope,* 116.

58. Ibid., 114.

# Contributors

John Milton Cooper Jr. is E. Gordon Fox Professor of American Institutions at the University of Wisconsin–Madison, *emeritus.* He is the author of several books dealing with presidents, including *The Warrior and the Priest: Woodrow Wilson and Theodore Roosevelt* (1983) and *Woodrow Wilson: A Biography* (2009).

Seth Cotlar is Professor of History at Willamette University. His book *Tom Paine's America: The Rise and Fall of Transatlantic Radicalism in the Early Republic* (2011) was awarded the James Broussard Best First Book Prize by the Society for Historians of the Early American Republic. His current book project is entitled "When the Olden Days Were New: The Cultural History of Nostalgia in Modernizing America, 1776–1860."

Edward Countryman is University Distinguished Professor of History at Southern Methodist University and has taught previously at the University of Canterbury, New Zealand; the Universities of Warwick and Cambridge in England; and Yale University. He won the Bancroft Prize for his first book, *A People in Revolution: The American Revolution and Political Society in New York, 1760–1790* (1981), and has written or edited more than a dozen books on American history, American identity, and film. He is working now on a reinterpretation of what happened between the earliest Atlantic contacts and the American Civil War.

KATHLEEN DALTON has taught at Boston University, American University, and Phillips Academy, Andover. She is the author of *Theodore Roosevelt: A Strenuous Life* (2002) and is working on a book about William and Caroline Phillips and their political friendship with Eleanor and Franklin Roosevelt.

JONATHAN EARLE is Dean of Louisiana State University's Roger Hadfield Ogden Honors College. He is the author of numerous books and articles, including *Jacksonian Antislavery and the Politics of Free Soil* (2005), winner of the Society of Historians of the Early American Republic's 2005 Broussard Prize and cowinner of the Byron Caldwell Smith Book Prize; *John Brown's Raid: A Brief History with Documents* (2008); and *The Routledge Atlas of African American History* (2000). He is the coeditor, with Sean Wilentz, of *Major Problems of the Early Republic (1787–1848)* (2nd ed., 2008), and, with Diane Mutti-Burke, of *Bleeding Kansas, Bleeding Missouri: The Long Civil War on the Border* (2013). He is currently working on a book on the election of 1860 for the Pivotal Moments in U.S. History Series published by Oxford University Press.

RICHARD J. ELLIS is the Mark O. Hatfield Professor of Politics at Willamette University. Among his books on the presidency are *The Development of the American Presidency* (3rd ed., 2018); *Judging Executive Power: Sixteen Supreme Court Cases That Have Shaped the American Presidency* (2009); and *Presidential Travel: The Journey from George Washington to George W. Bush* (2008). He is currently working on a book on the 1840 election for the American Presidential Elections Series published by the University Press of Kansas.

JAMES T. KLOPPENBERG is Charles Warren Professor of American History at Harvard University. He has been elected to the American Academy of Arts and Sciences and the executive board of the Organization of American Historians, and he has served as the Pitt Professor at the University of Cambridge and as a visiting professor at the Ecole des Hautes Etudes en Sciences Sociales in Paris. His most recent books are *Reading Obama: Dreams, Hope, and the American Political Tradition* (2nd ed., 2012) and *Toward Democracy: The Struggle for Self-Rule in European and American Thought* (2016).

Charlie Laderman is a Lecturer in International History in the War Studies Department at King's College, London. He was previously a Harrington Faculty Fellow at the University of Texas at Austin; a Research Fellow at Peterhouse, University of Cambridge; and a Fox International Fellow and Smith Richardson Fellow at Yale University. He is the author of *Sharing the Burden: Saving Armenia and the Anglo-American Search for a Global Order* (2019).

Elvin T. Lim is Professor of Political Science at Singapore Management University, and dean of the Core Curriculum. He is the author of *The Anti-Intellectual Presidency* (2008) and *The Lovers' Quarrel: The Two Foundings and American Political Development* (2014).

Jeffrey L. Pasley is Professor of History and Journalism, and Associate Director of the Kinder Institute on Constitutional Democracy at the University of Missouri. He is the author of *"The Tyranny of Printers": Newspaper Politics in the Early American Republic* (2001) and *The First Presidential Contest: The Election of 1796 and the Beginnings of American Democracy* (2013), a finalist for the 2014 George Washington Book Prize.

Rick Perlstein is a political journalist and essayist based in Chicago. He is the author of *Before the Storm: Barry Goldwater and the Unmaking of the American Consensus* (2001), winner of the 2001 *Los Angeles Times* Book Award for history; *Nixonland* (2008), a *New York Times* best seller picked as one of the best nonfiction books of the year by over a dozen publications; and *The Invisible Bridge: The Fall of Nixon and the Rise of Reagan* (2014), another *New York Times* best seller and a "best book" selection in publications including the *New York Times, San Francisco Chronicle,* and *Los Angeles Times.*

David Sehat is Associate Professor of History at Georgia State University. He is the author of *The Jefferson Rule: How the Founding Fathers Became Infallible and Our Politics Inflexible* (2015) and *The Myth of American Religious Freedom* (2011), which won the Frederick Jackson Turner Award from the Organization of American Historians.

David Waldstreicher is Distinguished Professor of History at The Graduate Center of the City University of New York. He is the author of *In the Midst of Perpetual Fetes: The Making of American Nationalism, 1776–1820* (1997); *Runaway America: Benjamin Franklin, Slavery, and the American Revolution* (2004); and *Slavery's Constitution: From Revolution to Ratification* (2009). As editor, his books include *A Companion to John Adams and John Quincy Adams* (2013); *John Quincy Adams and the Politics of Slavery: Selections from the Diary* (2016); and the two-volume Library of America edition *The Diaries of John Quincy Adams, 1779–1848* (2017).

# Index

*Italicized page numbers refer to illustrations.*